# THE
# SCARLET
# SISTERS

My nanna's story of secrets and heartache
on the banks of the River Thames

# HELEN BATTEN

EBURY
PRESS

1 3 5 7 9 10 8 6 4 2

Ebury Press, an imprint of Ebury Publishing
20 Vauxhall Bridge Road
London SW1V 2SA

Ebury Press is part of the Penguin Random House group of companies
whose addresses can be found at global.penguinrandomhouse.com

Penguin
Random House
UK

First published by Ebury Press in 2015

www.eburypublishing.co.uk

A CIP catalogue record for this book is available from the British Library

ISBN 9780091959692

Printed and bound by CPI Group (UK) Ltd, Croydon, CR0 4YY

MIX
Paper from
responsible sources
FSC® C018179

Penguin Random House is committed to a sustainable
future for our business, our readers and our planet. This book
is made from Forest Stewardship Council® certified paper.

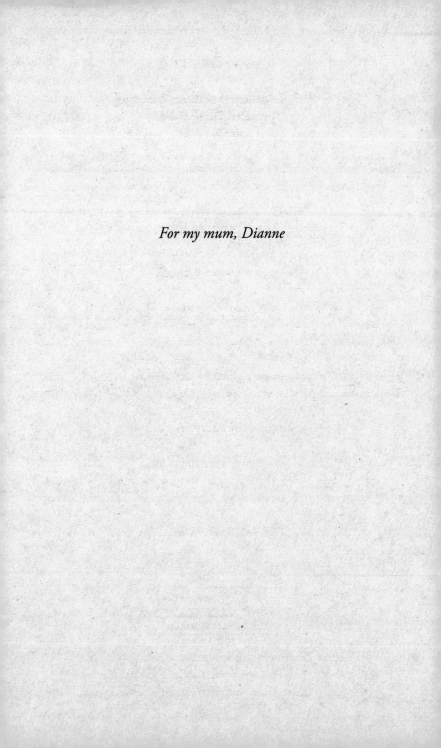

*For my mum, Dianne*

*'This year, this year, as all these flowers foretell,*
*We shall escape the circle and undo the spell.'*

C. S. Lewis

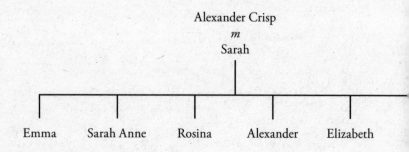

Alexander Crisp
*m*
Sarah

Emma　　Sarah Anne　　Rosina　　Alexander　　Elizabeth

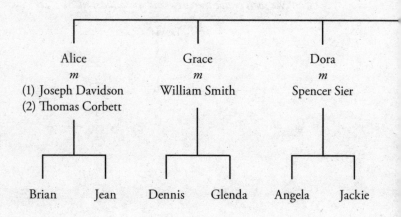

Alice
*m*
(1) Joseph Davidson
(2) Thomas Corbett

Grace
*m*
William Smith

Dora
*m*
Spencer Sier

Brian　　Jean　　Dennis　　Glenda　　Angela　　Jackie

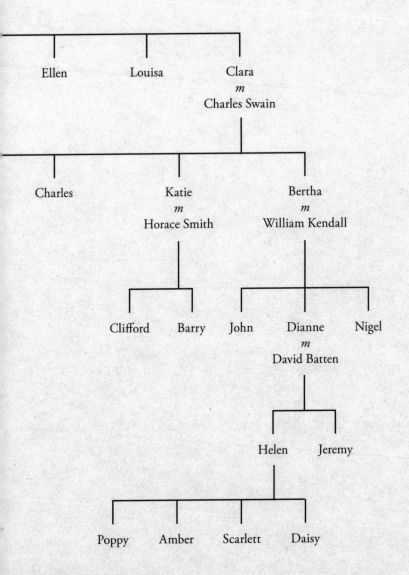

Ellen

Louisa

Clara
*m*
Charles Swain

Charles

Katie
*m*
Horace Smith

Bertha
*m*
William Kendall

Clifford    Barry

John

Dianne
*m*
David Batten

Nigel

Helen    Jeremy

Poppy    Amber    Scarlett    Daisy

# CONTENTS

# PROLOGUE
# The End

I knew it was the last time we were going to see each other, and she knew it was the last time we were going to see each other, and we both knew each other knew. Of course neither of us said anything, but it did make a difference. Our conversation was less flippant, more direct, and in between our bursts of talking, I held her hand tight, stroked it, kissed it and told her I loved her over and over again.

I'd got the phone call from Mum first thing in the morning: 'You'd better go and see Nanna quick. I think this is it.'

Mum went on to fret because it wasn't visiting time, but I'd had plenty of experience of hospitals and nurses: 'No one's going to stop me from seeing Nanna. Just let them try.'

I was eleven weeks pregnant with my third child and as sick as if I was a tiny boat tossing around in an ocean storm. But I dressed with care. If I didn't hurry Nanna might die before I got there, but then I knew the sight of a messy granddaughter would do nothing for her state of health. What if her last sight of me was looking unpressed? I worried about hauntings. I took out a designer pencil skirt that I had purchased from a West London charity shop, and I was relieved when I managed to zip my new bump into it. Then I added a plain, stretchy black shirt, and completed the outfit with red wedge sandals. Sophisticated and understated – it was not necessarily my normal look, but I knew it would please her.

And, as I walked into the intensive care unit, feeling at home with the beeping monitors and resuscitation unit stashed in the corner, glaring at the nurses and daring them to stop me, Nanna took off her oxygen mask and looked me up and down with a smile. 'Hello, dear. Well, you do look smart, I must say.' She paused, took my hand, pulled me closer, and said in an earnest whisper, 'Always keep your hair short, Helen.' I nodded. And then, satisfied I'd got the message, she nodded too.

She looked down and gestured at her hospital gown. 'What do you think of this?'

I looked at it thoughtfully and said, 'It's pretty, Nanna. I noticed it when I walked in – the little blue flowers are exactly the colour of your eyes.'

'Oh, really, dear? I guess you're right.'

And she put her oxygen mask back on, once more satisfied.

And it *was* the thought I'd had. Nanna had very blue, periwinkle eyes and they were exactly the colour of the sprigs of blue flowers in her rather superior hospital gown.

Looking her best and, in fact, all of her descendants looking their best, was very important to Nanna, but there was method in her vanity. She had been the youngest of five sisters, growing up in poverty. All she'd had were her looks. Nanna had always put a great deal of effort into standing out from the crowd. She was a master of unusual colour combinations and not afraid of a clash. I often heard her friends make comments such as, 'I would never have thought to put red with purple, but it really works. You are so clever, Bertha.' She loved accessories: hats, gloves, beads, scarves in jewel colours wound around to create a stir. She had an air of glamour about her, although the money her husband had made had all been lost by the time I came into the world. So it was left to her children and eventually her grandchildren to indulge her. With one of my first pay packets, I bought her a scarf from Liberty's. I thought its swirly autumn colours would look beautiful against her fair skin. The next time I saw it, it was wrapped around my nanna's head as an elaborate turban. She'd chopped it up, taken a sewing machine and some stuffing to it, completed the look with a brooch and feather, and used it to create a splash at my brother's wedding.

Nanna's hair was her trump card. All of the five Swain sisters were blessed with thick wavy hair of differing shades of red – the Scarlet Sisters. When they stood together it was like a wood in autumn. The third sister, Dora, had the darkest hair. It was a kind of rich brown chestnut. Then came Grace, a lighter chestnut; Katie a bit auburn; and the eldest, Alice, a sort of strawberry blonde. Nanna was the youngest of the sisters, and her hair was the brightest. She was the only one who had really inherited her father, Charlie Swain's, traffic light for a head. By the time I knew her it had turned a beautiful glossy, snow white, but she still had a bit of the brightest red in a layer underneath, at the back. As a little girl I used to sit on her knee and stroke this silky, red seam in awe and wonder. My own hair was fine and mousey. My cousin Elisabeth had inherited Nanna's red hair and I was most jealous.

Competition was a bit of a theme in the family: there was nothing the Swain sisters wanted to do more than outshine each other. Their back-handed compliments were legendary and went on until the end. Typical was the stir Nanna caused at her sister Grace's funeral. As they lowered her coffin into the ground, Nanna peered down and then turned to her sisters, and Dora's daughter, and said loudly, 'Did they lower your mum on top of your dad at her funeral, Jackie?' Then she went over to Grace's granddaughter, who held out her hand in greeting, but Nanna bypassed it and took a lock of her hair instead. She felt it and said loudly, 'Is this your own colour, dear?'

Which leads me on to what happened next. As I knew it was the last time I'd see Nanna, I felt compelled to tell her about my new baby. I took courage and launched straight in. 'I'm pregnant again.'

She looked shocked and then took off her mask. 'Are you sure?'

'Well, yes. Eleven weeks and I'm feeling really sick, so yes, pretty sure.'

'Oh.'

There was an ominous silence.

'Did you mean that to happen?'

'Um, well … Nanna!'

'What I mean is, are you pleased?'

'Yes, yes, of course.'

I don't know why I said 'of course'. There was no 'of course' about it. My first pregnancy ended tragically and being pregnant was not a happy, healthy state for me. I knew that this was what she was thinking and she knew I knew, but as in so many of my dealings with Nanna, the uncomfortable, painful thing was left unspoken.

'Girl or boy?'

'I don't know yet. I'll find out, but that's at the twenty-week scan. I haven't even had the twelve-week one yet.'

'Hmm. Yes, but what do you think? What do you want?'

'Oh, I really don't mind. A healthy baby and I'm not just saying that. You know that.'

A look of recognition passed between us.

'Another girl, though, Helen.' She sighed. She seemed to know something I didn't, but I decided not to question the premise.

'Well, I like girls.'

'Do you?'

'Yes, of course! Girls are best. Come on, Nanna, you like girls too.'

'Sisters, though. Awful.'

'Awful?'

'Yes, all the fighting and the jealousy. Sharing a bed. Yes, dear. Three girls. Too many.'

Three girls? I was confused. I only had one – my two-year-old, Amber.

Then she said, 'You were so lucky to have a brother.'

Suddenly there was a ghost in the room. Nanna had had a brother, one boy slap in the middle of the five girls, but he'd died and, so the story goes, broken their father's heart. Charlie Swain never recovered from being a lone man surrounded by six women. Apparently he would put his head in the gas oven, and took to drink. More than that I didn't know. Now I was tempted to ask, but Nanna had put her oxygen mask back on and I was suddenly aware of the intensive care machinery around me.

Instead I kissed her hand again and stroked her forehead. 'I love you,' I whispered in her ear. Nanna closed her eyes, looking tired. 'Her heart's giving out,' I thought. She was ninety years old. Apart from having her children, this was the first time she had ever been in hospital. The doctors said there was nothing wrong with her: her heart was just worn out with all the years.

I studied the back of her hand. The shape of her fingers and nails was so familiar to me, as were the big freckles. Images flashed through my mind – those hands teaching me to knit, holding her cards playing bridge, smoothing her hair, waving her elegant tortoiseshell cigarette holder with her one-a-day Silk Cut cigarette, grabbing the bowl of dish water and throwing it over the fire I'd started in her kitchen when I accidently knocked a bottle of turps down the back of the fridge, and dissolving into laughter when we ran outside to escape the billowing smoke: 'Oh, Helen, I've never seen your face so white. You're a ghost!'

She'd cried with laughter despite the fact I'd sent flames licking up the walls of the kitchen and she had to have it redecorated. How she paid for it, I've no idea. But that was the thing – she only ever made me feel incredibly loved.

And I couldn't believe that this hand that was so familiar wouldn't be there any more. Here in front of me was Nanna, so sharp, so herself, it was difficult to believe that within days she would be gone for ever.

My mobile phone rang. It was my husband, worried about Nanna and about me. I put his mind at ease and then we fell into our usual banter. Nanna opened her eyes and watched me carefully. I was suddenly self-conscious and felt maybe I was crossing a line, being too flippant. I hung up.

Nanna took off her mask. 'Is he good to you?'

I was slightly taken aback. 'Yes, Nanna, he is.'

She looked at me. She didn't seem convinced and I was surprised. He was a singer and so was she. He made her laugh. He was short and stocky and had lovely chestnut, wavy hair. The sort of man she said she always fell for. A man that was a bit like her father, Charlie Swain.

She changed the subject. 'It's Maundy Thursday, isn't it?'

'Yes, I suppose it is.'

'Can you get me a radio? I'd like to listen to the *Messiah*. It'll be on this afternoon.'

Well, I tried. I fiddled with the radio beside her bed. I summoned the nurse. I am hopeless at technology. I promised I would ask Mum to bring a radio in later. But in the chaos of morning sickness and having a small child and a noisy husband, I forgot. The *Messiah* was her favourite piece of music – she'd sung it in choirs every Easter since she was a child. Now when I sing it with choirs, I sing it to her with an apology. Playing it at her funeral was not enough.

It was time to say goodbye. I leant over and the words were out of my mouth. It seemed cruel but a bigger obligation was at stake. For the first time, I mentioned that name to her. 'Look after Poppy for me.'

Nanna looked scared and I wished I hadn't. I'd broken the rule and admitted I knew she was dying. She did nod, though.

I leant over and kissed her for the last time. 'I love you,' I said again. And then I walked out of the door. I stopped first and looked back. We stared at each other. And then I turned my back and carried on walking.

I couldn't take her with me. The universe had decided and was pulling rank. It felt unbelievable and yet weirdly right – the natural order of things. I had a feeling she was so indelibly printed on my psyche that she'd always be with me.

When my life started to unravel, years later, this last meeting with Nanna started to take on a new level of significance. Nanna had never been known for her psychic powers and yet something about her hovering between this world and the next had seemed to give her the power of prophecy: the questions about my husband, her anxiety about my three daughters – because I did indeed end up having three daughters and my husband was not good to me – in the end he was very bad for me, and I had to ask him to leave. And as I thought more about Nanna and her life, I realised I really didn't know anything about her. Yes, she had been such a presence in my early life, I could still feel her around me. But who was it I thought I knew? Nanna could talk and she loved to keep a room entertained, but she never talked about her childhood, and her four sisters were strangers to me.

One day, while studying for a history degree and writing an essay on working-class Conservative voters between the wars, I had asked Nanna how her father had voted. 'Because you were working class, weren't you, Nanna?'

'Well, dear, I wouldn't say that.'

'What would you say, then?'

She looked unusually annoyed.

'I don't remember.'

'Oh, come on, Nanna.'

She pretended not to hear.

But I wasn't giving up. I had an essay to write and I was lacking inspiration. 'Mum told me your grandpa used to drive Gladstone to Parliament in his hansom cab and he lived off the Old Kent Road, so I reckon that makes you working class and I know you always vote Tory.'

'Look, there was working class and then there was working class. All I'll say is on election day, there were those that wore red rosettes in the playground and those that wore blue, and me and my sisters always, always wore blue.'

'Really? That's fascinating. Why?'

'I'm not talking about it any more.'

'But you are an electoral phenomenon! The Conservative Party has been in power more years than it hasn't because there has always been a significant, solid, working-class Conservative vote. Help me, Nanna! I've got to write an essay on why.'

But she had closed her eyes and absolutely refused to engage any further with me.

The only time I ever met one of the Scarlet Sisters was when her twin, Katie, flew over from New Zealand. It was the last time Nanna ever saw her. They had a few sherries and started telling stories of their hapless father in cockney rhyming slang and giggling till the tears started rolling.

I watched in fascination. Normally Nanna spoke like the Queen Mother.


After twenty-four years of being with my husband, I suddenly found myself a single mother of three daughters. I had by accident found out that he had been seriously and serially unfaithful and everything I thought was so, wasn't.

It seemed I had been a bit naïve. I knew something had fundamentally changed (and not in a good way) when I became pregnant with our last child, but I couldn't put my finger on it. When I gave him a set of cufflinks which said 'If Lost' on one, and 'Return to Wife' on the other, I was only half joking. He had always been the International Man of Mystery but he suddenly became a bit more mysterious, travelling the world and not answering his phone. When I said to an older male friend of mine, 'I did ask him many times if he was having an affair and he always said no,' he had looked at me, astonished. 'Well, what did you expect him to say? He was hardly going to say yes, was he?'

'Wasn't he?'

'No.'

Of course having four children in six years meant I had slightly taken my eye off the ball. But he had never been a womaniser – or so I thought. He had always seemed such a devoted husband. He had started sending me flowers (stupidly, I forgot what he used to say: 'A man who sends a woman flowers, sends lots of women flowers.') He started picking me up from nights out with my girlfriends. 'He's very possessive, isn't he?' they said. 'He never used to be,' I'd replied, not really questioning why he started being so solicitous. 'He loves you so much,' my girls said to me. But I think you can sense when it's an act.

And that niggling doubt sometimes became a feeling in the pit of my stomach and I thought of the parable of the house built on sand. At times I felt as if I was going mad: the blurring of truth and untruth, the endless ever-more complicated excuses, the shifting realities. He just didn't touch me like he used to and even when he was there, he wasn't. There was an absent look in his eyes. I can spot it now: 'The Eyes of the Cheating Man'. I think I see it sometimes in certain husbands' eyes at parties. So when I started to emerge from that new baby madness, I made an ultimatum and we had a year of couples counselling.

'Sometimes I see people and it's very clear, but I don't understand why you two don't work,' the counsellor said.

Yes. That's because he neglected to mention he was having an affair. I was the child of divorced parents, so I knew exactly how devastating the break-up of a family was. Without having a very good reason, how could I press the nuclear button and then look my children in the eye? And he wouldn't give me that reason. So I was stuck. And I felt not just stuck, but trapped.

But, finally, I did find that reason and with that revelation everything I had believed about my past, my present and my future was blown apart. Who do you think you are? I knew who I thought I'd been, but suddenly I had no idea.

I no longer had a narrative for myself.

I came across an article that suggested that suffering could be inherited. The research had concentrated on traumatic life events such as bereavement and abuse, and had shown them repeated down generations of mothers and daughters and shared among sisters. There's a name for it: trans-generational trauma. I read the article slowly and carefully. It might be that this is a physical inheritance – research has shown that trauma affects and changes DNA; it equally may be a psychological phenomenon where trauma affects the relationship you develop with your children and in turn the relationships they go on to make.

It may not matter how it happens, just that it does.

I knew so little about Nanna, practically nothing about her sisters and as for my great-grandma, just a name and a location: Clara Crisp from the Old Kent Road. I decided that while I would probably never know why my husband did what he did, I might be able to make some sense of why I chose him and why I stayed with him. It felt important for me to understand where I found myself, and to find a new narrative. Not to repeat, but to fall in love with someone better next time.

And, most crucially, so that if there is a traumatic inheritance, I might be able to stop it at me.

I started to talk to the family. Nanna and her sisters are long gone but their children – my mum, her brothers and her seven cousins, are still very much with us. I wrote to them, telephoned and then eventually went to see them. They fed me food and stories, got out old photo albums, and scoured their attics specially, finding new information, things they didn't even know themselves. And a story started to unfold.

Late one night I felt compelled to draw a family tree with a difference. I took the normal diagram with its births, marriages, deaths and descendants, and I plotted the trauma. It didn't feel a healthy thing to do and not something I'd necessarily recommend, but once I'd had the idea, I had to follow it through. With a glass of wine in one hand and a pen in the other, I overlaid all the things that we don't talk about.

It was pretty sobering. I saw a pattern, as if one of my ancestors had forgotten to invite the Wicked Fairy to the christening, and we had all been condemned to live difficult lives ever since.

I made a resolution there and then – to do everything I could to stop the cycle being repeated with my three precious daughters. I wanted to break the spell. But how? It seemed important to locate the original problem – the source of the curse, if you like.

Some things we know for certain about our families – the big, official stuff: births, deaths and marriages. And then the internet is an amazing thing. I was just a few clicks away from all sorts of information – war records, criminal records, workhouse records and the census results – information that even ten years ago would have been quite an effort to find. Now secrets that have lain buried for generations – our ancestors probably thought for ever – are being dug up. Family myths are being shown to be just that: myths. Often the truth is more interesting, and in my case, a bit darker.

But what lies behind these official happenings: the feelings, conversations and actions? This is harder to pin down. For a start, all the main protagonists were no longer with us, but I was blessed with a family that helped me piece together the history.

Some anecdotes were just part of the universal family folklore. I'd grown up with them, woven into my memory along with my DNA. The fact that these stories were so embedded in the extended family consciousness, despite often seeming insignificant, seems important. For example, Nanna was brought up on Carnation's condensed milk, while her twin sister, Katie, was breastfed. Everyone told me this, but I knew it already. Why did I know? Scratch the surface, though, and it's obvious. Because these much-repeated stories are small keys that unlock much bigger truths.

Then there were the gaps. With the paper and electronic trail ominously quiet, they had all us descendants scratching our heads. But I've researched enough now to know the general historical terrain, and I know the personalities involved. I'd also discussed the options with the wider family and had the benefit of hindsight. So I've made a stab at what might, if not probably did, happen in those missing years. And I hope my ancestors are not spitting at me from the heavens ...

On other occasions I heard the same anecdotes, but with different beginnings, middles or ends and, indeed, protagonists: 'No, that was Katie' 'No, I'm sure it was Bertha ...' etc. Then sometimes I heard something that no one else had told me, or which was in complete opposition to what I'd heard from someone else. So I had to make my own judgement.

I guess that goes for the whole story. It's my interpretation of our family history. It's subjective, as is all history, and I was looking to break a spell. Put it this way, if another member of my family wrote this book, it wouldn't be the same. We all have our own version of the truth, and our own reality.

So this is what I found.

# CHAPTER ONE
# The Hero

My great-grandfather, Charlie Swain, was blown into my great-grandmother Clara Crisp's life with a strong westerly wind on an autumn afternoon in 1897.

He was standing on the doorstep of the small terraced house in Lant Street SE1, a flutter of copper leaves dancing around his ginger head, with only a wicked grin on his face and his worldly goods in a rucksack slung over his shoulder.

It was my great-great-grandmother, Sarah Crisp, who greeted him on the doorstep. 'Here's trouble,' she thought, and with her seven daughters in mind, felt a twinge of apprehension.

'Mrs Crisp? I'm your new lodger.'

'Oh. Not too tall, are you?'

Charlie was indeed pushing to reach five foot four, but he was strong, and he had a sense of humour. 'Charlie Swain, pleased to meet you. Hasn't anyone ever told you, Mrs Crisp, that nice things come in small packages?'

'Yes, well, so does poison, young man. Guess you'd better come in, then,' she said, struggling to stop a smile, and ushered him into the kitchen where the baby of the family, my great-grandmother, Clara, was busy making biscuits.

They looked at each other over the kitchen table.

It wasn't love at first sight, at least Clara didn't think so at the time. But Charlie did make an immediate impression. Years later, when pressed by her daughters, all Clara could say was, 'He seemed to fill the room, like the westerly wind had blown in something exotic,' which would send them into a chorus of giggles because, by that time, the last thing Charlie seemed was exotic.

But, back then, when he was only nineteen, what Charlie did brim over with was confidence, his wide, freckly face open to the world, just daring stuff to happen.

Which piqued Sarah's curiosity. 'So, take a seat then, Charlie Swain. Tell me, how come you've landed in the lovely borough of Southwark? You're not a Londoner, are you? I can sniff it.'

'No, Mrs Crisp, your nose is right. I'm not a Londoner. I'm a black sheep that has been cast from the flock as a result of a large misunderstanding and a small amount of high spirits.'

'Oh, dear, I sense a tale,' Sarah said, sitting herself down and getting comfortable – gossip was oxygen in this house of eight women.

'A tale that is not to be told. Sorry to disappoint, but I'm turning over a new leaf and drawing a line under. I'm sure you understand. I've travelled away from the scene of my alleged crime, and left it behind. I'm starting tomorrow at the brewery, next door. I'm an engineer. I'm good at fixing things.'

'Well, that'll be handy, won't it, Clara?' Sarah said, glancing in the direction of her daughter.

Clara had kept her head down, busy with her biscuits, but not a crumb of this conversation had passed her by. She was determined to carry on with her work – she was kneading the dough and cutting out shapes – but Charlie Swain's gaze seemed to be having a wobbly effect on her fingers.

'Come on, Clara. Cat got your tongue?' Sarah said.

Clara looked up. 'Yes. Handy, indeed.' She had her sleeves rolled up, showing her dainty wrists, while a tightly tied apron showed off her waist. The look was completed with a light dusting of flour on her cheek.

'I hope I can be of service,' Charlie said, and once again Sarah felt uneasy.

'Well, we'll see about that, young man. Anyway, Clara's handy at making pastries and cakes and all sorts of treats for the bakers around here, aren't you, my dove?'

Charlie could see she was blushing as she started cutting out shapes in the dough once again.

'Save some for our Rosie Lee. I'll make you a cup. You must be parched,' Sarah said.

Charlie was only too happy to settle himself down, but the cockney rhyming slang confused him a bit. Also, he was finding it difficult to concentrate on Sarah Crisp when her youngest daughter was doing such pretty things with her hands. Her fingers gently but firmly pressed the dough into dainty shapes: butterflies, shells, crowns and flowers. Intricate yet effortless. Charlie was slightly mesmerised, and he got a familiar impulse to make a shy girl smile. While Sarah had her back to them, he found himself grabbing a small corner of the dough and fashioning it into a heart, then sliding it without a word back to Clara, who looked up, astonished.

Charlie and Clara were exact opposites. But when this couple of nineteen-year-olds looked at each other – Charlie's dazzling sharp periwinkle eyes looking into Clara's brown, gentle eyes – they felt like they had met before. Without thinking, just as her mother turned around, Clara hurriedly put the heart into her apron pocket and looked back at Charlie. They held each other's gaze.

Why do opposites attract? Hearing my mum and her cousins talk about Charlie and Clara makes me think of magnets pulling towards their polar opposites, as if we can be repelled by partners whose personality is too similar and hopelessly drawn to those who are different. Perhaps we choose people who appear to give us the very qualities we lack, as part of a natural quest for completion. Or perhaps it's just a recipe for marital disaster …

In any case, the instant attraction of opposites that were Charlie and Clara is a key piece of the jigsaw puzzle that made the Scarlet

Sisters; or, putting it another way, that's how the Scarlet Sisters became a twinkle in Charlie Swain's eye.

Later on, while Charlie was settling himself into his room, Clara was bursting with questions for her mother. 'Do you think Dad'll approve?'

'I think he'll rather admire that young man's nerve. Your father always appreciates a bit of confidence. And if high spirits are his problem, I think they'll hit it off.'

After a pause, Clara asked the biggest question on both their minds: 'What do you think he did?'

'Hmm … if I had to put money on it, I'd say it involved a lady. It's that look in his eyes. Anyway, I'll find out, love, don't you worry.'

But Sarah never did find out, and neither did anyone else.

Where does the story of one's own existence start? Sometimes it feels like a chain of random collisions between people – lots of events happening simultaneously in different parts of the world that are working towards the appearance of a new life on the planet. They seem to come out of thin air, haphazardly, by chance. But sometimes the opposite happens – it feels as if there are too many coincidences, and if they start to pile up, then events start to feel like fate – or perhaps 'destiny' is a better word …

It was only recently that I found out my connection to Lant Street SE1. Searching the 1891 census for a record of my great-great-grandfather, I saw Alexander Crisp's name and his eight children – seven daughters and one son (large families of girls are a bit of a theme here) – and the address of 68 Lant Street SE1. The name rang a bell.

I googled the area, and there it was: the Gladstone pub, nestled in the corner of Lant Street, right next door to the Crisp family home. I'd been to Lant Street before. Only once, as it's a long way from where I live in West London, but my one night in the Gladstone was one of those turning points where the gods are rolling the dice, the plates collide, and life spins off in a whole new direction – because the

Gladstone pub in Lant Street was the location for my first date with Mr D, a date and a person which were to have a huge significance for me.

As soon as I saw the address in the census, I picked up the phone and asked him why, out of all of the pubs in London, he'd chosen that one as our first proper date.

'I just thought you'd like it,' he said.

And yes, he was right – I did like it. And I liked him too.

The day of that date, I'd had a busy day trying to work and be a mum, dashing around in the chilly March rain, getting wet over and over again, ruining my hair and dampening my clothes. I'd had to feed the girls, and leave instructions with the babysitter, and of course the most difficult thing, wrench myself away from them. By the time I'd done all that I was not in the right zone at all – I was an exhausted, harassed mother, yet somehow I needed to turn myself into someone more chilled, more playful and definitely more foxy.

I was close to giving up, but some words of the immortal Nora Ephron came to mind: 'Be the heroine of your life, not the victim.' What would the heroine do? She would go on this date … I put on Beyoncé's 'Crazy in Love' loud and started to get in the mood.

What to wear? I picked the first thing in my wardrobe that caught my eye. That night it happened to be my short denim skirt and tight black shirt; the same one, in fact, that I was wearing the last time I saw my nanna. And remembering this, I listened to Nanna's voice in my head, and decided to counterbalance any potential tartiness with thick black tights and my patent Doc Marten shoes. After countless drenchings that day my hair was irredeemable so I put it in plaits (my hair now having grown very long, and here an apology to Nanna). Crazy for a forty-two-year-old, but I questioned the mirror and it didn't seem to object.

Despite the protestations of my children, I launched myself into the cold, wet London night, and as I strode off towards the tube with each step I felt myself metamorphosing, getting lighter; by the time I got off the tube at Borough I no longer felt nervous – just the right amount of fizzing anticipation. I felt *good*, my instincts telling me I had set off on an adventure that was about to have a happy ending and, anyway, I really had nothing to lose.

I wandered around the streets getting slightly lost, but not alarmingly so, and I soon came across Lant Street. 'It's like something out of Dickens,' I thought, which was bang on because Dickens *had* lived there: it was where he wrote *Little Dorrit*. In fact, St George the Martyr church around the corner was where Little Dorrit got married, and was also the church my great-great-grandparents had married in. The Gladstone pub is in his novels.

Lant Street was dark and cobbled, the terraced houses different to the ones I was used to in West London – early Victorian as opposed to late Victorian – darker brick, smaller windows and doors. And there, nestled in the corner, was the Gladstone, lights beaming onto the street, a friendly hum getting louder as I approached. And it was then that I must have unknowingly walked right past the house where my great-grandfather Charlie Swain had first been introduced to my great-grandmother, Clara Crisp. As I walked, in fact, I must have been walking in the footsteps of my great-grandfather as he walked towards his future wife.

How often does this happen – that we walk in the footsteps of our ancestors without knowing it, their ghosts tailing us, egging us on? As Charlie walked, over a hundred years earlier, were his (literal) whiskers telling him something was about to happen that was going to change his life?

The street must have looked the same, except murkier, with gaslights instead of the few street lamps. There still is a slightly deserted, desolate air hanging in the ether around the back of Borough station, which used to characterise the streets south of the river. As London grew, the Thames marked a natural barrier between the city proper on the north side, and the badlands of the south where the outlaws, gangsters and prostitutes sought refuge. It was wilder, poorer and edgier. The area was famous for its odours – the smells of jam, beer and butchery were ever-present in the gloomy smog. It was also where London's debtors traditionally fled – Lant Street is on the edge of the Mint slum, where debtors were given compensations. And it was handy for the Marshalsea prison, too.

So, how did my first evening in Lant Street go? As I opened the door of the Gladstone, the warmth and noise of the friendly pub hit me. As it happened, I didn't need to look around to find him: Mr D was sitting right opposite the entrance, a pint in front of him already half-empty (I was late, but not catastrophically).

He spotted me straight away and I had no time to collect myself. He had a quizzical, shy grin on his face, which I couldn't quite read. And when it came to the point of the evening, around 1 a.m., where we'd drunk all we could drink and filled ourselves up with pies and talked and talked, and a decision had to be made one way or the other, he said: 'Well, we could stay here, or we could go to a pub near me, or we could just go back to my place. What do you think we should do?'

My blue eyes looked into his brown ones and I felt like I knew him and I knew I could trust him, and I knew what I wanted to do, but instead I replied, 'What do *you* think we should do?'

And again we looked into each other's eyes and held each other's gaze and he said, 'I think we should go back to my place.'

And my stomach looped the loop and we did some more gazing as I savoured the anticipation of the moment before the point of no return … and then I said, 'Yes, I think we should go back to your place too.'

And he grinned at me again, his shy, boyish grin making a six-year-old out of the forty-something, and I'm sure I must have grinned back.

And the rest, as they say, is history …

*

Charlie landed on his feet in Lant Street too. Disowned by his own family, he was quickly adopted by the Crisps. Respectability was far less of a premium in this family, which earned a living ducking and diving on the edgier side of London society.

My great-great-grandfather, Alexander Crisp, was the Victorian equivalent of a black cab driver: he owned a hansom cab. This light carriage, with two wheels and two horses, was perfectly designed to nip in and out of the London traffic, and they were the fastest way to get anywhere, often going so fast they bumped into pedestrians – usually killing them. Rifling through the criminal records, I was astounded by the number of pedestrian fatalities – several every month in the Borough of Southwark alone.

Alexander set out from Lant Street every day, smartly dressed in bowler hat and greatcoat. He sat perched high on a seat above the carriage, and whizzed backwards and forwards over the great bridges connecting the south and the north side of the Thames: Blackfriars, London, Westminster and the new Tower Bridge. Sometimes he even ventured into the East End.

He communicated with his passengers through a little trap door at the back of his seat. This trap door was very important, not just because it was through this that he received his directions and payment, but it also gave Alexander the opportunity to charm his passengers. Because Alexander wasn't just any old hansom cab driver – he was cabbie to the stars, or the late Victorian equivalent. These included the Prince of Wales, whom he took to see his mistresses, especially Lillie Langtry; but it was the politician and four-times prime minister, William Gladstone, who was his most loyal customer.

This put Alexander in an interesting position. Gladstone was one of the most overtly moral and religious politicians of the Victorian era. Alcohol, or rather the dangers of it, was one of his pet topics. As Gladstone got into Alexander's carriage outside the Houses of Parliament, he would hold forth about its evils: 'You know, Crisp, the devil works through the demon drink. When I brought in the licensing laws I lost the 1874 election. I was borne down in a torrent of gin and beer – literally, as it happens.'

'Indeed, sir. The devil punishes those who are brave enough to take him on,' Alexander replied.

It was a good job Gladstone couldn't see his cab driver's rueful smile – only the week before the landlord of Alexander's regular pub had changed its name to the Gladstone, to honour the fact that one of his regulars was this most distinguished politician's driver. Alexander comforted himself with the thought that what Gladstone didn't know, couldn't hurt him.

He also didn't worry too much about probity with regards to Gladstone, as Alexander regularly took him to Whitechapel to 'rescue' fallen women.

Alexander would go home and, as was his habit, put a gold sovereign on the mantelpiece for his wife. 'There's your housekeeping, Sarah, courtesy of the greatest politician of our time.'

'Very pleased, I'm sure. I hope he appreciates just what you do for him,' she would reply knowingly.

'Don't worry, my dear, we're doing just fine,' and Alexander would pat her comfortable behind rather cheekily until she clouted his head.

But it was true – that shiny coin was the equivalent of a week's wages for most working men. Each week, Alexander's children would stare at it sitting on the mantelpiece and marvel at the company their father was keeping.

Alexander started taking Charlie for a pint in the Gladstone. One night, seated in the corner by the fire, after one too many ales, Alexander put his arm around Charlie's shoulders and gave him a bear hug of a squeeze.

'You're like a son to me, Charlie. I don't know what you did back wherever you come from, but you know I don't care. Sometimes you're more like my son than my own son, if you gets me drift.'

'Thank you, Alexander. It's an honour. And you are like a father to me too.'

'We all makes mistakes and we all needs a chance to start again. I won't judge you – not for your past – only for what I find before me now. And what I find before me is a young man I'm proud of.'

Charlie was quite overcome, not being used to praise from his elders. 'Thank you, sir. Thank you. And I shall not disappoint you, I swear on Mr Gladstone's life himself.'

'Let's leave the venerable gentleman out of it, eh? He's what keeps the roof over our head.'

'Whatever you say.'

At which point Alexander found himself saying something a bit unexpected: 'One thing I want you to promise me, Charlie – if anything ever happens to me, will you look after the girls?'

'But nothing's going happen to you.'

'I don't know. Maybe it's because I see things, you know, out and about. You never know what's around the corner, do you?'

'No, indeed. That's why I think we should drink while we can!'

At which point Alexander laughed, clapped young Charlie on the back and shouted, 'Another round for the philosopher here!'

But it was only a week later that Alexander found himself driving through the streets with a vague sense of unease. This was not unusual. The older he got, the more he saw, and every so often a shiver would run through him, like going over a hill too fast. Alexander worried about his reliance on the patronage of the fickle creatures that made up London's smart set. He cracked his whip and drove faster to shake the shadow clutching on to his greatcoat tails.

Alexander's next customer was known in the Crisp household as 'the Posh Puppy'. As he drew up to a grand front door in a Belgravia square, it swung open and the young lord skipped out. Alexander had been driving him around at the request of his father (with specific orders to keep him out of mischief and report back) since the young fop had gained facial hair.

But the trainee playboy was hard to tame. 'Evening good, Crisp! The Haymarket for now. There's a certain bricky actress I need to know better.'

'Bricky, m'lud?'

'Yes, indeed – she's the jammiest bit of jam.'

'Well, m'lud, you are a right gal sneaker, you are, and that's the truth.'

The Posh Puppy blushed with pride. 'Very well, Crisp, if you say so.'

Alexander, all existential angst banished for now, smiled to himself, gently flicked his horses with his whip and headed in the direction of the West End.

Disraeli once described hansom cabs as the gondolas of London. But while it's possible to crash both a gondola and a hansom cab, the results tend to be more catastrophic in a hansom cab – they go faster, and the landing is harder. Alexander was not a reckless man. He was all too aware that all his capital was tied up in that carriage and the three horses he used to pull it (two working, one resting, in rotation). And there was no insurance. But sometimes you can't allow for other people.

As they started on the downward slope towards the Strand, a cab drew alongside them, the curtain at the door opened and one of the Posh Puppy's so-called friends stuck his head out.

'Evening, my Lord Gigglemug. Off to see that saucebox at the Haymarket?'

'Might be, might not be!'

'It's just I've half a mind to pay a visit myself. Everyone's been doing the bear with her.'

At which point everything started to happen very fast. The Posh Puppy shouted at Alexander to drive faster and lose his 'friend'. Alexander whipped his horses and picked up speed, but this was early evening in the West End and there wasn't much room for manoeuvre. Worse, the friend's cab picked up speed too, and tried to pull alongside them again.

'Mind the grease!' Alexander shouted at the other driver, but in an instant they found themselves head-on with a carriage coming the other way. One of Alexander's horses stumbled on the cobbles and fell forward, and he lost his grip on the reins. The horse then picked itself up and the two dashed straight into the cab on the other side. The next thing Alexander knew, the cobblestones were hurtling towards his face.

When he came to he was lying on the ground, a crowd of faces peering at him.

'Are you all right, mate? Here, have a swig of this.'

Someone passed him a bottle with some strong liquor in it. It burnt Alexander's throat but it gave him a bit of his stuffing back.

'Thank you, thank you.' He heard himself saying, and then he realised he was crying.

'It's all right, mate. You ain't gone down to old nicky yet.' A kindly old woman was stroking his back.

And then a thought hit him: 'The horses?'

And he could tell by the look on her face.

He scrambled up unsteadily, a couple of arms shooting out to help him, and he limped over. What remained of his carriage lay on its side, mangled, with one of the horses underneath; still alive but bleeding, its legs all pointing in contrary ways. It was making whinnying noises and shaking. Luckily someone came over and shot it.

Alexander staggered and retched and sunk down on the pavement again, where several people, including the old woman, put their arms around him. As he sobbed, people around him had to get their hankies out too; his despair was difficult to witness.

In his grief, Alexander had completely forgotten about the Posh Puppy, who had emerged from the upside-down carriage unscathed, except for a few cuts and bruises. He had apparently pressed half a crown into the nearest policeman's hand saying, 'Make sure the driver gets this, eh? Got to dash. It's curtain's up in five,' and skipped off, never to be heard of again, even after Alexander's son, Alexander

Junior, wrote to the Puppy's father explaining that with no horse or carriage, Alexander now had no means to earn a living, and could he contemplate lending Alexander a small amount, which he would pay back with interest? There had been no reply, and no reply either from the other rich patrons that Alexander Junior wrote to.

'You know what the problem is?' Sarah said to her son. 'Your father knows too much.'

It was a dark day for the Crisp family when they finally had to accept that Alexander was never going to work again. The remaining horses had been sold and the money had run out.

After a year of struggling, Alexander was admitted to the Constance Road workhouse, classified as destitute.

My great-great-grandfather's swift fall from grace and health has felt like a cautionary tale. It haunted me for a while, because Alexander's fate was truly miserable.

Workhouses offered a home to the destitute, but not a home into which you would ever wish to go. They were like prisons: huge, forbidding buildings, where your clothes and belongings were taken away and you had to put on a heavy, itchy, sackcloth uniform. The inmates slept in draughty dormitories; the food was monotonous and portions kept small, and they ate in long lines on benches in communal dining halls. There was no privacy or dignity. Discipline was harsh – food would be withdrawn for two days if you were caught swearing. There is a reason why Dickens wrote *Oliver Twist*. How many of us are alarmed at the thought of going into an old people's home? It's a ghost of Christmas future that I imagine does not sit comfortably with many people. But a hundred years ago, workhouses must have been an even more frightening final home for the elderly.

There was also a real stigma attached to going into the workhouse: somehow you had failed in the most fundamental way – that is, to work hard enough to support yourself and your dependents. It was a mark of shame if one of your extended family members ended up in there too: as if, somehow, all of you had failed. None of us know why Alexander's family allowed him to go to the workhouse – he had eight grown-up children, all working. Except seven of them were women, and in those days the low-skilled jobs they were doing would not have brought in a living wage. Clara always talked about her father with great pride and respect. He was the big man of the family. All I can think is that he insisted on going into the workhouse himself. With no means to earn any money anymore, he would have been a drain on their scarce resources. Perhaps he saw this as the only way to save the rest of them from this terrible fate.

Within a year of entering the workhouse, Alexander was dead. The Crisps were told he had a massive seizure one night and by the morning he had gone. Meanwhile, unable to pay the rent on the Lant Street house, the remaining Crisps had done a moonlit flit a couple of miles down the road to cheaper rooms in Peckham. This meant Charlie could no longer show his face at the Gladstone's brewery and so he had decided to temporarily make ends meet by helping Clara and her mother, working as a confectioner.

It's strange the places you can find yourself. Making cakes was not something Charlie had envisaged earning a living from – he would have preferred to have oil on his hands rather than flour, and yet he was haunted by his conversation with Alexander in the Gladstone.

But even with Charlie's help, they were still struggling. Charlie watched as Sarah got up later, sat down more and forgot to put the filling in her pies. Her pastry was suffering and Charlie knew she was having secret talks to move in with her eldest married daughter. Added to this, Louisa, Clara's elder sister, was sweet on a boy and it seemed like only a matter of time before she would move out too.

Although she didn't mention it, Charlie could see that Clara was aware of her looming predicament. And, as a good engineer, when

Charlie saw a problem, he felt duty-bound to fix it – he turned over
different alternatives in his mind until he came up with the solution.

The day after Alexander's funeral, the Crisp family was back at work.
Unlike the first time Charlie had set eyes on Clara, he was now wearing
an apron too, while his own hands and cheeks were covered in flour – it
was playing havoc with his black mourning clothes.

He looked down and saw he was a mess. No matter. He looked over
at Clara's back as she stirred the filling for the pies on a pot hanging
over the fire. She was sniffing again.

Charlie felt a rush of blood to his head and a familiar feeling of heat
in his ginger blood taking control of the wheels of his brain. He picked
off a tiny corner of dough and, like a child, rolled it into a snake, then
curled it round and joined the two ends. He went down on one knee,
sending a mist of flour dust around the room, and tugged Clara's skirt
so she turned around. Then he took her left hand gently in his and
pushed the dough ring onto her third finger, saying, 'Clara, don't cry.
Marry me instead!'

'Oh, Charlie!' She laughed, wiping tears away with the back of
her hand.

'What sort of answer is that?'

'Well, what are ya like?'

'I'm like yer husband. Marry me, Clara! I mean it!'

'No. Stop it, you big ramper.'

'I'm not a ramper. I'm the opposite. Look, what are you going to do?
What am *I* going to do?'

'You'll be all right.'

'Well, maybe. But this way we'll both be all right.'

'Are you serious?'

''Course I am, you. Have you ever known me not to be serious?'

Clara gave him a quizzical look. 'Never ask a question you don't
want to know the answer to, Charlie Swain.'

'All right. This is how serious I am.' And he stood up and grabbed Clara and kissed her straight on the lips.

At which point Louisa walked in. 'What the bleedin' heck?'

'Louisa, I want to introduce you to my future wife.'

Louisa stood stock-still with a mouth wide enough to fit her daddy's old hansom cab in. ''Ave you gone nicky?'

Charlie turned to Clara.

'Have I?' he asked.

Clara looked back defiantly at her big sister.

'No, he hasn't. We're getting married,' she said.

And Charlie picked Clara up and spun her around and then they kissed again with Louisa's mouth still hanging wide open.

Later that night, in the bed they shared together, Louisa tackled Clara.

'You're a dark horse.'

Clara ignored her and pulled the blankets over her head, but Louisa wasn't giving up. 'Never thought Charlie would be your knight in shining armour.'

'Shut up. I ain't got no choice.'

'You could go into service.'

'You jolly well go into service.'

'I'm marrying Harry.'

'Exactly. And I'm marrying Charlie.'

There was not very much Louisa could say to that because she knew Clara was right. Like every woman in 1900, she was a second-class citizen with no political and very few legal rights. She was essentially the property of her parents or, failing them, her siblings, unless or until she married. And, like nearly all working-class women, Clara had no qualifications or professional skills, so the opportunities for her to earn enough money to keep herself were very limited; in fact, going into service was really the only way she could have been housed and fed independently. But there was no history of service in the Crisp family, and it would have felt like a backwards step.

And then there was the huge stigma attached to being a spinster. Clara was twenty years old. It was expected that a woman of her age would marry and have children, and if she didn't, there must be something wrong with her. Charlie had offered Clara a way out, and a future.

Five months after Alexander's death, on 20 October 1900, Charlie found himself hosting his own wedding breakfast (or, in this case, tea) in the small living room of their Peckham lodgings. It was just family, or rather the Crisp family. But they still made a jolly gathering, despite their black mourning clothes and the lack of food and alcoholic refreshment.

As Charlie got up to make his speech, he suddenly felt quite emotional and unusually nervous. 'Ladies and gentlemen, today is the twentieth of October. Of course this is my wedding day, but it is also my twenty-first birthday. It seems strangely fitting that I should be getting both the key to the door and the key to my wife.'

Most of them laughed.

'I want to say thank you, not just to Clara for doing me the honour of becoming my wife – and very beautiful she is too' – at which point a chorus of 'Hear, hear' broke out –'but I also want to thank you all. Because you have become my family, not just by marriage but long before that, from the day I first came to Lant Street. I arrived somewhat in disgrace, and I shan't dwell on that. But I was lucky – I had another chance. And it was all of you, but especially your father, Alexander, may his soul rest in peace' – here there were murmurs of agreement – 'who took me in. You always made me feel welcome and you became my family. Today has just made it official.'

At which there were more murmurs of agreement. Except for Sarah, who just stared at her plate.

'I can never repay this second chance you gave me, but I do hope to prove your trust and love was not misplaced. I am going to look after Clara and be a good husband to her. And on that matter I want to announce that I have a new job. Chief engineer of the Wethered's brewery in Marlow. Clara and I are going to live by the River Thames!'

There was a collective gasp and then loud cheers from various family members. Clara's sisters came over and kissed her. It was indeed a great opportunity for Charlie and Clara. A new start.

When I found the record of Alexander's death in the workhouse I could have shouted, 'Eureka!' Had I stumbled across the Original Sin?

Like Eve biting into that apple in the Garden of Eden, Alexander's downfall put Clara in jeopardy, and a train of repetition was put in motion: his female descendants thereafter condemned to a life of searching the world for a man to rescue them.

I chuckle at my own melodrama, and yet—?

In the dark of the night, with my three daughters tucked up, safely sleeping upstairs, I sit at my desk with my fire on, just the desk lamp illuminating the beautiful, appropriately Victorian room which is my study, and I start to plot a pattern – well, not really a pattern – a spiral that goes down. I see fathers who, through their own actions or an act of fate, are catastrophically absent for their daughters, who are then rescued by a hero: Charlie rescued Clara, and my grandfather rescued Nanna, and then my father rescued my mother, and then when my father left my mother, I suddenly looked at my boyfriend with new eyes.

And it really was like that. I remember it. We were just having fun, but when everything crashed he seemed like a rock. He went up in my estimation. That was the point when I started to take him seriously. And I used to tell people this, like it was a good thing.

But now it doesn't seem such a good thing at all. Now I think I entered into my marriage *needing* rather than wanting him. I didn't know that at the time, and I felt like I loved him – I didn't walk down the aisle under false pretences, just with a sense of unease. The first time he proposed I said no. Straight off, just like that. It was nothing rational; it was my deep intuitive, instinctive response. But I wasn't strong enough to walk away.

I am filled with compassion for Clara. She had no choice. But I did have a choice. I was not a second-class citizen, I did not need a hero. I had the means to be my own hero, the heroine, in fact, of my own story, and I wonder why, at that crucial moment, I didn't have the courage to follow my instinct.

Because marrying a 'hero' is a risky way out of a crisis: in the end, you are still dependent on someone else – in a way, you might just have jumped from the father's frying pan into the marital fire. Even the hero has a shadow, and perhaps the greater the capacity to be heroic, the greater the capacity to be destructive.

Because another thing Clara was clear on was exactly the moment her marriage started to go wrong, and Charlie Swain the hero turned back into Charlie Swain, the black sheep.

# CHAPTER TWO
# The Crippler

*Charlie Junior, Alice and Grace*

I am staring at a photograph on my desk of three children. Its faded sepia tones can't hide the look of mischief in the eldest girl's face as she peers through the bow covering half her head, at someone standing to the right of the camera. Maybe it's her mother, Clara. 'There's trouble,' I think. She makes me smile and I know without needing to read the inscription on the back that this is my great-aunt, Alice, the eldest of the Scarlet Sisters, Charlie Swain and Clara Crisp's children. I can't see the face of their second daughter, Grace. She's looking down at a book on Alice's lap. But I can see her beautiful, shiny, thick ringlets, pinned back from her face by two huge bows. I wish the photo had been in colour so I could see the famous chestnut shade of her hair. Both girls are dressed beautifully, as I would expect from Swains about to have their photo taken: big, fluffy, white dresses with many layers, and an overkill of lace and embroidery. I know what nimble seamstresses the Scarlet Sisters were, and I wonder whether they inherited their talent from Clara. They certainly don't look poor – they've all got beautiful ankle boots with buttons up the side.

But the person I study longest is the boy, Charlie, who was named after his father. With his chin on his fist and his mouth turning down at the edges, Charlie looks a bit cheesed off, as if he'd rather be running around outside. He's got a big moonface like my nanna and what looks like sandy hair. I turn over the photo and read the inscription. It says: 'Charlie, Alice, Grace 1910' and I feel a chill.

It's the date – 1910. Now the photo has taken on a whole new significance.

It was a warm, sunny day at the height of the particularly languid summer of 1910. Three children were trying, and largely failing, to spin their hoops along the towpath by the banks of the River Thames in Marlow. It was not an obvious location choice for chasing hoops – the wider, flatter street outside their house in Station Road would have been better. But nine-year-old Alice Swain had fallen foul of their neighbour and local busybody, Mrs Dossett, and was still smarting from the clipped ear she got for playing 'Knock Down Ginger'. This was a popular pastime for bored Edwardian children and involved knocking on a neighbour's door and then running away. Being Charlie Swain's daughter, Alice could never resist a wager, and when Johnnie Best bet her she couldn't do it to the 'Old Dossett Dragon', she had been put in an impossible position. Nor was she helped by the fact that when Mrs Dossett went to answer the door and found no one there except the hem of a gingham smock poking out from behind her front wall, and then chased the gingham smock down the street, Mrs Dossett's currant buns were left too long in the oven and burned. All of which meant Alice got an extra blow from the belt of her mother when she got home.

So now Alice had taken her little sister, Grace, and the baby of the family, Charlie, down to the banks of the River Thames and out of harm's way – or so she thought.

'Oi, Charlie, look out, yer great lump!'

Charlie was standing right on the edge of the bank, peering over at the perilous eddies which swirled around where the water plunged over the top of the weir. But the sound of the rushing water at Marlow lock swallowed Alice's shouts, so she threw down her hoop in frustration and ran over to where five-year-old Charlie was teetering on the brink, as if mesmerised by the whirlpools. Alice had a vision of him tumbling into the water, ginger head first, his loose shirt all untucked, button-up boots following the knee britches that she'd watched her mother make with such pride.

Charlie was blessed with his elder namesake's ginger hair, freckles and fair skin; his sisters, however, were a little darker: Alice did have strawberry-blonde hair, but her skin was more golden, while Grace, like her mother, Clara, had been blessed with the most extraordinary mop of chestnut ringlets, which today were elaborately tied up in big floppy lilac ribbons. Only a month into the school holidays, her skin had already turned the colour of toast on a grate.

Alice's stomach lurched. Sometimes there were advantages to being the eldest, but today the responsibility was making her feel ill. In a family that only seemed to produce girls, the only son was treated like they'd found the needle in the haystack.

She pulled Charlie back from the edge and pinched his arm. 'You great nincompoop! What are you doing? Do you want to get me thrashed?'

'What?'

'What's wrong with you?'

Charlie gazed back at her with glazed eyes. She pinched him harder, but for once he didn't hit her back.

'Is 'e all right?' Alice's sister, Grace, had trotted over and was peering at him too.

Charlie's eyes were rolling slightly. Despite the hot day, his pale, greyish face was reminding Alice of the trout she'd seen pulled out of the river, and he was sweaty.

'Dunno. It's like he's gone all balmy on the crumpet.'

The sisters looked at each other and giggled. They were both aware of the comical effect of too much drink. Their father, Charlie Swain, had a habit of crashing into their bedroom after a long night in the Two Brewers, collapsing on the bed and proceeding to tell them all, but particularly his son, how much he loved them.

'Maybe he's had too much sun?' Grace was only seven, but she was already practical.

'Yeah. Crikey, I'm hot.' Alice mopped her brow and, in a movement her mother would not have approved of, undid the sash around her waist, dropped it on the ground, picked up the hem of her pretty smock, and vigorously waved it up and down in an attempt to cool down.

'Alice, don't! I can see your drawers!'

'Keep your wig on! No one can see.'

'I can and that's enough.'

'Stop cheeking me, Gracie. Respect your elders.'

At which point Charlie, who'd been forgotten in the frequent, small-scale warfare between the sisters, collapsed to the ground.

Alice squealed. 'Oh, lordy! Charlie!'

Grace snatched up Alice's sash, dipped it into the river, and put it on his brow. But Charlie still didn't wake. His eyes were rolling and he'd gone all limp.

'Quick, go and fetch Mum. 'E's not right,' Grace pleaded with her sister.

Alice set off at a pace to the shop just off Marlow High Street that her mother owned.

A hundred years ago, it was a badge of pride to be able to stay at home and dedicate yourself to being a wife and a mother – a signal to the world that your husband (and, by marrying him, you) had made it.

But Clara was not like most women. She had experienced the shame of a family running out of money and she was quietly determined to do everything possible not to find herself in that position. And so, despite the fact that Charlie was doing well at the brewery, she had taken on extra baking and needlework and saved up enough money to take a lease out on a small shop around the corner from their house. Darn It! was her pride and joy. As well as basic needles and thread, she had filled it with beautiful ribbons, unusual fabrics and knobbly wools. It was a shrewd move. Marlow's high street did not yet have a department store, and most women still made their family's clothes. Clara had a steady stream popping in to make little purchases. As she walked around the town she got a sense of deep satisfaction when she spotted people wearing the distinctive fabric and ribbons from her shop.

Alice flung open the shop door, making the bell ring urgently. 'Mum! Quick! Charlie ain't right. He's lying on the ground and we can't get 'im up.'

'What? What have ya done?'

'I ain't done nothing. Honest. One minute 'e was up, next 'e was down. Please come quick.'

Luckily no one was in the shop, so Clara tore off her apron and hurried out after her daughter.

By the time she reached the river, Grace's ministrations with the sash seemed to be working. Charlie was still lying on the ground, but he was awake.

'Charlie, what's the matter?'

Charlie looked dazedly at Clara and mumbled, 'I wanna go home.'

She felt his forehead. He was hot and clammy.

'Yes, love. Let's get you home.' Clara was short but strong. She picked her son up and carried him the quarter of a mile down the road, Grace and Alice trotting behind in a sombre silence. Every so often she'd bump into a neighbour or a customer: 'Ohhh, little Charlie don't look too good.'

'No. Just getting him home, Mrs Waites,' she would reply, a fixed smile on her face.

'What's the matter with him?'

'Just a bit hot.'

She hoped Charlie was just a bit hot. A visit from the doctor cost the equivalent of a day's wages.

As she turned the corner to Station Road, old Mrs Cadwallander stopped scrubbing her doorstep and looked up. 'All right, Mrs Swain?'

'Yes, he's just got a bit hot.'

'It's that red hair of his. Pity he took after his father, eh?'

Clara ignored this comment and quickly opened their front door and shut it behind her. Her reluctance to join the street gossips and persistence in getting her own shop, not to mention the fact that she came from 'that London', had not endeared her to the female community.

Charlie spent the next couple of days in a made-up bed in the front room. He seemed to have the 'flu. Clara went to the chemist and bought him some Beechams Powders and left him in the care of his squabbling sisters but, back in the shop, she had to work hard to keep a smile on her face for the customers.

It didn't matter how much she told herself Charlie only had the 'flu, Clara had a very strong feeling that she wanted to be back in the house watching over him, as if just by being there the sheer force of motherly love could fight the image of the Grim Reaper that insisted on appearing in her mind.

Over the next few days, Charlie would seem to be on the mend and Clara's world would be all right again, but then he would worsen and that feeling of dread would come back.

'The house is so quiet. It's horrible,' Charlie Senior said when he came back home from the brewery. He kept catching sight of the small wooden train engine he'd made his son for Christmas lying abandoned in the corner of the kitchen. 'It's odd, isn't it – you spend your whole time telling him to shut up, and then when he's not here it's too quiet.'

Clara nodded. Having a son had made a disproportionate impact on the noise level in the house.

'Let me take the poor mite his supper.' Before she knew it, Charlie had taken the tray she was preparing and was heading off to see his son in the front room.

On the third day, Clara managed to persuade Charlie Junior to get off the sofa. He swung his legs round and tried to stand up but as he took a step, he buckled over and collapsed.

'What's the matter? Lost the use of your legs?'

'I don't know, Mum. I can't feel nuffin' in me leg.'

'What do you mean?'

Charlie started to sniffle.

'Come on, Charlie. You've just not used them for a while. Let's 'ave another go.' Clara picked him up and held his arm. She noticed that his baby fat had all disappeared. It was like holding on to a twig. 'Come on now. There we go.'

Charlie took a little step with his left leg.

'If you don't use them, you lose them,' she said and then wished she hadn't. He couldn't move his right leg, and she had to stop him from falling over again. She moved it for him, but it seemed to have no strength.

'Dear Lord, he's like a stuffed toy without any filling,' she thought.

'Mum, I can't.' He sniffed again. 'I feel real dizzy and my head … it's got a hammer in it.'

'All right, let's get you back to bed.'

Clara kissed the top of his sandy head and gently lifted him back onto the sofa. As she tucked him up, he closed his eyes and seemed to sink into an exhausted sleep.

Clara sat beside him and stroked his forehead. The Crisps had never been a religious family but at this point she found herself saying a prayer, and surprised herself with the words that came tumbling out:

'Dear Lord, I know I have been greedy. I have wanted too much. I have been too proud. But please, please save my son. Make him better. Let him walk again.'

Then she started whispering in Charlie's ear: 'Charlie, you need to get well. There is so much for you here – running on the grass, climbing the trees, all your little friends and your sisters ... I know they're a bit bossy, but they love you. Come on, son, for your dad. You make his world go around.' Then she heard her daughters fly in the front door, fresh from playing, all a-clatter. She quickly wiped her tears and hurried out to prepare tea.

Although Clara put on a brave face, Alice and Grace watched anxiously as she dropped the pan; and they rolled their eyes at each other when they tasted her stew. Normally it was delicious; today it was awful. There was a battle going on: Clara's head was telling her it was just 'flu, and her intuition was telling her it wasn't.

Her sense of panic had got so acute that when Clara opened the door to the front room after tea, she half expected to find Charlie dead. What she found was an alive Charlie, but not in a condition that put her mind at ease: he was unconscious, sweaty, and lying rather stiffly on the couch. His soaking hair had lost its ginger sheen and looked almost black, his skin a corpse-like grey. He seemed shrunken. But it was his raspy, irregular breathing that sent Clara shouting: 'Quick, Alice, go and fetch Dr Pincus! Tell him he needs to get here right away.'

Stunned, Alice hesitated at the threshold.

'Just go!' Clara yelled.

Alice had never heard her mother shout like that before. She fled.

Half an hour later, Dr Pincus was in the Swains' front room, examining Charlie Junior closely. He asked Charlie to move his legs or his arms, but by this time the little boy was beyond taking instructions. He couldn't seem to bend his neck and was moaning as if he was in pain. After five minutes examining him, Dr Pincus shook his head and said,

'Mrs Swain, I'm sorry to have to tell you this, but I think we need to get young Charlie to hospital. We need to check that he hasn't contracted something called polio. Have you heard of it?'

Clara suddenly felt very calm, as if Dr Pincus was telling her something she'd known all along. She nodded. The newspapers had been full of news of 'The Crippler' sweeping the country. Only a week before she had overheard a couple of mothers talking about a child who had died of polio a few miles down the road in Bourne End. It had been her first thought when Charlie buckled over.

For hundreds of years children had been catching polio, but only a small number went on to develop the more severe forms that led to either being crippled, or death; but, by 1910, better sanitation and hygiene had left the population vulnerable in a new way to this old disease. Polio is passed through contact with infected faeces. Children used to be exposed to the polio virus when they were babies and still had some immunity inherited from their mothers. Now, because people washed their hands and there was an effective sewage system, there was a generation who had far less immunity. Polio thrived in hot weather, so the balmy summer of 1910 proved the perfect incubation ground for a major outbreak of the disease.

Charlie was taken away in a horse-drawn ambulance to the local hospital. Clara was not allowed to go with him. As she watched the ambulance rattle down the road and turn the corner out of sight, she felt disconnected, unreal. She was determined not to lose control in front of the neighbours, so ignored the seemingly friendly shouts of enquiry from across the street, nodded a greeting, and went indoors. It was when she caught sight of the abandoned bedding that she collapsed on the sofa, holding the blankets that still smelt of Charlie close to her face and crying visceral sobs.

In those days, hospitals were places you rarely came back from.

In the corner, unnoticed, Alice and Grace held each other and watched in horror.

*

For the next two weeks Charlie Junior fought for his life in the little isolation ward in Wycombe cottage hospital. The doctors performed a lumbar puncture on his spine, and found that Charlie did indeed have polio. As the virus attacked his spinal cord and the command centre that controlled his lungs, Charlie struggled to breathe. Alone in a dark ward one night, Charlie hovered on the threshold between life and death … but when the nurse came round in the early morning, she found that the fever had broken – the signal that the virus had run its course in his body. Charlie was going to live.

Now the issue was going to be the damage that it had left behind.

Just over a month later Alice and Grace were skipping in the street outside their house in Station Road. Alice had no choice but to brave the wrath of the Dossett Dragon because her mother had given her strict instructions to keep watch for the ambulance that was bringing her brother back home. It was turning out to be just another strange day in a very strange month for the girls.

At the start, there had been more food at mealtimes and more time to eat it, without the constant distraction of their brother pinching stuff from their plates, kicking them under the table, generally being a pain, and, as far as the girls could see, getting away with murder. They also got more sleep without Charlie wriggling in the bed they shared.

But then the novelty had worn off. They had started fighting with each other over the bed blankets, which ended in the usual kicking, hair pulling and insults (spoken in hisses, because if they woke their mother, she'd come in and clobber them).

'Do you miss him?' Grace asked her sister one night.

'Suppose so. Wobbleface …'

'Yeah.'

Gracie tried to do an impersonation of Charlie's frown and trembling bottom lip when he was just about to cry.

'Ahhh. Bless 'im. He's only little,' Alice said, stroking Grace's head.

After years of practice, she had pretty much perfected her impression of her mother. The girls started to snigger and this turned into uncontrollable laughter and then they had to stuff the blanket in their mouths to keep quiet. Fits of giggles were endemic and infectious, and the Swain sisters were infamous for them.

Once they'd got themselves back under control, Grace piped up, 'Suppose there's going to be lots of wobbleface now.'

'Oh, Grace! Don't, that's horrible! We don't know that.'

'Well, it don't look too clever, does it?'

'Hmm.'

As usual, no one had told them anything, so all they knew was what they'd managed to learn from bits of conversations – and the scene in their backyard the day before, when they'd found their father hard at work, making what looked like a small coffin.

'Crikey, is that for Charlie?' Grace had said, peering out of the window.

'Holy Mother of Jesus!' Alice had crossed herself enthusiastically. She'd come under the influence of a nun who'd started teaching at their local school. The ritual and performance of high church appealed to her sense of drama, although most things to do with church were very much frowned upon in the Swain house.

'I didn't know he was gonna die. Do you have to make your own?'

'No, look, it ain't a coffin, you juggins. It's got metal levers and straps and things. Coffins don't have nuffin' else inside.'

'How do you know?'

'Jamie up the road took me in to see his nan.'

'Ooh, Alice, you didn't tell me.'

'No, and you still ain't heard it, right?'

'What she look like?'

'Like the cat that got the cream.'

'What?'

'Well, you know how miserable she was? Wasn't she lying there with a grin fit for the Cheshire cat 'imself.'

'No! Alice Swain, you're pulling my leg.'

'No, I'm not. Ask Jamie. No, actually, don't ask Jamie. If you do, you'll get one in the eye from me, because it's a secret. Now shut up. What's he doing?'

'Why don't you ask him?'

Alice looked around at her sister in amazement. 'You jolly well go and ask him!'

'You're the eldest.'

'Yeah, and I'm old enough not to be that stupid.'

'If you don't, I'll tell Mum about you kissing Archie Beard.'

At which Alice grabbed her sister's long chestnut ringlets and gave them a good hard yank.

Grace squealed and their dad looked up and shouted, 'What's going on in there?' and the girls ran.

Part of the reason they were free to snoop on their dad was that the girls had been left to their own devices pretty much all month. Most of the time their mother was busy in Darn It!, trying to earn as much money as possible to pay Charlie's hefty hospital bills. When she was home, she was very preoccupied. On the one hand this was good because she didn't notice Grace stealing biscuits from the tin, but on the other it was bad because the slightest noise or light squabbling between the sisters would bring out their mother's wooden spoon. Whenever the sisters thought their mother was in a bad mood they would mimic a couple of horns on their forehead and mouth 'Blue', which was their code for their mother having 'a fit of the blue devils'. They had done this just about every day since Charlie had been taken to hospital.

Meanwhile their dad had become more elusive too. There was a certain day when Alice was sent to get Charlie Senior from the brewery because he was late for lunch. She waited outside the big iron brewery gates sniffing the familiar smell of hops coming from the chimneys and peering, on tiptoe, trying to spot her father's familiar red hair. In the end she plucked up courage to tug the sleeve of one of Charlie Senior's mates. 'Excuse me, Mr Waters, have you seen me dad?'

'Hello, Alice. Yes, I think he's down the pub.'

'Oh, right … thanks.'

Alice was a bit perplexed. She was used to having to retrieve her dad occasionally from the Two Brewers for tea, but she'd never known him go down there before his lunch. Well, maybe on a Sunday, but never during the working week.

She went home and told her mum, and saw the frown on Clara's face deepen, and then her mum took her dad's plate off the table and scraped the food back into the pot with special rigour.

So the Swain sisters didn't know quite what to expect when the clip-clop of the horses' hooves finally heralded the ambulance's arrival.

Charlie was lifted into the house on a stretcher. He looked like their brother except the moonface they used to tease him about had gone. He'd sort of shrunk. Suddenly shy, the girls couldn't say anything and watched as Charlie was carried past, staring back at them, his eyes haunted and hollow.

He was taken into the front room and Clara shut the door firmly behind her so they couldn't see what was going on. The ambulance men left and then, five minutes later, their mother came out and shut the door firmly behind her again and leaned against it, just to make sure. 'Now, listen, girls. You are not to go in there, right? And you are not to talk to no one about Charlie. He's our business and no one else's. If anyone asks, you say he's still in hospital. Got it?'

The girls nodded solemnly at their mother. But like Eve with the apple, how long can children resist the forbidden fruit, especially when they have a brother behind a closed door, who they haven't seen for a month and who shows no sign of ever coming out? Often the girls paused on their way through the hall and listened at the door. Sometimes it was silent but sometimes they could hear Charlie crying. Once or twice they heard him shouting for his mum, which sent Clara scurrying into the room. Meals went in and out. Mainly soup or things cut up small. A chamber pot also came in and out a few times a day.

One day, Alice suddenly realised she had not seen her father go into the room since Charlie had come back. In fact, he had hardly been in the house at all.

The Two Brewers seemed to be his new home.

A few days later, their mother was out and Alice and Grace were listening at the door of the front room again.

'Alice pinched Grace's arm. 'Come on, I'll go in if you come too.'

'Lordy, do you think we should?'

'No. But it's the best chance we're going to get.'

'She's not gonna come back, is she?'

'No, not for ages.'

'Go on then!' Grace pushed her big sister and they both giggled.

'Stop it, Gracie. Now be quiet.'

Alice grabbed her sister's hand, slowly turned the handle with her other hand, and then pushed gingerly at the door. It opened a crack and Alice stuck her head round.

She couldn't help taking a sharp intake of breath, and Charlie looked up, straining to catch sight of her.

'What is it? Let me see,' Grace whispered, tugging on her sister's sleeve.

But all Alice could do was stare. She could now see what the coffin was for. It was on the table in the middle of the room, and Charlie was lying inside, all strapped up, with leather buckles around his waist and chest and a complicated system of metal levers and splints attached to his legs.

Grace pushed Alice into the room, stuck her head round the door, and broke the spell with a loud exclamation of, 'Crikey, Charlie, what's goin' on?'

'Alice? Gracie?'

'Yes, Charlie.'

Grace walked straight in and over to Charlie in his box. Without thinking, she leant over and kissed his forehead. 'Oh, no, Charlie! What are they doing to you?' And she took his hand, which was strapped down, and immediately huge tears started rolling down her cheeks. Alice now found the courage to come over to the other side of the box and take Charlie's other hand and kiss his forehead and before she knew it she was crying too, and then Charlie started crying and suddenly they were all sobbing and talking over the top of each other.

'Charlie, you poor, poor thing!'

'Oh, Charlie, this is awful!'

'Let me get you out. Surely Mum don't want you in here?'

Charlie, buried in a river of the girls' hair and tears as they leant over his face, struggling to speak in between sobs, said: 'I can't get out. It's me legs. I can't walk no more.'

At which a fresh round of wailing broke out from Alice.

Grace stopped stroking his forehead and moved down to the far end of Charlie's box. She gently prodded his legs. They were there, but a bit shrivelled.

'Can you feel this?'

'No. Can't feel nuffin'.'

Grace pulled a face at her sister and started examining the splints and levers that encased both his legs with interest.

'So, what's this for then?'

'It's to keep me legs growing, 'cos they won't do it by themselves no more.'

'Crikey!'

'If they keep growing then surely they're gonna work again?

'Don't fink so.'

'Come on, Charlie. Where's ya spirit? Dad'll get them working again. He can fix anything.'

'Don't think engines are quite the same thing as human beings, Gracie,' Alice said, then stopped as she saw Charlie starting to cry again.

They both started patting him and kissing him.

'I've got to stay in this box for ever. It's like I'm dead.'

'Ohhh, Charlie, no, you won't! You'll get out one day,' the girls chorused together.

Then Alice spoke up: 'Look, Mum says we're not allowed in here. But we'll find a way to come and see you every day, won't we, Grace?'

'Yes, we will. And we'll bring you things.'

'And we'll tell you what's going on.'

'It'll be fun.'

'We won't forget about you.'

Which sent Charlie into howls of tears again and earned Alice a kick from her sister. Alice was about to hit back when she stopped. 'Shhhhhh!' The sound of their mother's footsteps could be heard coming down the pavement, heading swiftly towards the house. The girls ruffled Charlie's hair and got out just in time.

From then on they used to creep in and kiss Charlie like he was their pet. There was always at least an hour between coming home from school and their mother arriving home from Darn It!, which they could spend with him. They saved sweets, picked flowers and drew pictures for him. Sometimes they'd read stories from their Grimm's fairytales book, or Alice's favourite – compose rude rhymes. But what Charlie liked most was to hear the gossip – who had hit who, who was kissing who, who was in trouble with the Dossett Dragon that week.

What the two sisters didn't tell their brother was that the greatest amount of gossip was about themselves. The Swain family had come under the community spotlight because of their amazing disappearing child ...

'Where's Charlie, then?' Johnnie Best would call after Alice. And when she ignored him he'd start saying worse. 'Lost a brother, then?

What, is he a mentalist? A spaz? What you done with him? Put him in the loony bin?'

And they'd all start laughing so that one day she was so sick of it she turned around and said, 'He's dead, so you may as well shut up.'

They had all gone quiet. Alice had fled home and scrabbled in her drawer for the secret rosary the school nun had given her and there, on her knees, her shaking fingers rubbing the beads shiny, she had asked for God's forgiveness for saying such a dreadful thing.

'But, in a way, Lord, he is dead. The old Charlie is dead. But we have a new Charlie, so thank you, Lord.'

And she had cried with her head pressed into the covers of her bed, leaving a wet patch her mother would puzzle and tut over later.

Nor was Alice the only victim of wagging tongues.

Clara was hurt but not surprised when the likes of Mrs Waites and Mrs Cadwallander gave her a wide berth in the street. It was like the parting of the Red Sea – no one wanted to get too close, as if she was infectious. Customers no longer lingered gossiping in the shop. Takings were down. One day she saw Mrs Brookes whisper in the ear of a lady with a young toddler who had just come into the shop, and gesture at Clara, and the lady had scooped up her little boy and hurried out.

That night she couldn't help but blurt out the story to her husband, but all Charlie Senior would say was, 'You can't blame them. It's like the plague, innit?' And then he had grabbed his coat and walked out, off to the Two Brewers, as if he thought she might be infectious too.

Left on her own, Clara stared into the kitchen fire and thought about the stories she'd heard of what rich people did with their crippled children: they were sent to special homes in the countryside hundreds of miles away and effectively hidden. Sometimes the family even pretended they had died. It sounded a bit cruel, but was it? It meant the child was looked after properly and the family could get on without the terrible shame of a child who wasn't right. Well, it wasn't an option for people like them – all they had was the front room.

It was at this point that Clara suddenly had an idea of another option that was open to her, which didn't involve money – well, not at the start anyway. If it felt like her life was unravelling, perhaps she needed something to glue it back together – to make her husband stick to his home as opposed to the side of his beer glass, to bring her family back together, to fix together the broken pieces of her heart …

I look at the dates on the birth certificates of Charlie and Clara's children and I am impressed: three children born exactly two years apart, starting from two years after their wedding day. And then the children stop. It's in sharp contrast to the spacing of Clara's own siblings, and indeed both the Swain and Crisp families generally, who seem most prolific and to have had children straight away for years, without a break, and with no heed of their financial situation.

It seems Clara, and maybe Charlie too, had made a choice to limit their family. In this they were not so much unusual for their time, as slightly ahead. Long before the invention of the birth control pill women had found ways to prevent conception, but because sexual intercourse was such a taboo topic, it's difficult to know exactly how or why people started to practise birth control, although it's thought the working classes generally relied on abstinence, withdrawal or the safe period. What is known is that during the Victorian period the average size of a family was between five and six children, but this had fallen to 2.2 by the 1920s.

From 1902, children had to go to school until they were fourteen, which meant that, financially, there was much less advantage to having a big family. The fall in the death rate also meant that more children were surviving to adulthood. For Clara herself, she had watched her mother struggle with eight children, and in the end their existence had not stopped Alexander ending up in the workhouse. So, once she had had her son, she had decided to stop having children and concentrate on her other requisite for a contented life: a successful business.

But now that Charlie was crippled, Clara's world looked very different. As she went about Marlow, she was alarmed to find she was a bag of new, unpredictable and powerful emotions. She hid it well, but 'unhinged' was the word that kept coming to mind. One day she saw Mrs Best ruffle the dreadful Johnnie's hair and she wanted to go over and spit. Little Billy Waites bumped into her chasing his marbles and it was all she could do not to push him into the road into the path of a cart. It was the *injustice*, the temerity of them being alive and well and healthy when her own precious son was lying in a box all twisted and broken in her front room. She had an even stronger reaction to baby boys. One of their neighbours had just had a baby boy and Clara had to walk past her neighbours admiring him in his perambulator in the street. She had never been particularly fond of babies except her own, but she found herself experiencing such a wave of envy she couldn't even bring herself to go over and have a look.

Clara could only see one solution – she had to have another son. People would stop gossiping about the missing one and look at the new one; Charlie would stop seeking solace in the pub. And, most importantly, the new baby would snatch the reins of her senses back from the malevolent fairy. She was finding it impossible to live with the physical ache in her heart.

So it was, almost a year to the day after Charlie fell ill, that the next baby Swain arrived in the front bedroom. But when the baby slipped into the capable hands of the local lying-in lady, Mrs Coates, and she said, 'A girl, Mrs Swain!' Clara was dumbfounded. Despite the fact that in both the Crisp and Swain families, girls outnumbered boys by a ratio of six to one, everything about her pregnancy had screamed 'Boy!' – her hair was glossy, her skin was dry, her bump was low, and she hadn't felt that sick. Most importantly, when she had lain down on her bed, hung her wedding ring on a piece of thread and dangled it over the bump, the ring had gone round in circles. The ring had never lied before, so why now? Someone was taunting her.

Charlie had walked out in disgust.

It was not the best start for the third Scarlet Sister, baby Dora, but Clara was determined not to be defeated. On her first outing with Dora in the pram, she walked down Marlow High Street and straight into the elegant, gothic All Saints church that sits gracefully by the Thames. Not daring to look around, Clara pushed the pram straight up to a statue of the Virgin Mary in the side chapel. She took a candle, lit it and placed it in front of the Virgin. She didn't kneel or close her eyes. Clara stared straight at Mary and for the first time felt a real connection. 'Yes, you know what I'm talking about, don't you? You lost your only son. I understand that. Help me now. Help me to get him back.'

And she found herself bobbing a small curtsey, taking the handle of the pram and marching out with her head held high.

On 27 May 1913 Clara went into labour again. It was exactly thirteen years to the day since her father, Alexander Crisp, had died in the workhouse. It was a sign – Clara felt almost elated.

The birth progressed quickly and within hours a baby appeared, healthy and screaming. The lying-in lady, Mrs Coates, smiled and exclaimed, 'A girl, Mrs Swain!'

Clara was flabbergasted, but before the despair had time to hit Mrs Coates said, 'Hang on! What have we here? We have another baby coming, Mrs Swain. Twins! Prepare yourself!'

Under normal circumstances Clara would have been horrified, but today of all days, she felt only a huge wave of relief and excitement – her deal with the heavens was about to be fulfilled and God had answered her prayers after all.

Within minutes another baby was entering the world: 'Oh my goodness – another girl, Mrs Swain!'

At which point Clara's usual iron composure broke and she screamed, 'No! That's not the bloody deal!'

Mrs Coates was used to all sorts of interesting things being said, or indeed screamed, during childbirth, so she ignored Clara and proceeded to chatter away about how wonderfully healthy both girls were and how they were fortunate to have each other, that they would always have a friend – and other such 'helpful' comments.

Clara couldn't hear her. She felt utterly exhausted and defeated. For the first time the thought entered her head that she had made a massive tactical error: of course, the Virgin Mary's son had never been replaced. Well, this served her right for being so presumptive.

And that is how my nanna, Bertha Swain, entered the world. Her sister, Katie, was the first twin, and Nanna was the second and indeed last Scarlet Sister to be born.

Clara vowed there and then to give up trying to have a boy.

Later on that morning, after Mrs Coates had left and all was quiet, Clara looked down at the two girls, tightly swaddled, asleep in the box that served as a crib on top of the chest of drawers. Twins, yet completely different: one big, bonny, rosy cheeked; the other tiny, with translucent white skin and bright red hair.

She felt nothing … except guilt for feeling nothing. By an unlucky coincidence a photo was propped up beside them: 'Charlie, Alice, Grace, 1910'. Clara picked it up and stared at it for a few minutes and then flung it across the room with such force that the frame dented the wall. Nothing stirred. Not even the babies.

Clara sat down on the bed, shocked. A shaft of early morning sunlight shone through the window and hit her face. A story she'd been told came to mind: the man who had made himself wings and flew too close to the sun. He fell down in a ball of flames. Yes. Clara went over and picked up the photo of her perfect family and put it away, underneath all the clothing in her bottom drawer. She'd learnt her lesson.

She would never look at it again, and she would never have any photos taken again.

One hundred years later, this photo is finally out and on display. It is sitting on my desk and, as I look at it, I feel its pathos – although the cheek in Alice's eyes amuses me too. I can look at the photo of Clara's family that wasn't to be, and yes, I feel sad, but it doesn't mock me as it did her.

I can't, however, look at my own family that wasn't to be. I have my own photos at the bottom of a drawer: a photo of a precious baby with unfeasibly long legs and a mop of golden curls in a hospital incubator; a photo of a young girl in a big hat and her new husband in his velvet suit with confetti swirling around their heads; a party in a garden with bunting hanging from the tree and a husband playing his guitar with his three daughters dancing around him.

Will it take a hundred years, three generations and a great-granddaughter before the pain has melted enough to allow these photos out again?

# CHAPTER THREE
# Fighting on all Fronts

*Charlie Senior*

Is it normal to feel so at home with a long-lost relative?

I went to see Grace's son, Dennis. I stood on his doorstep and I wasn't nervous at all. From what Mum had told me, I knew we were going to get on: he'd published a book on the spirit world – of course we were going to get on!

Dennis opened his front door and we shook hands, and then we both laughed and hugged and kissed, genuinely happy to meet. It was, inexplicably, instantly emotional.

'Helen, you are the image of your mother. It's wonderful to see you,' Dennis said, taking a long look at me.

I was struck by his eyes. It was those blue Swain eyes again – that true periwinkle blue. And Dennis is quite old – in his eighties, although you wouldn't know it. He looks sixty and is as bright as a shiny pin.

'We must be second cousins,' I said.

'Yes, I think that's what we are. You are your mother. I love it when that happens,' he said, squeezing my arm.

From my unscientific observations, it seems that when people who have been adopted meet their birth family, it's either as if they have never been apart, or they feel like strangers to each other. Why? I wonder if there is something about the way the genetic dice land that means that if you share enough DNA, you smell like family. If that's the case, then I must be quite a Swain. Certainly, sitting in Dennis's front room was like putting on a familiar old slipper, which resulted in lots of laughing, but also an honest sharing of the sad stories. Dennis's walls are covered in pictures of poppies too.

I had come to find out more about Charlie Swain Senior. As the second eldest grandchild, Dennis had precious memories of his grandfather: 'He died young, you know, Helen. Terrible really. Well before his time. Gassed in the First World War. He was underneath a truck, mending it, when a canister rolled underneath and exploded next to him, right next to his face. He was sent home and he was never well again.' And then he exclaimed, 'Oh, I know! I've got something that might interest you.'

Dennis started rifling through a cupboard. 'Here, have a look at these.' He took out a very old British Home Stores bag. 'Dead German soldiers,' he said, as he tipped it up.

Before the chill had time to start running down my spine, ten pocket watches and five cigarette cases had spilled out onto his rug. 'Grandpa gave me these. He got them from the Front during the First World War … he took them off dead German soldiers, apparently.'

'Oh, I see! I wondered what was going to appear there. You gave me quite a turn!'

We giggled.

I picked one up. It was a thing of beauty: heavy, substantial, with intricately carved vine-like leaves trellising around the case. I opened it. 'But, Dennis, this was made in London ...' I picked up another one and opened it. 'London, too!'

Dennis peered over my shoulder. 'Oh, yes. How strange.'

'And this one ... and this ...'

'Well, I don't know how to explain that.'

'Unless it wasn't dead German soldiers, Dennis – it was English ones.'

Dennis and I looked at each other again, and this time there was no laughing.

I decided Charlie's war career needed some more investigation.

On a certain lunchtime at the end of April 1915, Charlie Swain was on his usual bench in the Two Brewers pub. Well, I say he was on his usual bench, but rather than sitting on it, he was actually standing on it and conducting a chorus of 'Colonel Bogey'. He had sworn an oath to volunteer to go to the Front that very afternoon, and he'd commanded the pub to sing along and follow him down the street to enlist. Which, loving Charlie, many of them did.

Charlie had got into this position from the right motives. The First World War was in its eighth month and Ypres was under siege. The British had expected to win the war by Christmas, but the Germans had proved rather intractable and the troops had become embedded in the trenches in Northern France and Belgium. By the end of April 1915 reports had started to come in of a new weapon being unleashed on the Allied troops – chlorine gas. Charlie's friend, Bill, came into the pub with the latest copy of the *Daily Mail* under his arm and proceeded to read from the paper: '"... the cloud of smoke advanced like a yellow wall, overcoming all those who breathed in the poisonous fumes, resulting in a slow lingering death of unspeakable agony."'

Bill stopped and shook his head.

'Blimey, that's bad. Bastards.' Charlie said, drinking fast.

In the sombre silence that followed, a fresh round of drinks was bought and consumed. Then Charlie started the debate: 'You know, if that's their game I think we've got to get the gloves off and start teaching them a lesson.'

'Bunch of bloody macers,' someone shouted from the corner.

'I heard somewhere the boys are having to piss into their hankies and cover their faces to stop the smoke,' Bill said.

'What? That's disgusting!' Charlie grimaced.

'No. I read it too. Something in your piss stops the gas,' Bertie said.

'Blimey, they can't let this go on.'

'Well, it's all right for you to say, Charlie, sitting there with your beer in your hand,' Alfie shouted across the public bar.

A hush came over the room as Charlie got up and slowly walked over to where he was sitting. He looked down at Alfie and simply said, 'Meaning?'

Alfie chose his words carefully. 'Well, you seem to be implying that you don't think the Tommies are doing their best.'

Charlie pulled a face and slowly shook his head, scratching his chin slightly melodramatically. 'No, I'm not saying that. I think the boys are. But I think as a country we're not. I think the Hun needs a proper kick up the backside.'

Alfie grinned. 'And we're not doing that, then?'

'No, because if we gave it our best we'd beat their bleedin' backsides so hard they'd fly from France all the way to China.'

There was laughter, but Bill was looking nervously at Charlie, because there was history there.

Alfie had never forgiven Charlie for being brought from London to be the brewery's chief engineer; in Alfie's opinion, he would have made a more reliable – and sober – job of it himself. And the most lingering insult was when Charlie had rescued the brewery from going up in flames.

The Swains' garden backed onto the brewery premises and, early one evening, while having a cigarette in the back garden, Charlie had noticed smoke coming out of one of the brewery's windows. He promptly threw down his fag, tore off his jacket and vaulted over the back fence, shouting to Alice to alert the men down the street. He had managed to break down a side door, run into the building and, through the smoke, ring the alarm bell. Then he dashed out again and organised a bucket chain as the men came running. The fire was quickly put out with only a minimum amount of damage. In short, Charlie's quick thinking and bravery had saved the brewery and the men's jobs.

Even more galling, the brewery bosses had decided to show their thanks by hosting a dinner in Charlie's honour. It was quite an occasion, with plenty of fine food and excellent wine, to which Charlie helped himself magnificently. At the end, the boss made a speech and presented Charlie with a medal.

Despite the best efforts of his friends, Charlie of course couldn't resist getting unsteadily to his feet and replying. 'It is a very great honour to receive this fine medal, sirs, and I just want to say that the next time the brewery burns down, I will do exactly the same.'

To which the boss retorted, 'There's not going to be a next time, Swain. Now sit down.'

Faced with a pub full of expectant faces, it was no surprise when Alfie asked, 'Alright then, Charlie, since you think you're the bleedin' prime minister, what would you do about it?'

And Charlie started on a road that could only lead to one place: 'Well, I'd get all us lot out of this pub and onto the frontline for a start. I mean, look at us. We're able, fit men.'

There was laughter and shouts along the lines of, 'Bill's only good for the knackers!' but Charlie was on a roll. 'No, I mean it. If you took every man who's sitting in a pub right now and put a gun in his hands and pointed them at the Hun, they'd be back in Berlin tomorrow.'

'Why don't you do it then, Charlie? Put your money where your mouth is,' Alfie said.

'Come on, Alfie. Leave it out. That's enough,' Bill said, putting his hand gently on Charlie's arm.

But Charlie couldn't help himself. 'All right then, Alfie, that's exactly what I'm going to do. I'm going to join up. In fact, I'm going to do it right now.'

A cheer went up around the pub but Bill was a little more sober than everyone else. 'You're doing your bit, Charlie. You're keeping the morale of the nation up. Brewing is a vital part of the war effort.'

'Well, you're never going to hear me say beer's not important, obviously.' Charlie paused and looked around at his audience for effect. 'But I think Alfie's got a point. I'm needed somewhere else more. I think we're all needed and, to prove it, when I've finished this pint I'm going down to the recruitment station. I'm going to lead by example.'

There was a huge roar of a cheer. And Charlie didn't just finish his drink, but a whole host more that were bought for him in a swell of affection and excitement, the end result of which was Charlie standing on the bench and leading the chorus of 'Colonel Bogey', before falling off and stumbling away towards the recruitment station.

When Alice came to collect Charlie to bring him home for his lunch (complete with a wheelbarrow – when Charlie was that late, it invariably meant he was going to have to be wheeled home) she peered through the window to find his usual place on the bench deserted. She had to wheel the barrow home empty.

Clara looked at it and sighed. 'No sign, you say?'

'No, Mum.'

'Did you go inside?'

'No, but I could see it was empty. There was no Bill nor Bertie neither. It was real quiet.'

'That's strange.'

After sixteen years of marriage, Clara was used to Charlie's adventures. If something was happening then she knew her husband was probably right in the middle of it.

Sure enough, as Clara pondered the empty wheelbarrow, Charlie was trying to talk himself into the Army. It was quite difficult. At the age of thirty-six, he was only two years below the cut-off age, and at five foot four and a half inches, he was an inch and a half below the minimum height. However, by this time the government had realised they were going to run out of men unless they relaxed their rules, and Charlie's skills as an engineer meant he could be useful keeping the trucks rolling. So Charlie found himself attached to the Army Service Corps.

Meanwhile, in all the excitement, he had forgotten the real reason why enlisting might not be such a good idea: it was only as he filled out his enlistment form and got to the bit where he had to list the names and ages of his children, and he found himself putting: Charles Swain, 9, and then the girls in age order: Alice, 14; Grace, 12; Dora, 4; Katie, 1; Bertha, 1, that he wondered how on earth he was going to break the news to Clara.

By the time he made it home, Charlie's lunch had been redistributed among the hungry Swain girls, and now Clara was preparing a stew for supper.

'Where have you been?' she asked, stirring the pot vigorously with her heavy iron ladle.

'My dear, prepare yourself. Things are going to change around here.'

'What?'

'I've joined up.'

'Dear God!' Clara sank into one of the kitchen chairs, still holding the dripping ladle.

'You'll be proud of me. I can't stand by and do nothing any more.'

'Nothing?'

'Yes. You know they've started gassing them.'

'I don't bleedin' well care.'

This was not going well. Clara was working class but respectable, and she rarely swore.

'It's my duty.'

'Duty? What duty? What about your duty to your family?'

'Sometimes there is a greater duty.'

And then the normally calm and collected Clara exploded. With a roar she jumped up and flung the ladle at Charlie's head. He ducked and it smashed into the wall with such force it created a small dent, and remnants of Clara's dumplings splattered across the whitewash.

'Get a hold of yourself, Clara! Look, you've made a hole!'

'A hole? How dare you! What about the hole in my heart, you idiot!'

'What? What are you talking about? You've lost it!'

'Lost it? Six children, one in a box, two under two, never a sixpence to rub together! I'll give you lost it, Charlie Swain! How do you expect me to keep this family going while you are doing this "greater duty", then? Come on, tell me how?'

'The same way everyone else is. We're at war and we're going to lose if we don't all make sacrifices and do our bit.'

'Everyone is *not* doing it. Not them that are thirty-six years old and have six children.'

Charlie kept quiet. There wasn't a lot he could say.

'What if you get killed? What do you think is going to happen? You don't mind your children going to the workhouse?'

Charlie knew he was in trouble now. The workhouse was never mentioned in the Swain house, so he said, 'I'm not going to get killed.'

'Oh, yeah, you know that, do you? Who are you then, God?'

'No! The war's going to be over soon.'

'You just said we're going to lose.'

Charlie decided to change tack. 'You know they've started giving white feathers?'

'I don't care! I'd rather have a white feather than a husband in a coffin.'

'Where's your pride, woman?'

'I don't care about pride. I care about our children and feeding them. I wish to God I'd married someone who felt the same way.'

'I'm not listening to this.' Charlie stormed out of the kitchen, slammed the front door, and marched past his playing daughters, back down the road to the Two Brewers, which was just about to open for the evening. Here he would be guaranteed to receive a hero's welcome, and he would drink enough to forget how guilty he felt.

Because it was true – they had six children and they were struggling, and although Charlie couldn't admit it to anyone else, he was starting to feel pretty bad.

Clara sank back down into the kitchen chair and put her head in her hands. She felt like a refugee, trapped in the gilded cage of this peaceful market town on the banks of the Thames. She had a sudden longing for her six big sisters, down river. She knew there was nothing she could do and she was going to have to think of a plan, but first she allowed herself just a little time to be angry.

Yes, she *was* angry with Charlie, but most of all she was angry with herself – she had chosen him, after all. Charlie had been the hero, but since his son had got ill, he seemed to have lost his stuffing. She often found herself gazing at him while he kept her awake at night with his drunken snores, a question running around her head: 'Why can't you be a proper husband and a proper father?'

It hadn't taken long after Charlie Junior had come back from hospital for Clara to notice that Charlie was avoiding going into the front room – before, he had been in there all the time.

One day, as Charlie walked down the hall, she said, 'Why don't you pop in and see Charlie? He's been asking for his dad.'

And he had swung around and hissed, 'Don't you ever, *ever*, say that to me again. I don't want to see him now. Not like that. I want to remember him the way he was.'

'But you talk as if he's dead.'

'Well, he may as well be.'

'Charlie ... don't ...'

But he had slammed one of his hands over her mouth and pointed a finger at her. 'No you don't. Don't you *dare*.' And he'd marched out of the house.

Since then Charlie had taken refuge in beer. And the problem was, that cost money. After Dora was born, the amount Charlie gave Clara from his weekly wage packet began to dwindle, and after the twins were born, sometimes the money didn't appear at all. Worse, he ran up gambling debts. Clara felt the absence of every penny as if it was one of her own toes.

Clara's best and oldest friend had always been the heavy, bound ledger in which she did her accounts. She inhaled its leather, library smell as if she was smelling a flower. It was weighty and solid, giving security like a baby's blanket. She also had a special, black tortoiseshell ink pen she had bought herself with her first week's takings from Darn It!, and she carefully drew her numbers in beautiful, clear loops. But, bit by bit, the ledger no longer felt like a friend and Clara dreaded taking it out, because it had started to whisper, and then shout, something that was devastating – her business was going under. Too much money was going into the housekeeping and bailing out Charlie. She could no longer pay her suppliers; worse, she could no longer pay the rent not only for her shop, but also for their house. Clara knew they were facing her father's fate if she didn't do something quickly.

She shut the shop. As she closed the door on Darn It! for the last time she made a vow which she said over and over to herself: 'One day I will open a shop again, and this time it will never close.'

For ever etched in Clara's mind would be their strange, moonlit procession through Marlow on the night they had to flee their home. As the light faded, a brewery wagon that Charlie had managed to 'borrow' pulled to a halt outside. A few of Charlie's mates arrived with it. They shambled in, touching their caps respectfully at Clara, not really knowing what to say.

Clara only had sympathy from the local menfolk – Charlie was great company, but you wouldn't want to be married to him.

Clara tried to break the ice. 'Thank you for your help, Bertie, Bill.'

They nodded but avoided eye contact and started loading the wagon as quickly and as quietly as possible. Alice and Grace, with little Dora clamped to them, stood at the side of the house and watched wide-eyed.

'Why have they left the gap in the middle?' Grace whispered in her big sister's ear, pointing at a space on the back of the wagon.

'Why do you think, dummy?' Alice rolled her eyes.

Grace shrugged.

Alice pointed at the front room: 'Charlie's box.'

'Really?'

'Shhhhhh …' Alice hissed as their mother shot them a look.

When all their belongings were loaded, Clara came out with the twins, still practically newborn, in the large perambulator. Never light, now weighed down with pots and pans hanging from the sides, it was quite the little tank.

There was one thing missing. The men went inside and carefully carried out Charlie Junior in his box. The little boy was turning his head, looking slightly wildly from side to side. It was the first time he'd been outside since he was carried into the house from the ambulance.

'It's all right, Charlie. We'll get you down in a moment,' his father whispered. Face to face with the reality of his son, Charlie couldn't ignore him any more.

The box was loaded carefully into the middle of the wagon. Charlie got up onto the wagon and leant down so the two Charlies' faces were almost touching. 'It'll be all right, son. We'll be at our new home soon,' he whispered.

Then he stood up and leapt off the wagon and the procession started moving slowly down the back streets of Marlow. It was a cold night.

The wagon went first, followed by the men, and then the three girls, with Clara bringing up the rear, pushing the pram. She didn't dare look around, but kept putting one foot in front of the other. They reached the river. She noticed the tide was taking the water up to London. If she jumped in, maybe it would wrap her in its watery embrace and carry her to Borough, to home, and away from all this.

Charlie dropped behind and walked alongside her. She didn't look at him. Eventually he squeezed her arm. 'I'm sorry, Clara. I'm really sorry.'

She didn't respond. Charlie had another go.

'It'll be all right. Really, it will. It's a nice little cottage. You'll see.'

She carried on walking.

'Aren't you going to say something?'

Clara didn't reply, and then all she could manage was, 'I thought we'd left this behind in Lant Street.' She was thinking about the night they had to make a run for Peckham.

'Well, that was a bit different.'

'Was it?'

Charlie stayed quiet.

Clara stopped pushing the pram and turned to look at him. 'On our wedding day, you said that you would look after me. You promised, in front of my whole family.'

They stared at each other. The procession carried on moving forwards, away from them.

Clara turned away from Charlie and resumed her slow, steady walk.

They gradually made their way through the centre of Marlow and then out the other side. The shops dwindled and ran out, the rows of terraced cottages got smaller. Now there were gaps between dwellings, and fields either side.

'Are we ever going to get there?' Grace asked her sister.

'Are we nearly there yet?' Dora joined in.

'You're not helping, you know,' Alice snapped.

'But the houses have run out.'

There was one more row of houses left, before the lane they were on descended into black countryside. Alice decided if it wasn't one of these, they would be living in a field.

The wagon came to a halt at the second to last cottage.

Clara stopped and looked at it. It was a sweet cottage, safely sandwiched in by the homes either side. A plaque with the brewery arms was in the centre of the row. To Clara it seemed like a proclamation that the Swains were going to be looked after. She would make this work. It wasn't so bad. Charlie was right – it wasn't quite Peckham … yet.

On the morning that Charlie set off to war, as he stood in the kitchen in his huge greatcoat (made to withstand the Russian front) almost brushing the ground (him being so short), Clara didn't feel so confident. It seemed to her that every time she had just got used to her new, reduced circumstances, Charlie threw in a new grenade of horror.

'Aren't you coming to see me off?' he asked.

'No.'

'That's nice.'

'I've got things to do. No one else is going to look after these children, are they?'

As if demonstrating her point, Dora clung to Clara's skirts and started to cry, but with a twin on each arm there was not much she could do. And then Charlie Junior started calling for her from the front room.

'No time to hang about,' she said, brushing past him. 'You'd better go … you're no use here,' she muttered under her breath, but just loud enough for Charlie to hear.

Clara knew it was wrong. She knew she might never see him again but, damn it, she felt so angry she could quite easily do some serious damage to him herself.

Charlie walked out, his heavy boots clumping, and started off down the hill towards the main street where the new recruits were gathering. He hadn't got far when he caught sight of Alice and Grace.

'Dad! Are you going?' they called out.

'Yes. Yes, I am.'

The two girls ran over and hugged him tight, burying their heads in his body. He kissed their heads and when the familiar smell of his girls' warm red hair, and home, hit him, his tears started to fall.

'Oh, Dad, we're going to miss you,' Grace said.

'Look after your mum,' Charlie replied and then, lifting up Alice's chin to look in her eyes, he said, 'And you, little miss – you be good … if that's possible.'

She nodded and gave one of her mischievous smiles. 'I'm going to pray for you every day, Dad.'

Charlie laughed. His eldest daughter's enduring love for the Almighty never ceased to amuse him. 'You do that, my very own fairy cake, and remember also to say a prayer for your mother.'

'And for little Charlie, too?'

Every time it pierced him like a knife.

'Yes, princess. And Charlie, too.'

And with that he had to go. He wriggled out of their embraces and started off again, down the hill.

'Don't die, Dad,' they called after him.

He started to walk faster, but the girls followed him. That familiar itch to have a drink made his fists clench. But soon Charlie saw the crowd in the distance – soldiers, men, women and children, flags waving. He could hear a band playing, and people singing.

Charlie rushed forwards and lost himself in the middle of it. Before he knew it, his friends were calling out to him and slapping him on the back. He started to join in the singing – 'Pack up your Troubles in Your Old Kit-Bag' – and then they were marching off to the station. People lining the streets were cheering, and his grief was overtaken by excitement. Yes, he was not proud of how he'd been since Charlie Junior had got ill. He had a strong feeling he'd failed a test. But this war had given him a chance to redeem himself: he was going to come back a hero.

Just as he got on the train he turned and looked back, and he thought he caught sight of two little red heads jumping up and waving.

Meanwhile, Clara had rushed to answer Charlie Junior's call. She firmly detached Dora from her skirt and closed the door in her face.

'Mum?'

'Yes, son?'

She bent over and kissed him. He reached up and touched the side of her face, tracing the line of the tears still on her cheeks, both of them ignoring Dora's mewling on the other side of the door.

Charlie was anxious. 'What's the matter?'

Clara lay face down, on the sofa, exhausted. Ever since Charlie Senior had announced he was going to war, she had felt as if she had lost her foundations.

Charlie may have been unreliable, but he did exist. Clara moved through the world as a capable, confident woman. But in her head she was still the baby of a family of eight, with indomitable parents. When they had faltered, Charlie had stepped in.

She had never lived on her own before – it was her Achilles' heel.

Charlie tried again. 'Mum?'

With a sigh she said, 'Your father's gone off to fight.'

'Who?'

'The Germans, of course!'

'Oh, yes, of course … Wow!'

Dora's mewling suddenly stopped, which meant the sound of Clara sniffing became more obvious.

Charlie Junior was a sweet boy who, in the absence of any other calls on his intelligence, had developed a fine attunement to his mother's emotional needs. 'I mean, oh no!'

The sniffing got louder.

'I suppose he's going to be all right, isn't he, Mum?'

'Yes. The devil looks after his own. It's us that I'm thinking about.'

'Oh, Mum!' And then, all of a sudden, Charlie started to hiccup and sniffle.

Clara's tears were trumped by her boy's distress, and she jumped up from the sofa and took his hand. 'Oh, Charlie, what is it?'

'Well, I should be the man of the house now, shouldn't I? If I wasn't like this, I could look after you all.'

Clara stroked Charlie's forehead. 'Oh, Charlie – box or no box, you're still a little boy. And such a brave one at that. No, I'm just being silly … we'll manage! Let's face it, your dad was never here much anyway, and when he was, well, he wasn't much good, was he? I mean, who does all the work around here anyway?'

'You, Mum!'

'Exactly!'

And just as she reassured Charlie, Clara found she was starting to reassure herself. After all, wasn't it true?

Charlie piped up: 'And Alice and Grace help too.'

'Yes, we've got Alice and Grace too.' And it was at this point that a plan started to develop in Clara's mind. 'We shall still have Dad's soldier's wages. They won't be as much, but maybe there's something we can do about that. Don't worry, Charlie, I have an idea.'

And with that she kissed him on his head and bustled out, scooping up a shaky Dora on her way.

Later that evening, she packed the little girls off to bed and beckoned Alice and Grace to sit down at the kitchen table. In front of her she had a piece of paper and a pencil.

'I've been thinking. It's going to be hard to keep everyone fed and the rent paid with your dad away.'

A look of horror came over the girls' faces. Alice and Grace had been holding whispered meetings in their bed at night. They had had an idea that their dad joining up was going to cause a financial crisis of some description, and had seen an obvious, if ghastly, solution: in those days, when things got tight, it was common to ship spare children off to the extended family.

Alice burst out: 'Don't send us to stay with Aunt Louisa! I promise I'll be good. I'll help. Grace and I won't eat so much.'

'Eh?'

Grace waded in: 'They're ever so common, Mum!'

'Who?'

'The aunts.'

'Grace Swain! How dare you? You show some respect. They're my sisters and your aunts and if they're common, then we're common too.'

'No! We're not like them!'

'How do you work that one out then?'

'Well, we wear knickers for a start.'

'Grace!'

Alice nudged her sister – they were for it now. But Grace wouldn't be deterred. An indelible image had been placed in the girls' minds during a visit to their Crisp aunts, Katie and Louisa, in London. In keeping with the Victorian tradition they had been born into, the older Crisp sisters were still wearing bloomers. These consisted of two separate leggings reaching from the knee and tied at the waist, but open from the thigh up. In the old days ventilation was considered hygienic and also necessary because of voluminous skirts – impossible to use a chamber pot otherwise. But Grace was more interested in propriety than history. In her world, she had only known ladies wear the closed briefs which had become popular since the turn of the century, when skirts became shorter and less full, and the closet had taken over from the 'po'.

'Mum, they took us to the park and they just crouched down and peed right there in public. It was so embarrassing!'

'Grace, if you're not careful I'm going to get the soap and wash those words right out of your mouth.'

Now Grace looked scared. It wouldn't be the first time she'd tasted her mother's carbolic.

Alice felt it was time to rescue her. She jumped in quickly: 'Yes, Mum. Sorry, Mum. Grace doesn't mean it, not like that. We just don't want to leave you.'

Clara looked at Alice's distraught face and felt a sudden wave of affection for her eldest daughter.

'Yes, well, I don't want you to leave either. Don't worry, I'm not going to send you away … ever. If you'd just give me a chance to tell you – I don't need to send you away, but I do need your help. Both of you.'

Darn It! had taught Clara that paying suppliers made her vulnerable. She would do better if she could sell things that she made herself, and if she didn't have to pay rent on a shop, either. So she explained her plan. 'Girls, I'm going to declare a war on poverty. I'm the Commander-in-Chief. Alice, you're my general, and Grace, you're the brigadier. We might promote Dora to colonel but she'll have to shape up a bit. The twins are going to be privates for a while, but in time, who knows? We're going to draw up a plan of action.'

Clara picked up her pencil and tapped the paper in front of her.

'From now on, we are going to start selling things – anything we can think of. Things we can grow, things we can make. Now, any ideas what we might sell?'

The girls looked at each other, and then Grace turned to her mother and said, 'One of the twins?'

At which point Alice dissolved into giggles and Grace joined in and then in a flash they were clutching their stomachs, howling.

Clara tapped her pencil and then banged the table and shouted, 'For goodness' sake, girls, this is serious! Shut up!'

But it was no good – she'd lost them.

Alice gasped: 'Which one?'

And then both hiccupped simultaneously: 'Bertha.'

Which set them laughing even harder.

Clara was caught between the desire to clobber them over the head and the rising hysteria in her stomach. They'd inherited their giggling from Clara and her Crisp sisters. The more their father, Alexander, had shouted at them, the more hysterical they'd got until he'd either literally knock their heads together or, if it was really bad, go and fetch his horse whip and start flinging it around threateningly. That always worked.

Giggling fits *en masse* – an occupational hazard of being in a family packed with female Swains and their descendants – I know this only too well.

A certain performance of Stainer's *The Crucifixion* in the Chapel of St John's College, Cambridge, where I was a student and singing in the choir, took place, and I had invited my family. As I walked out and took my place in the front and found myself directly opposite my nanna, Bertha, and my mum, in the front row of the audience, my heart sank. I knew exactly what was going to happen.

Sure enough, they caught my eye and they started to giggle. I saw my mum's face crinkle in contortions; Nanna just grabbed Mum's hand and used the other one to cover her face in her handkerchief. I put my face down and dared not lift it for the whole production, my music shaking in my hands as I tried desperately not to catch their hysteria. It was totally inappropriate in this august setting, for this sombre work, and of course that was the whole point. I also knew part of the problem was that Nanna never expected to find herself in such an exalted place, nor my mum. Nor me, actually.

In the end, desperation caused Clara to stand up, pick her iron ladle out of the stew pot, and fling it at the wall, leaving a dent just as she had done two weeks previously when Charlie had announced his intention to go to war. Not a subtle tactic, but an effective one.

'This is serious. Do you want to starve?'

'No, Mum. Sorry, Mum,' they said, wiping the tears from their faces.

'Good.' Clara sat back down, picked up her pencil and started again. 'So, what can we sell?'

Grace made a second attempt: 'How about vegetables from the allotment?'

'That's more like it.'

One of the advantages of their move was that they found themselves next to some allotments. Clara had wasted no time in renting a little plot and had been growing peas, potatoes, cabbages, carrots and onions. They also had a couple of plum trees and a small apple tree that gave them very tasty fruit in the autumn. Clara had been using the extra produce to barter for things with her neighbours, but if she put her mind to it she could add some more produce and make some money. Selling things made in the kitchen was a common way to make an extra bit of pocket money for the working-class woman; indeed, if Charlie Junior had not been in his box, Clara could have opened up her front room as a shop. But the kitchen would have to do for now.

'Alice? Any ideas?'

'Well, Mum, I could go and get eggs and milk from Handy Cross.'

'Good girl,' Clara said, scribbling on her paper. Handy Cross Farm was a five-mile round trip, but the farmer was friendly and Alice was a fast walker. 'I can make pies, bread and cakes,' she added.

'We could all make jam and pickles.' Alice wriggled with enthusiasm.

'We'll have a real shop again,' Clara said, clapping her hands. 'We'll have a shop again, but we're going to have to work hard. You're all going to have to help me around the house. You especially, Alice. It's going to mean missing some school this year. Of course, next year you can help me all the time and perhaps we can do more, maybe even rent a place properly.'

With the girls' help, Clara drew up a list of responsibilities, and then she drew up their plan of action.

Just a week later, Alice was putting notes through the doors of the neighbourhood alerting them to the fact that Swain's Kitchen was now open for business.

Clara's war on poverty was successful from the start. Most women shopped every morning for the food that they would be needing that day. Clara's little kitchen enterprise was very convenient, as many of the local women had taken the jobs that had become available as the men went off to the war, and now they didn't have time to go to the shops or cook themselves. Clara's pies, bread and cakes were a special hit.

Meanwhile, thirteen-year-old Alice was happy to be skipping some of her lessons. By 1916, education was compulsory up until the age of fourteen, but many children still missed school to help out at home or earn some extra pennies. Alice was bright, but not a fan of school. The headmistress of the secondary school was a rather formidable Miss Packer, who made the children line up in the playground at the start of the day to be inspected. They all had to stretch out their hands to check they were clean, and nails scrubbed, shoes shiny, hair neat, with a fresh handkerchief in their pockets. Many of the children rarely had a bath, but as long as they looked clean, that was all that mattered.

Alice had usually been up for several hours helping her mum before she even got to school, and her hands would often be dirty. Miss Packer would immediately call her out and rap her palms with a ruler. Grace had an even more difficult time, due to the particularly unruly nature of her chestnut curls: by the time she had run to school, her head could resemble a medium-sized furry animal. Miss Packer would beckon her out of the line, grab her hair and swing her around by it. Alice couldn't bear to watch.

Added to this, much of what Alice was being taught she knew already. She could read and write and she was good at sums. There were extra lessons in sewing, cooking and general housekeeping: how to do the laundry, how to polish the brass and bath a baby. But Alice had been doing all of these under her mother's firm eye since before she could remember. Which meant she was only too happy to miss school and set up shop instead.

Of course there were some teething troubles. Five-year-old Dora had been given the responsibility for collecting the fruit and vegetables from the allotment. Dora was a whimsical, creative child. She loved stories, she also loved making up stories; so vivid was Dora's imagination that sometimes the line between fact and fiction could become blurred. This posed a serious threat to Swain's Kitchen early on, when Dora was sent to collect some peas from the allotment but came home empty-handed. She flew in through the back door screaming: 'Mum, Mum, there's planes!'

'What?'

'I was bending down and I heard this growling sound … grrrrrrr … and I was looking up and there was this big German babykiller, right above my head!'

'Well, I didn't hear anything,' Clara said, wiping her floury hands on her apron and striding outside. She searched the sky but, as she suspected, there was nothing except some starlings and a few puffy clouds. She walked back into the kitchen but Dora had disappeared.

A little voice came out from under the table. 'It was going to land on my head. There was a soldier grinning right at me, holding a gun.'

Clara bent down and looked underneath the table at her daughter. Her little shoulders were shaking.

'Don't be daft, Dora. There's nothing there. You was just imagining it, you little juggins.'

'No, Mum. I ain't coming out and I ain't going down the allotment again.'

Clara realised she had to nip this in the bud. 'The growling was next door's dog, lovey. Those airships only get as far as the coast. Come on, let's go back there and I'll show you.'

'Nope, I'm not getting out, no way. I tells you there was a plane.'

Dora started to howl, and Clara inwardly cursed Alice for bringing back an old newspaper telling horror stories of the 'babykiller' German Zeppelins that were raiding the east coast of Britain.

From then on, trying to get Dora to go to the allotment was a daily torment. It was a combination of cajoling, bribing and sometimes, when Clara ran out of patience, sheer brute force.

As Clara watched her tiny legs tripping down the garden path, she couldn't help but feel guilty about Dora's emotional fragility – the pregnancy full of grief as the extent and permanency of Charlie Junior's disability had sunk in. Clara had an image of a toxic weight of sorrow sinking through her body and down the umbilical chord to infect the fledgling Dora that nestled in her stomach. Alice and Grace whispered about their mother's tolerance of her highly strung third daughter, but Clara felt that Dora hadn't really had a chance.

Of course she could have just let Dora off the vegetable patch, but really there was no one else to do it – Alice was the only one who could manage the long walk to Handy Cross, while Grace was in charge of supervising the twins.

It wasn't that the three-year-old twins were particularly difficult: Bertha was very biddable and Katie keen to be one of the big girls and help her mother with household chores – like cleaning the front step. Small, round and rosy-faced Katie would insist on commanding the brush and scrubbed away with the most tremendous vigour. Meanwhile the pale, delicate Bertha was more than happy to sit beside her, looking beatific with her bright red hair shining like the Virgin Queen. It was a happy, functioning dynamic. Katie and Bertha were the most unlikely twins – they were opposites, but somehow together they made a whole – the yin and yang of Marlow.

But Katie was a bit of a busybody. Sometimes she would take matters into her own hands. And where Katie went, Bertha, the willing foot soldier, followed. It meant that they could find themselves in rather compromising situations. Like the time Katie decided that they should help their mum by sneaking through the hedge into old Mr Smith's garden and picking up his fallen apples. They were brought back by an irate Mr Smith, and received a sound hiding – Clara had had a difficult time persuading Mr Smith that she hadn't put them up to it for her new kitchen enterprise. Most embarrassing. Another time, Katie took Bertha to pick up spare coals from the railway line. Luckily they were spotted by a man walking his dog before the 5.15 express from London came steaming through. And then there was the time Katie invited their neighbour, Mrs Talbot, to tea. She called at the door and said, 'Mum would like to have you over.' Mrs Talbot duly turned up later that day on the doorstep in her best dress, much to Clara's mystification and then complete mortification. There was another spectacular hiding after that one.

So while Clara was stuck with the daily ordeal of trying to get Dora to the vegetable patch, the actual selling itself gave her little frissons of joy, particularly those things that she had made herself.

Clara had seen a picture of an alchemist in a book that one of Alexander's customers had left behind in his hansom cab. It had been an old man with a long white beard and wizard's robes gazing, puzzled, at a big glass vial. Intrigued, she had asked her father what he was doing.

'He's turning lead into gold, my pippin.'

'How?'

'Oh, you can't do it really, although there's many that's tried. There's a legend that there's a secret recipe. Imagine if you found the recipe, you'd be rich for ever. You could buy anything you wanted – the whole world!'

Sometimes, when Clara was at her kitchen table mixing all her different ingredients and transforming them into something that was much more than the sum of its parts – something that would indeed bring them gold – she felt like that alchemist (minus robes and beard). Yes, cake into gold. It was something she'd been doing since she was a toddler in Lant Street, hanging round her mother's skirts.

But that was in the broad light of day. In the witching hours of the night, Clara had a recurring dream that she was with Charlie Junior and he was turning into a skeleton, crying for food, and she couldn't feed him and was helpless. They could be in different places: in a boat on the river, in a railway carriage, often in the back of her father's hansom cab; but no matter what the setting, the dream always ended the same – she was left holding a skeleton. Clara would wake up suddenly, her heart thumping, and sit up in bed feeling alone. She would tiptoe downstairs and steal into the front room to gaze at her son lying in his box – not a skeleton, not dead, only sleeping. And in the morning, the witching hour broken by the rising of the sun, she would wake and shake off the dream and come downstairs to her kitchen enterprise, her optimism restored.

# CHAPTER FOUR
# Playing the Hand

I picked up the telephone to speak to Great-Auntie Dora's daughter, Angela. I was slightly nervous – we'd never met or even spoken before. But I was only slightly nervous because by this time I'd encountered enough of my Swain cousins to guess the sort of reception I was going to get. And I wasn't wrong.

'Oh, hello, dear. It's so nice to speak to you. You're Dianne's daughter?'

'Yes.'

'Oh, lovely! How is she? How are you? When are you going to come and see me? It's SO lovely to speak to you.'

Angela was excited, and I could feel the hug down the telephone. Once again I was struck by how my mum and her cousins were so fond of each other. They had spent a lot of time together as children but as adults distance had kept them apart. We started to natter and we couldn't stop. I was telling her things she didn't know, and she was telling me things I didn't know, and there were lots of exclamation marks flying around:

'Ooooooooh, you don't say!'

'Noooooooo! Never!'

'Ooooooooh, he *was* bad!' (I'll let you guess who we were talking about.)

I recognised the love of melodrama in Angela, but I also felt a bond of sadness: 'That poor, poor little boy – and the only son too,' she said.

It wasn't the first time I'd heard it; in fact, every Swain relation had said it and I was beginning to think that it probably wasn't a coincidence, but a phrase that the cousins had inherited from their mothers, who had probably inherited it from Clara or Charlie, or both, or indeed any of the adults around them as they were growing up. There was also a shared sense of humour. We chuckled over watches from 'dead German soldiers' that were made in London. 'What was he like?' she said.

Indeed.

Light and shade, sunshine and showers. Our conversation felt a bit like a spring day in April.

The time whizzed by. I glanced at the clock and realised I was already late picking up my girls from school. Angela let me hang up on condition that I promised to come and visit her soon, but not before she told me two things that would linger in my mind: 'Well, of course Charlie kept cutting the line.'

'What?'

'Yes. He can't have been a very nice man, can he?'

'But what do you mean, "cutting the line"?'

'Well, the washing line, of course.'

'What?'

'Dreadful thing to do. After she'd worked so hard hand-washing all those clothes for all those girls – five girls, imagine! – and there they are, hanging out all clean on the line, and him coming home from the pub and cutting it, so they landed in the dirt.'

'What a strange thing to do. Why would he do that?'

'Yes. Wicked.'

Angela didn't have an answer for the washing-line sabotage, but she went on to say something even more disturbing.

'Have you heard how they all got sent in to see the little boy after he died?'

'No.'

'I don't think my mother ever got over it. She suffered from nerves all her life.'

'Oh, dear!'

'Yes, well, I'm not surprised really. The sisters were sent in and he was lying there, dead, and there was still a tear wet on his cheek.'

I didn't know what to say. It seemed strange for the girls to be sent in to see their brother after being kept away, except attitudes towards death and mourning were different in those days. Laying out the dead and paying your respects were an important part of the mourning ritual. But then the whole story of Charlie Junior is really difficult.

Early in 1916, Clara's nightly sense of doom started to intrude into daylight hours.

Charlie Junior was often very uncomfortable. With limbs strapped taut in metal and leather harnesses in a vain attempt to stretch them into a normal shape, the aches and pains of living in a box were sometimes unbearable. Alice's nun had told her about the torture of the sixteenth-century Jesuit priest, Edmund Campion, who had been put on the rack until his bones popped. Sometimes she gazed at her little brother and wondered whether his bones were going to pop too. She used to smuggle in her mother's bottle of 'Mrs Winslow's Soothing Syrup' and give him a swig. It was pretty effective, despite the fact that it was primarily designed for teething babies. This may have had something to do with the large amount of morphine in the syrup. What Alice didn't realise was that her mum was also giving Charlie doses too. He could be remarkably giggly and at times show signs of an imagination to rival Dora's. But then even Mrs Winslow stopped working as Charlie started moaning about a new pain between his shoulder blades, which was odd because that was one bit of his body that had been free and straight. Then he stopped eating.

As Charlie shook his head and turned away from the soup she'd made him, Clara remembered the skeleton she nursed in her dreams. And that night she had that dream again, except this time it was Charlie Senior and Charlie Junior who were lying in his box together.

When Clara woke up, she shook herself and crept downstairs. Instead of sleeping peacefully, Charlie was awake and tossing fitfully.

'Oh, Charlie. Are you all right?'

'No, Mum – I'm burning.'

She moved swiftly over to him and felt him. He had such a fever he was soaking in sweat. 'My poor boy! It's all right. Let me cool you down and dry you off.' Clara rushed off to find towels to dry him and cloths to put cool water on his forehead.

When she got back, Charlie looked at his mum. 'I don't know what's wrong with me. I don't feel right. My back – it hurts so much.'

'Show me where, darling.'

It was difficult, but he managed to point between his shoulder blades: 'Here.'

Clara put her hand up the back of his shirt, and then she felt it – a sort of lump. It wasn't big, but a kind of mass of hardness filling the usual space between the shoulder blades.

Clara sat back, fighting an urge to be sick.

'What's the matter, Mum?'

'Nothing, son, I'm just thinking.'

She squeezed his hand and walked out of the room into the kitchen, where she leant over the sink for a few minutes. In the end she collected herself, splashed cold water over her face, took a deep breath and went back in.

'It's all right, Charlie. You're all right. There's nothing there, but I'm going to get the doctor. He hasn't come to see you for ages, has he? He might have some ideas how we can make you more comfortable. Time we had a visit. Now, let's see if we can get you to sleep.'

Clara stroked Charlie's hand and forehead and sang quietly to him, and her exhausted boy was soon asleep. But Clara didn't go back to bed. She sat next to him, staring as the moonlight came in through the uncovered window and gave Charlie's fragile face an ethereal air.

The next day, Charlie Junior had a visit from Dr Pincus. The girls watched as the old gentleman with his ominous, black leather bag went into the front room.

Grace turned to her big sister. 'What do you reckon 'bout Wobbleface, then?'

'Not sure,' Alice replied.

'He's gonna die.' Dora was hanging on to Alice's arm, her eyes as round as the buttons on her shirt.

'Shut up, Dora.' Grace gave her a cuff around the head. 'Wasn't asking you.'

'Ow! I'm gonna tell Mum on you.'

'Yeah, and she'd hit you even harder. Saying that about your brother! What are you like?'

'I'm not saying nothing that ain't true. He's gonna die.'

'And how'd you work that one out?'

'I dreamt it.'

The big girls groaned and rolled their eyes. Sharing a bed with a prophetess wasn't a recipe for a good night's sleep; but still, this time Dora's divination made a shiver run down Alice's spine.

'Dora, do us a favour – keep your mouth shut. I don't want to know, and Mum certainly doesn't. She's got enough on her plate without you coming over all Cassandra – got it?'

'Yeah, that goes for me too. I don't want to know about any of your dreams – not about Wobbleface, nor no one,' Grace couldn't resist adding.

Dora looked up at her big sisters, saw that any further protest would just end up with her being hit, so she ran up the stairs and hid in the wardrobe.

When Dr Pincus emerged from the room twenty minutes later, he retired with Clara to the kitchen and the door was closed firmly behind them.

Later on, the girls found their mother busy scrubbing the kitchen floor. Alice looked at her face for a sign, but she just carried on scrubbing hard. That in itself didn't signify anything – Clara always operated on a 'need to know' basis.

In the end, it was Grace who couldn't resist. 'What did the doctor say, Mum?'

'Nothing, nose ointment. Now get those twins ready for their tea.' And that was that.

But as the days went on, Alice wasn't convinced. She noticed her mother seemed to have lost the war spirit and when she looked into her eyes, there was a strange, two-dimensional deadness there. Clara's hair, normally mercilessly pinned back and controlled, had, all of a sudden, got a life of its own: the chestnut brown waves had escaped and were getting into her eyes. Alice was a bit embarrassed in front of the customers. She looked a bit wild. Added to this, the pastry suffered – crisp pastry always suffered when the maker was upset.

Some nights Alice heard Charlie crying out and her mother creep down to him. At mealtimes, Alice noticed that her mother came back from the front room with the bowls of soup still full, bread left on the plate. Then Clara started to pop out on 'errands', leaving Alice in charge of Swain's Kitchen, which Alice loved, but she was puzzled; until one day, Grace came back from taking the twins for a walk and said she had spotted their mother.

'She was just sitting on a bench, looking at the river.'

'How strange. On her own?'

'Yes, like she had all the time in the world.'

'Well, that's not like her.'

'Yeah. Not when there's customers to be served.' They grinned at each other.

'So what did she say?'

'She didn't see us. I don't know why, I felt like she was doing something secret. Like she wouldn't want to see us. Alice, what's going on?'

'I don't know but I feel all a jumble, like the wind's about to change.'

That afternoon when her mother went 'out' again, Alice slipped in to see Charlie with the bottle of Mrs Winslow's syrup in the pocket of her pinafore.

He looked awful – unbearably thin, sweating, and he seemed to be developing a lump on his back like the Hunchback of Notre Dame. It was all happening so quickly.

'Ohhhh, Alice, it hurts so much!'

'The back again?'

'Yes.'

'Poor Charlie. Here, have a bit of this.'

She held up Mrs Winslow and he took a swig. She stroked his head.

There was a little boy down the road, whom they unanimously agreed was spoilt on account of him being an only child. He had been given a guinea pig as a pet. With the war on and food scarce, having a guinea pig was seen as a bit of an indulgence, if not a scandal. Clara muttered that if it wasn't careful, it would end up in the pot. However, the girls, curious, invited themselves to go and look at Sidney. Dora wouldn't go near him, but the twins squealed delightedly and poked him until one of them got bitten and they had to leave under a bit of a cloud.

Stroking Charlie in his box now put Alice in mind of Sidney the guinea pig in his cage: not for the first time, she wondered what the difference was, except Sidney seemed to be thriving, whereas Charlie seemed to be wasting away. Alice worried about Charlie's future. Was he really going to have to spend the rest of his life in this box, and who would look after him if anything happened to their mother?

Then, as if reading her mind, Charlie sprung a terrible question. 'Alice, am I going to die?'

'No, Charlie. No, you are not! What a silly thing to say.'

'But look at me. You know, sometimes I wish I was dead. It hurts too much.'

'Oh, Charlie! Don't say that. Please. Look, have another swig.'

She pushed the bottle of Mrs Winslow on him and within minutes he had fallen into a restless sleep. Alice watched her little brother and for the first time wondered whether he was right, whether he was in fact dying. And then, horrified at where her mind was taking her, she rushed out and upstairs to reach under the pillow where she kept her rosary beads, and once again prayed for forgiveness for her wicked thoughts, and then prayed fervently that her brother's pain might stop and that he would get better.

But for once her prayers didn't bring her any peace. That night she tossed and turned, until Grace told her to pack it in. She stole downstairs to find her mother sitting in the chair by the range in the kitchen.

'Alice! What are you doing? Get back to bed.'

'Mum, please. Can I talk to you?'

Clara didn't answer so Alice pulled a chair close to her and sat down.

'I can't stop thinking about Charlie. He's dying, isn't he?'

Clara looked, startled.

'She's searching for words,' Alice thought.

And then Clara came out with it. 'Yes. Yes, he's dying.'

'Oh, Mum!'

'He's got Pott's Disease. TB on his spine.'

'The hunchback?'

'Yes.'

Alice started to cry, saying, 'Poor Charlie,' over and over.

Clara put her arms around her saying, 'I know, I know.' And then she said something that shocked her. 'It's for the best.'

And Alice stopped crying, sat up and really shocked herself by saying, 'I know.'

Suddenly there was a cold calm in the room. Both of them thinking very quickly, and then Alice asked, 'Are you going to tell him?'

'No. What would be the point?'

Alice thought about it. There were reasons to know and reasons not to know. Actually, she reckoned Charlie knew anyway. What good would it do? Her mother knew best. Probably. But what if he asked her again?

As if reading her mind, Clara said, 'I've told Charlie that he's just got a bug. A cold in his back. Nothing to worry about, but he'll feel a bit poorly for a while.'

'Yes, Mum.'

'So you are not to say nothing to nobody. Dr Pincus says there's nothing can be done and it's not going to take long. There's no point in upsetting everyone. Not when there's nothing to be done.'

'But what about Dad?'

'What about him? He's fighting Germans. He wouldn't be any help even if he was here.'

Clara grabbed Alice's hands and stared deeply into her eyes. 'It's taken me a while and a lot of thinking but whichever way I look at it, I come round to the same thing. You and me are going to have to be strong. Really strong. Stronger than we've ever had to be. For Charlie. To help him through.'

'To the other side.'

'All right, if you want to put it like that. To the other side. There will be time enough to cry afterwards. For now, we've just got to get through.'

Alice nodded. It was horrific, but it made sense.

'I wasn't going to tell you, but you know, I'm glad you're with me. I could really do with your help.' And with that Clara finally started to cry.

Alice got up from her chair and put her arms round her. 'I love you, Mum.'

And Clara nodded. 'I love you too.'

It was the first time she'd been embraced by her daughter rather than the other way around, and it felt really good. It wasn't until that moment that she realised how truly lonely she had been.

From then on Clara and Alice were closer than ever. Bound together by the shadow of their knowledge, the Commander-in-Chief was under no illusions how much she relied upon her general. Because Clara was appalled at what she was about to witness. There was one part of her that knew it was a blessed relief, but a huge guilt came with that thought. And a nagging, evil little devil every so often whispered in her ear that this TB had happened because there had been times when she had wished he had died of polio in 1910; that he wouldn't have had to suffer for all these years; and perhaps, more importantly, she wouldn't have had to watch this suffering, which constantly crushed her heart and made it impossible ever to be happy.

Those were the kind of thoughts that had been whirling around her head and had made her seek refuge by the Thames.

Because what sort of a mother wished for her child's death?

At the Front, Charlie Senior's thoughts of being a hero had long disappeared.

On 12 June 1916, he found himself stuck behind the wheel of a truck with German artillery shells hurtling down.

He was travelling in a convoy transporting ammunition, and he had been struggling to stay awake. Several times Arthur, in the passenger seat, had to poke him: 'Wake up, Charlie! For God's sake, we nearly went in a ditch! What's wrong with you?'

'I've had no sleep! I reckon I've had four hours in the last four days. It's doing me head in. As soon as I get back from delivering one load it's, "Oi, Swain, get your arse back in your truck! We need you to take this lot up to wherever."'

Arthur nodded. He'd had the same treatment. 'Well, the brass hats are up to something, aren't they? There's got to be a reason why we're taking so much up there. It's not as if there's a battle going on.'

'No, but I reckon there's one about to start, poor blighters.'

Charlie was spot on. In exactly two weeks, the British Army planned to start the massive artillery bombardment that would be the prelude to the Battle of the Somme.

Charlie, however, was not destined to take part in the offensive, which would turn out to be the bloodiest encounter in human history; just as he was nodding off again, he was brought to his senses by a huge shell hurtling down from the sky and landing on the road in front of them. It narrowly missed the lorry at the front, but it had to swerve and then it skidded and rolled over.

Charlie slammed on his brakes and just missed hitting the truck. The two men shouted expletives and ducked down in their seats as their truck was rocked to and fro by the force of the bombardment. They were trapped, and had no choice except to sit tight and pray, even though Charlie had an aversion to prayer. If God did exist (which he doubted), then he felt he'd sold his soul to the other bloke a long time ago. Instead, he reached inside his rucksack and with shaking hands brought out a bottle of rum he'd nicked from a load destined for the officers' mess. He took large gulps and then passed the bottle over to his companion.

Charlie suffered from major ambivalence when it came to military life. On a good day he felt as if he had been rather lucky: the ASC was known as 'Ally Slopers' Cavalry' – Ally Sloper was a cartoon character famous for his rent-dodging, wheeler-dealer, work-shy nature. 'Dodgy' would be the best word to describe him. The soldiers in the Army Service Corps rarely saw frontline action, as they were dedicated to getting supplies from the British mainland to the front. Charlie's engineering experience meant that he was drafted into the Motor Transport Corps and trained to drive the trucks, which were a vital link in the supply chain. As a result, he didn't have to fight and he lived in a permanent camp in a pretty town in northern France. He had access to all the best luxuries, including the spirits meant for the officers, and Charlie regularly helped himself. The locals were also a great source of food and liquid refreshment. When Charlie finished a jug of *vin rouge*, singing in the local bar with his arm around a comely village girl, he regularly consoled himself with the thought that it could be worse.

But then, on a day like today, as another shell landed, blasting his eardrums, showering him in dirt and generally shattering his nerves so that he had to grab the bottle back and take more long gulps, Charlie felt he was trapped in hell. The Germans deliberately targeted the British supply lines. He may not have been at the frontline, but during the long hours he worked without a break, he still saw plenty of action.

At times like these he resented the lack of respect given to the ASC. Only the week before Charlie had been at the depot when the Germans had started shelling it. As the place went up in flames and explosions, a band of British infantry passing through had cheered and sung, to the tune of 'The Church's One Foundation':

> '*We are Fred Karno's Army*
> *We are the ASC*
> *We cannot fight. We cannot shite,*
> *What fucking good are we?'*

Charlie's ginger blood had boiled up to its formidable top temperature and he had run over to them and shouted, 'Whose bloody side are you on?'

To which all he'd got back were jeers and, 'Yeah, not yours, you robbin' bastard!'

Charlie had backed off at this point because the jibe had hit home. Because, as well as the pilfered rum inside his rucksack, Charlie had a collection of 'souvenir' items: watches, cigarette cases and a couple of signet rings that he was planning to try and sell on when he got back to base.

Soldiers at the front regularly scoured the battlefield salvaging whatever they could – boots, ammunition, binoculars, brass shell cases – anything that could be recycled by an army desperately short of supplies. However, a fallen soldier's personal belongings were supposed to be handed in, and the punishment for keeping them was high. But this was completely ignored by most of the soldiers. The British Tommy was notorious for helping himself to souvenirs from both the enemy and his friends – he didn't discriminate.

The problem was that the soldiers were at the frontline, away from the (strictly unofficial, of course) market for this sort of merchandise, which was safely back behind the lines. And that market couldn't get to the frontline. The only people who had access to both the supply and demand were the soldiers of the ASC, and many were only too happy to buy cheap from the front and sell on at inflated prices back at base. In fact, a few were so entrepreneurial that they were able to retire on the proceeds once they got home.

Charlie was not quite in this league, but he was managing to stash away a useful little nest egg. On his darker nights he consoled himself with the thought that even if he didn't go home a hero, he might arrive back relatively comfortable.

After ten minutes or so, the shelling stopped. No one dared move and then cautiously, one by one, the men emerged from their vehicles.

Charlie and Arthur looked at each other. Arthur cocked his head towards the door: 'You first.'

Charlie rolled his eyes and opened the door. It needed a bit of a shove and he fell out onto the ground. Arthur couldn't help but giggle – the dark humour that comes with dangerous places.

Unfortunately, Charlie had fallen at the feet of his superior, Sergeant Ashby.

'Come on, Swain. All hands to it.' He gave Charlie a gentle kick with his boot, and shot a dirty look at Arthur, who was cowering in the well of the truck, still with the bottle in his hand. Lucky for him, Sergeant Ashby decided there were more important matters to hand – namely, getting the front lorry moving again and the hell out of this trap. They were like sitting ducks for the time being.

The men gathered around the overturned lorry as Ashby issued orders to find some ropes. Once they were secured to the lorry, they lined up and started heaving.

Charlie stood watching in a daze.

'Swain, come here! Grab this rope. Look sharp! What's the matter with you?'

Charlie was struggling. The fresh air had hit him and he was feeling uncomfortably light-headed, sick. He staggered towards a rope and grabbed hold of it.

The man in front of him turned around and stared at him. 'You all right, Charlie? You're not looking too clever.'

Charlie had caught sight of the lorry's driver. He was lying by the side of the road with blood pouring out of his head. Half his face was missing. Charlie's head spun and he slumped to the ground and blacked out.

He came to with the sensation that he was standing in a waterfall. He opened his eyes to find Sergeant Ashby standing over him, pouring water over his head. 'For God's sake, Swain – you're drunk!'

At that moment there was the familiar hum and whizz of an artillery shell flying through the air towards them: 'Take cover!' the sergeant screamed.

Charlie closed his eyes tight and put his hands over his face, resigned to death. Instead, he felt himself being dragged over the ground and shoved underneath a truck.

As the shells whistled around them, Sergeant Ashby, lying next to him, hissed, 'You're a liability, Swain! I don't want you here any more. I'm bloody well going to make sure if any of us make it out alive, you're going home. Dead wood, that's what you are. I don't care if you're a danger to yourself, but when you risk the lives of other men—' He stopped as Charlie turned over and threw up, luckily just missing him.

One month later Charlie was back in England and walking up the hill towards the cottage and home. He was wearing his army greatcoat and looked like a proud soldier. What couldn't be seen was the bag of booty in his rucksack, the pound notes stashed in his socks, and the dismissal papers in his pocket which gave the reason for his departure from the army as '*Indigestion*'. This was a common euphemism used by the army to let go soldiers who were a liability in some way: drink problems, or mental health problems, were classic examples. Charlie had been dismissed in an instant. It was not the first time he had come to the attention of the authorities for his high spirits and liking for liquor. Moreover, army command had been given instructions to do a general cull of any soldiers who were a liability in the weeks leading up to the great offensive on the Somme.

Charlie was all too aware that this left him with a bit of a problem. In the fevered atmosphere of July 1916, to be sent home for 'indigestion' would make him a laughing stock among his friends and an object of derision among the wider community. He had shamed not only himself, but his whole family. The idea of facing everyone made him feel sick.

He had had thoughts of disappearing completely – his fantasy was making a dash to the West Country, growing a beard and becoming a fisherman. But still, he knew that he would be regarded with suspicion wherever he went. By now, Kitchener's Army was in full swing and every man of his age was expected to be away fighting. More importantly, whenever he indulged in this fantasy, he saw two little red-headed girls jumping up and waving at him at the station.

It was the inability to solve this problem that had kept him from writing to Clara and telling her he was on his way home. It was going to be a bit of a surprise. In fact, Charlie still hadn't made up his mind what he was going to say when he walked into the house.

He bumped straight into Dora, who screamed.

Clara came rushing out. 'What the—? Oh, Lord!'

Charlie put out his arms. 'I'm home.'

Clara just stood still, frozen.

'I'm back for good.'

And immediately, the question he dreaded: 'Why?'

And before he could stop himself, an answer came flowing out: 'I was gassed.'

'What?'

'Yes, I was gassed.'

'How?'

'How do you think?'

'Well, I don't know.'

'I was under a truck … fixing it … it kind of rolled underneath.'

'What?'

'Yeah. The gas.'

'Rolled?'

'Well, it's in a can, isn't it? One came rolling underneath the lorry I was under and blew up.'

'Dear God! But you're all right? I mean, no one told me. You look all right. Shouldn't you be dead?'

'What sort of a welcome is that?'

'It's just I don't understand.'

'Well, I was very lucky …'

Clara waited and Charlie realised he was going to have to fill the gap. 'Yeah, the wind was blowing the other way …'

'Thank heavens for that!'

'Yeah.'

'But you can't fight no more?'

'No.'

'So you must be poorly?'

'Yes, it's me chest.' He coughed. 'Anyway, aren't you going to say hello?'

Clara went over and put her arms round him briefly and rather awkwardly, until Dora started to wail.

It wasn't many days later that Charlie caught Clara looking at him quizzically. 'Are you sure you was gassed?'

'What sort of a question is that?'

'It's just you don't look like Johnny Gardner up the road.'

'What do you mean?'

'Well, he can't breathe no more and shakes and stares into space.'

'What are you saying?'

'It's not just what I'm saying – it's what all sorts of people are saying.'

'Like who?'

'Like Alfie Walker's wife, in the queue at the baker's. She was asking me all sorts – how was your breathing, and "Is poor Charlie able to walk? I hear he's going back to the brewery." Questions I was finding difficult to answer.'

'Why's that difficult?'

'Because you look all right. Rather too well for someone who's been sent home 'cos they've been hit in the face by a tin o' gas.'

'What sort of a wife is it that says her husband looks too well?'

'One that's known you for nearly twenty years.'

Clara stared at him. Charlie was shocked by the coolness in her eyes. An image of a rat caught in a trap came into his head.

'I'm not going to listen to this.' Charlie grabbed his jacket and walked out.

As he sat on his usual bench in the Two Brewers and drank his first pint, then his second and then his third, the alcohol washed through him and soothed him, like a hungry baby when it finally gets its bottle. He reassured himself that if he just stuck to his story and told it enough times, no one could say different.

He might even come to believe it himself.

I sent an email to Dennis telling him what I'd found – in particular that Charlie was not gassed, but rather dismissed for 'indigestion'.

Dennis emailed back: 'But if he wasn't gassed, then he couldn't have died from his injuries from being gassed. Which begs the question, what did he die from? It's actually quite important for me to know.'

'Don't worry, Dennis,' I replied. 'I'm going to order his death certificate tonight. We'll know in a couple of weeks.'

\*

Clara wasn't convinced about Charlie's story either. He seemed far too perky. He had gone straight back to his old job in the brewery. And why hadn't she been officially notified, and what hospital had he been in? But with a huge secret of her own – that of Charlie Junior's rapidly declining health – she didn't feel inclined to press him.

Charlie had made no move to see his son other than: 'How's Charlie?'

'All right.'

'I'll go in and see him later.'

Except he hadn't, and things always seemed to get in the way.

For once Clara didn't mind. She was dreading the moment when he saw his son, because he would surely realise things weren't right.

Charlie Junior was fading fast. When Clara went in to see him he was usually asleep, or not conscious, anyway. The last week he didn't eat at all.

Alice would slip in and sit with him. She'd heard that when a person was dying it was important to keep talking to them – even if they seemed not there, they could still hear. So she would whisper little stories in his ear, the sort of gossip that had used to amuse him: 'Mrs Goodenough owes Mum half a shilling for a pie and now she says she doesn't, and there was a bit of a row. We was all watching. Mum got really angry and told her she's not welcome in our kitchen any more. You should have seen her!' And then she found she was telling him secret stuff. 'I've lost a shoe, Charlie. Don't know where it's gone. Mum's gonna kill me. I think that Dora's nicked it because I told on her for breaking the jug.' Sometimes she would find herself saying something more serious. Gaps were dangerous – dark thoughts seemed to fill them. 'I don't know. There's something odd going on. Mum doesn't seem very pleased to see Dad. I think she doesn't know what to do with him now he's back. And he seems to prefer being in the pub rather than being with us …'

And then she'd catch herself and think it wasn't fair to burden Charlie. Instead, she'd whisper how she hoped he was feeling better and she missed him and loved him.

Then one day she found herself saying, 'Look after me when you're in Heaven, Charlie.'

Where had that slipped out from? She said sorry and left quickly, looking for her mother. In a state, she blurted out: 'Mum, I've done something dreadful! I asked Charlie to look after me in Heaven.'

Alice braced herself for her mother's fury but instead, Clara was very quiet and just nodded.

That night Clara stayed up with Charlie. She lit a candle and kept it burning through the night. Somehow it seemed appropriate. At the very darkest hour Charlie opened his eyes and stared at his mum.

'They're calling me.'

'Yes, son. It's time to go.'

He nodded and closed his eyes.

At some point, as the sun rose, Clara fell asleep. When she woke up, the candle had gone out. The room felt different – still, and a little chilly. She looked at Charlie and realised he had gone. But he had only just gone: he was still warm, and there was a tear on his cheek. She kissed him and opened the window to let his spirit fly free.

Everything seemed right and appropriate except for that tear. That tear was to bother Clara for years to come. It seemed like a sign that perhaps Charlie had not wanted or had not been ready to go, and that really, really worried her. When he had cried that tear, she had been asleep.

He had cried it on his own.

# CHAPTER FIVE
# Poppy

I would love to talk to my great-grandmother, Clara, about Charlie Junior: what she went through and how she got through. Lots of questions – did she think about him every day? (I'm sure I know the answer to that one). What would she ask him if she saw him again? Was she ever the same again? Because I lost a child too, my first daughter, Poppy.

When I went for my twenty-two-week antenatal check-up, my blood pressure had gone up. I found myself having all sorts of tests and spending hours hooked up to machines, but I wasn't worried and my husband and the family even less so.

'What exactly is your blood pressure, then?' Mum asked.

'On average, I guess about 138 over 89.'

'Humph, that's nothing. How silly,' she said.

And part of me agreed. I was more worried about my holiday on the Italian Riviera. As a reward for bearing the next generation, my husband had booked a hotel in Positano and I had bought some special maternity wear to glide around in. The Scarlet Sisters would have approved.

But when I mentioned the trip to the doctor, she was unimpressed. 'Unless we are one hundred per cent sure that you are not showing the early signs of pre-eclampsia, you will not be getting on a plane.'

By the middle of April I was twenty-five weeks and four days pregnant and due to fly to Italy the following week. The tests had come up with nothing. Around ten o'clock one evening, I was on my own again. Pregnancy may have cramped my social life, but my husband was out, playing in the City. I kept tackling him: 'I'm so lonely. I never know where you are.'

'Look, there's nothing I can do here. I wish there was.'

'At least you could keep me company.'

'I can't. I need to keep doing my job and that means going out with clients. You know that.'

I didn't really have an answer to that so I ended up feeling slightly pathetic: 'But I never know where you are. You never answer your phone.'

'That's because I can't hear it. It's in my pocket and it's noisy in those wine bars.'

But I wasn't convinced.

Out of the blue the telephone rang and I jumped. I leapt up, and as I did, I felt something go, like I'd pulled a muscle in my stomach. More uncomfortable than painful, I struggled over to the phone and picked it up.

'Helen?'

'Nanna?'

'Are you all right, darling?'

'I was until you rang.'

'What?' (She was a bit deaf.)

'No, I mean, why are you ringing so late?'

'Oh, I'm sorry, dear. I just wanted to know that you're all right.'

'I'm all right. Are you all right?'

'Yes, dear. Where's that husband of yours?'

'Well, you know how he is. Out again.'

'Hmmmm. Well, as long as you're all right.'

'Yes, I had my scan today, and the results were good. I'm seeing the consultant tomorrow to be signed off.'

'Oh, that is good news. But you still have to look after yourself. It's a very important package you're carrying there.'

'Yes, I know, Nanna. I know.'

'You should be in bed. Goodnight, dear. Take care.'

'You too, Nanna. Bye bye.'

I hung up and cursed her for giving me such a fright.

I went to bed, but it was difficult to sleep. Waves of muscle spasms were hitting my body every few minutes. They were incredibly powerful, my whole body doubled up. At some point I staggered to the spare room and was relieved to find my husband lying there. He seemed the worse for wear, but at least I knew where he was.

I got on the bed beside him and looked at my stomach. It seemed to be growing.

'Please wake up. I swear my stomach is swelling.'

He did not seem unduly concerned. But, to be fair, I was seeing the consultant the next day anyway.

It went quiet. I tried to shake him awake but it was no good. I lay beside him in the darkness. I was really scared. Suddenly I didn't want to have this baby – I wished I could rewind the tape and never get pregnant. Just carry on with our lives the way they were before. I felt very alone.

The next thing I knew I was back in our bedroom and dreaming. I dreamt I had wet myself. I staggered to the bathroom and switched on the light. And that's the moment our nightmare started.

The bathroom was covered in blood. I screamed. It was inhuman, a scream to wake the dead. It even woke up my husband.

He came running as I sank to the floor. The next minute he was sitting beside me, talking fast to the hospital. They told him to dial 999 and get an ambulance. Of course I knew this was serious, but I was even more frightened by how serious they thought it was. Going around my head was the thought, 'I'm losing this baby' and then another strange little thought, 'How am I going to face everybody?' Even then I felt a twinge of guilt. Why did that matter?

I was bleeding everywhere, but the ambulance ladies were cheery. They merrily remarked away as we sped off: 'You're lucky, you know, this happening at three in the morning. No traffic. It's murder down here during the day.'

All I could do was nod and raise an eyebrow because I had an oxygen mask strapped over my face.

'First baby?'

I nodded.

'Know what it is?'

'Girl,' my husband replied. I noticed he was rubbing my hand hard. If he continued much longer it would rub away.

'Last quiet night you're going to get.'

'You call this quiet?' I tried to say through the mask.

The ladies laughed and I noticed a look of complicity pass between them. They looked to be in their late thirties. 'They've both got children,' I thought. I couldn't believe they were talking as if my baby was going to be OK.


We arrived at the hospital, where there was a midwife expecting me. Quickly she wheeled a heartbeat monitor over and strapped me up and before I had time to think about the implications, there was the rapid, *thump*, *thump*, *thump*, of a baby's heartbeat.

Poppy's heartbeat.

'Your baby's alive!' She sounded as surprised as I was.

'Really?'

'That's your baby's heartbeat.'

I couldn't believe it. It didn't seem possible.

'So now we need to get the baby out as quickly as possible.'

She went over to the phone and started making calls. I could hear the words 'registrar, theatre, anaesthetist and blood' and for the first time the words 'placental abruption'.

All the time Poppy's heartbeat was echoing around the room – *thump, thump, thump.*

A woman in a white coat hurried in, followed by some figures in theatre gowns. And then they were wheeling me out of the room. I caught a last glimpse of my husband, shell-shocked in the corner, left behind. Later he told me that the midwife had said:

'They usually manage to save the mother, not the baby.'

Suddenly I was plunged into an episode of *ER* with myself in the leading role. The trolley picked up speed and we went flying down the corridor, the anaesthetist running along, trying to keep level with my head: 'When did you last eat?'

'Not since last night.'

'No. I need to know what time exactly. Please try to remember, this is really important.'

'About eight o'clock?'

'And anything to drink?'

'Yes, a cup of tea a bit later.'

'Uh. OK, that should be OK … oh God, I'm sure there's something else I should ask you. Yes! Are you allergic to anything?'

'No. I mean yes – cats. But that's not relevant, is it?'

'No. Now, we're going to have to put you out very quickly.'

'You mean a general anaesthetic?'

'Yes.'

'I really would prefer a local anaesthetic. Can my husband be there?'

'No, I don't think you understand. This is not a matter of choice.'

'Please,' I begged. 'I really don't want a general anaesthetic. Is there any other way?'

'No. Believe me, this is serious.'

Within minutes, I was staring at the ceiling of the operating theatre. Everyone was shouting.

'Registrar is on his way!'

'Have you rung SCBU?'

'Paediatrician on the way!'

'Where's the blood? Why haven't you ordered the blood?'

They were shouting at a small junior doctor, who looked really harassed.

'I've got to get the consent form signed.' She waved a piece of paper in front of my face. 'You need to give consent for us to perform a hysterectomy.'

'But, hang on … I'm not sure …' I started to say.

'Look, this is to save your life. Otherwise you will die. You have no choice. For God's sake, just sign quickly.'

I signed the form. And the thought that went through my head was: 'Please God, just let me live. I must just concentrate on surviving and I'll worry about the rest of this later.'

The registrar walked into the room. He was pulling on his surgical gloves as he swept in. I saw a young face behind a mask. He rolled his eyes at me and shook his head as if to say 'What sort of a mess have you got yourself into?' He immediately started barking questions at the theatre staff, the numbers of which seemed to be growing all the time.

I noticed a large, complicated incubator being wheeled in.

'Right, I'm going to put you to sleep now. It's going to be a bit fast and a bit uncomfortable. I'm sorry – I'm going to have to press hard on your neck.' The anaesthetist put her thumb at the bottom of my throat, and started counting down: 'Ten … nine … eight …'

And I repeated over and over in my head: *I want to live. I want to live. I want to live.*

'Seven … six …'

Everything cut to black.

Six months after the surgery, I was left with my hospital notes by accident. They were impressively thick. I knew I shouldn't, but I started reading them and it was like going back to the start and reliving every step in gruesome, technical detail. I struggled a bit with some of the medical terms, but the impression I got was that I had been in a bad way when I arrived. I had lost a lot of blood – over a third – and it had been coursing around inside my body with the potential to wreak havoc for hours.

But it hadn't. I was in one piece. I did survive and they didn't have to perform a hysterectomy. At that critical moment the line of the Scarlet Sisters was saved – the daughter's daughter's daughter survived and thus went on to have more daughters.

Nanna and I never did talk about that call, the one that in jumping up to answer it caused my placenta to break away from my womb, with catastrophic consequences. Did Nanna anticipate or precipitate? Did she have a premonition I was about to be in trouble, or did she inadvertently cause it?

The senior midwife at the hospital said it had been an accident waiting to happen: 'You're just lucky you were safe at home and not on that plane to Italy. You're lucky to be alive.'

I came round from the operation as I was being wheeled from the theatre. I was lying on a trolley and crying with relief. Literally crying, as I woke up. The first thing I saw was my husband peering into my face as we moved through the corridors.

'She's alive, she's alive,' he kept saying.

'Who?' I thought. Then I thought, 'Ah, yes, but what about me? I'm alive. I'm alive too.'

'She's called Poppy,' he said. I was struck by his agitation. I had never seen him so ruffled. 'I hope you don't mind. We can change it to Daisy. But I had to call her something. They needed a name for labels and things and in case … well, I just thought it suited her. Is that OK? You don't mind?'

It crossed my mind that he had done it for me; he had wanted to call her Daisy. So I knew he'd called her Poppy because he felt he owed me. And I appreciated the gesture.

So Poppy she stayed.

*

'The darkest hour is just before dawn' is a line from a song by The Mamas & The Papas – 'Dedicated To The One I Love'. Every time I hear it, I see that room: the high dependency unit they took me to after the operation, the pitch-black after the bright lights of the corridors. Time is definitely not absolute, but bendy; and that night it stretched for ever.

I drifted in and out of consciousness. At one point I woke up to find my husband lying beside me, face down, sobbing, his thick curls shaking with emotion. We held each other and cried. There was nothing to say, just raw grief. I had never seen him cry like that. I knew why I was crying – for myself – and I wondered for whom he was crying. For me? For Poppy? For him? I still don't know the answer.

I woke up and daylight was pouring into the room. It was morning, and Mum was standing beside my bed. I was twenty-nine years old and I suddenly realised that there was no one else in the world I wanted more.

She grabbed my hand and held it tight and I felt the power of maternal love. 'How did it happen? I mean, I only spoke to you last night and you were fine and I went to bed reassured that you were doing well, and then I'm woken up by a phone call and you're in here and nearly dead and had the baby. I just don't understand.'

Poor Mum. I didn't understand it either.

My husband was in and out of the neonatal unit, phoning people, buying me a toothbrush, so it was Mum who sat with me and never left my side. She was there when the doctors swept into the room, the consultant in his suit surrounded by junior doctors.

'Morning, how are you feeling?' he boomed, and didn't wait for a reply. He launched into a summary of the whole situation and finished with the words: 'So it seems Mrs Batten was suffering from pre-eclampsia after all, but luckily we have a successful conclusion.'

The junior doctors all looked a bit shocked and there was silence.

Then Mum spoke up, in icy tones. 'It doesn't look very successful to me. A daughter who nearly died and a very premature baby fighting for her life. If you call that a success, I'd hate to see a failure.' My mum – the mouse who occasionally roars.

The consultant made a swift exit.

After the doctors came the express machine. The nurse wheeled this lumbering contraption over to my bed and told me I was going to have to try and express some milk. I had no idea what she was talking about. A woman milked like a cow? I was to connect that industrial radio transmitter to my breast? And turn it on? Mum and I got the Swain giggles as a rather serious nurse demonstrated its terrifying suction capacity. But something did come out in the end. Mum looked impressed; I was amazed. It's funny how you can be surprised by your body doing what it's supposed to do.

But there was something we were both avoiding – my baby. Up until the afternoon, there had been no suggestion that I should go and see her. Actually, I didn't want to. I think while I still hadn't seen her, I could pretend that this was only about me, and I seemed to be fine. Something told me whatever was happening down the corridor couldn't be good. All those hours Poppy had been deprived of oxygen, bleeding.

My husband told me the doctors had said she was OK. I didn't believe them.

When the medics had decided I was stable, it was impossible to put the visit off any longer. 'Right, time to get you up. Time to see your baby,' the nurse chivvied me along. She could see my reluctance.

My husband raced me down the corridors, pushing my wheelchair at speed. He explained the tight security, how you had to ring the buzzer to get into the unit, the special way you had to wash your hands before and after each visit, not to be scared by all the wires.

As he wheeled me into the room I felt self-conscious. The nurses were looking at me. Out of the corner of my eye I could see other mummies staring at me curiously. I felt vulnerable, in my wheelchair, hospital gown and catheter jangling alongside.

There were just four incubators in the room: two on the left and two on the right, and each was dwarfed by an amazing collection of machinery – drips, monitors, ventilators, wires everywhere. The room was brightly lit and noisy, the pop music coming from a radio was all but drowned by a cacophony of electronic bleeping and alarms. I was pushed up to an incubator right at the back.

I could just see a tiny body. She was lying on her front, wearing a little bonnet that was tied under her chin; then there was a smooth red back, a nappy, and a face with a tube coming out of the mouth – her ventilator.

I felt nothing.

No connection.

Here was my baby in front of me – believe me, a twenty-six-week-old baby is a proper baby; just very tiny, the size of two hands. Everyone was watching me.

'Shall I lift you up so you can have a better look at her?' my husband asked. He took my arm as I gingerly stood up from the chair.

I could see her better. Amazingly her eyes were open, but I still felt nothing. If you had asked me to pick out which of the babies was mine, I wouldn't have been able to.

The nurses came over and introduced themselves. Parvati was Poppy's key carer. She was the one who had collected her from the theatre and helped bring her back to life. She explained the monitors, the routine. She showed me the room where I should go to express my breast milk so they could give it to her fresh – the most important thing I could do for her. They already had a roll of labels with 'Poppy Batten' written on them, ready to stick on her bottles and pop into the fridge.

Seeing my baby's name, written like that … she had officially come into existence, and I couldn't get my head around it.

The one thing Parvati didn't talk about was Poppy and her prognosis – whether she was going to live or die. I felt they were avoiding the subject and I couldn't bring myself to ask. 'The paediatrician will come and talk to you about Poppy,' Parvati said. What she did tell us was to look after ourselves; that whatever the outcome, this was going to be a rollercoaster ride.

In the afternoon they wheeled me down to the ordinary postnatal ward. There were new mummies surrounded by flowers, balloons, excited relatives and each with a new baby in their arms. Everyone was casting me furtive glances, wondering where my baby was. I was stuck and it was messing with my head. My husband brought me a Polaroid photo the nurses had taken of Poppy to have beside my bed. I lay and stared at it. All I had was white noise going on in my head. I prayed for sleep and escape.

Mum was back with me by the time the consultant was doing his rounds the next morning.

He ignored her. 'Mrs Batten, the results of your blood tests have come back and it seems you are anaemic. You need to have another blood transfusion.'

I'd made a documentary about mad cow disease a few years before and a little knowledge is a dangerous thing. 'When you say I need another blood transfusion, do you mean that my life is in danger if I don't have it?' I said.

'No, not at all, but your recovery will be much quicker. If you have the transfusion now you will feel better straight away.'

'In that case I won't have it.'

'Why on earth not?'

'CJD, for a start.'

He was taken aback. 'What utter nonsense. You can't get CJD from a blood transfusion. You can't get anything from a blood transfusion. It is one hundred per cent safe.'

'I'm sure that's what they said before they discovered HIV.'

Now he did look cross. Actually, I couldn't believe my own contrariness. But I didn't trust him.

When he had left a tall, pale woman in a white coat strode over. 'Mrs Batten?'

'Yes.'

'I'm the physiotherapist. I've come to give you some exercises to help your body after your caesarean. Where's your baby?'

'Here,' I said, pointing to the photo beside my bed.

She walked over to the other side of my bed and picked up the photo. She stared at it for a few moments and then just handed it back with a sad expression on her face. 'I tell you what, I'll come back later to do these exercises,' she said.

And that was the last I saw of her.

'She thinks Poppy's going to die,' I thought.

I realised I still hadn't seen the paediatrician.

It was the woman in the bed opposite me who pushed me over the edge. She kept pestering the midwives about her baby.

'He's got bandy legs.'

'Don't you think he's cross-eyed?'

'I'm sure there's something not quite right.'

I couldn't believe it when, within minutes, a paediatrician appeared. Mum and I watched while he gave the little boy a thorough examination.

'I can assure you, you have a perfectly normal, healthy little boy.'

'But look, doctor. Look at his legs. They're bandy.'

'No, they're not.'

'Well, he's definitely squinting.'

'He's just been born.'

'Is that what they're supposed to look like?'

'Yes.'

It suddenly occurred to me that maybe no one had come to see me because no one had been to see Poppy. She was lying in her little incubator, forgotten, with just a few machines pumping away, keeping her alive.

I started to howl.

The midwife strode over. 'What's the matter with her?' she asked Mum.

'What do you think's the matter with her? My daughter had a very premature baby yesterday and not one doctor has come to see her to tell her how her baby is!'

'She hasn't talked to the paediatrician yet?'

'No.'

'Well, he was in here just a minute ago.'

'Oh, yes, we know he was here. But not to see us. He was seeing that lady opposite about her baby's bandy legs.'

The midwife got the message.

Five minutes later the paediatrician reappeared, full of apologies. There had been lots of crossed wires but Poppy was not forgotten at all. I forgave him because he was terribly nice and a little bit handsome. He sat down on my bed with a bunch of charts. I studied every move of his face.

The first prognosis was good. Unbelievably good.

Poppy was twenty-six weeks old when she was born. This was crucial. At twenty-three weeks, 90 per cent of babies die, but by twenty-six weeks, 80 per cent survive.

Ten years before, hardly any babies born before twenty-eight weeks lived. Their lungs didn't work and they were very vulnerable to infection. Then someone developed steroids that could be given to a baby in the womb which would activate the baby's lungs, kick in the immune system and basically prepare the baby to come into the world. And the results were amazing. Overnight survival rates rocketed. No one knew the long-term effects of these steroids, but so what? Babies who almost certainly would have died now had a fighting chance of life.

But Poppy didn't get those steroids. Moreover, all those hours with my uncomfortable tummy had meant that Poppy had been deprived of oxygen. In theory, she should not have survived at all. But somehow they had managed to bring her back to life and they had found a baby in excellent condition. A strong, healthy, fighter of a baby. Poppy was big – 2lb 1oz – the size of a twenty-eight-week-old baby, and all her vital organs were working.

Nor was there any sign of brain damage.

'She has an 80 per cent chance of making it,' the paediatrician said.

'What do you mean "making it"?' I asked. 'Just surviving, or growing up to be a completely normal, healthy adult?'

Deep down my absolute worst fear – a fear I could barely admit to myself – was that she was brain damaged.

'There is a very good chance that your baby will leave here completely well. Of course it will be months, if not years, before we will know for certain. But the first signs are very good. However, there is always the risk of infection. Premature babies are vulnerable because their immune systems are so underdeveloped. But we are very pleased with her. Poppy really is a miracle baby.'

And it was then that my attitude changed. Now that there was a fighting chance, I was determined my miracle baby would survive, and I was prepared to go to any lengths to make it happen.

I sent Mum off to tell them I would have that blood transfusion after all.

I remember the first time I saw Poppy. I mean, really *saw* her.

I'd had a row with Moira the midwife. The blood transfusion was taking hours. I was all wired up and unable to move as the blood slowly trickled down the tubes. In one of the beds opposite, I had watched as a new mummy was wheeled in. I could see through the curtains as she breastfed her baby for the first time.

I felt desperate. I rang my bell.

Moira marched in. 'You rang?'

'I need to go and express some milk.'

'You're not going anywhere. I can't disconnect you, not until this transfusion is finished.'

'And when is that?'

'Let's see – another six hours, at least.'

'I can't wait six hours! I've got to go and feed my baby.'

'She's not going to starve, you know. They've got plenty of milk in the neonatal unit. You can go when this is finished, in the morning. Why don't you just go back to sleep?'

'Look, my baby is fighting for her life in there. You know that. You know this is the only thing I can do for her right now. I'm going, even if I have to unplug this stuff myself.'

She stared at me over the top of her glasses, then shook her head and sighed. 'OK, but not until this bag is finished.'

About twenty minutes later she came back in. 'You'll have to go by yourself. I can't leave the ward.'

'Fine, I don't care.'

'No, I can see that.'

Silently she disconnected me and watched as I struggled out of bed.

I walked slowly along the hospital corridors pushing my lines, the only sound my drips clanging. I didn't care.

I walked into the ward. It was peaceful. Three o'clock in the morning, no visitors, no nurses, and for once the alarms were silent. I was on my own with four tiny babies and the gentle bleeping of their monitors. The lights were turned low. I shuffled to her incubator.

The most amazing sight greeted me. There she was with no oxygen mask on, breathing by herself. The joy! No one had told me they were going to take her off the ventilator. She looked so strong – her eyes were open, and she was waving her arms and legs in the air. It was the first time I had ever seen her face properly, without all those horrible wires. And she was the image of her daddy – lots of curls, and my husband's frown. For the first time I could see she was really my very own baby, *our* baby.

'My baby, my very own baby.' The words were going round and round my head.

She looked at me. I held her hand and the world stopped moving. She held on to my finger with a fierce grip, stared straight into my soul and waved her arms at me. At that moment there was no one else in the world but her and me. Tears poured down my face. Until that moment I had been walking in a dream, but now I was awake. The extraordinary miracle that my husband and I had made: a baby. The *joy* of that moment; I guess that's what they mean by bonding. But it was also more than that: for this was the first time that she looked like a real baby – incredibly small, but strong, alive, very much with us.

For the first time I thought she might actually make it. I took a leap into the unknown and dared to hope.

Parvati was right. It was a rollercoaster ride. Some of it was really bad but there were some amazing bits too.

It was Poppy's smell more than anything. I wanted to eat her. I poked my nose into her incubator and inhaled the smell of the most visceral basic love. Why hasn't anyone come up with a bottle of newborn baby perfume? Surely it is the smell of heaven and the angels? And it was lovely because, despite her traumatic arrival, underneath all the wires and machinery, that smell told me more than anything else that there was a real baby in there. My baby.

And she was cute. Well, she seemed so to me. The nurses said so too. We laughed at her huge frown and Churchillian features – Parvati called her 'the lanky chick' because of her unfeasibly long legs, which *were* rather curious considering how vertically challenged her daddy was.

As Poppy began to grow and thrive, the nurses were anxious that we should start doing things for her. 'It's time you changed a nappy,' they said to me. Back then I didn't know one end of a baby from the other, and I was terrified of doing anything that might harm Poppy. What if I dislodged one of the wires?

While I hesitated, my husband leapt in. 'I'll do it ... what do I do?' The nurses laughed. They loved him, of course.

With his usual deftness and confidence he got stuck in. I watched and marvelled and felt hopelessly inadequate.

The most amazing thing was hearing Poppy's voice for the first time. I hadn't really thought about it, but of course the ventilator had stopped her from crying. The first time I changed her nappy, she gave a yelp and started to scream. I jumped. Her little cry sounded a bit hoarse, but it was a proper baby cry. I said a silent prayer of thanks for hearing her.

Of course once she was able to cry we got a much better idea of her personality. Poppy didn't grizzle for nothing: she was quite content to look around the room and wave her legs in the air, but woe betide anyone who tried to bath her, or put her flat on her back. She let us know her disgust in no uncertain terms. I was proud of my Poppy. My cool, lanky chick. Of course I was her mum, but here was a baby I could do business with.

Like all the babies in the unit she wore a dinky woollen bonnet tied under her chin to keep her warm, and she had an old-fashioned crocheted blanket in bright colours. In the beginning they didn't put her in a sleep suit, so that they could get to her quickly in an emergency. It meant we could stroke her skin. It was pink and warm and the softest thing in the world. Her little fingernails were tiny but growing.

There's a phrase about 'seeing heaven in a grain of sand'. I held Poppy's tiny hands and marvelled at the miracle of creation.

When the nurses started to dress Poppy in proper sleep suits, I missed touching her skin, but it was another sign that she was getting closer to the start of normal baby life. I allowed myself to daydream about the outfits I would buy. Mum found an obscure baby shop which sold premature-baby clothes and sent a big parcel. Parvati and I discussed what colours suited her best. There was a light green and white striped suit that looked particularly fetching.

One day I looked around and realised that the other babies had accumulated lots of toys, photos, pictures drawn by siblings, even a few plastic flowers. To me their incubators looked a little like shrines covered in votive offerings – sort of Roman Catholic, ghoulish. Poppy's space looked neat and, most importantly, hygienic. However, maybe she just looked unloved?

My sister-in-law had been struck down with terrible 'flu and had kept away; instead, she had sent a fluffy bunny. At first I had kept the bunny to myself: what microscopic nasties were lurking in its fur? Could stuffed bunnies catch 'flu too?

'Don't be daft,' said my husband. So, one afternoon I slipped the bunny into Poppy's incubator. Then Nanna sent a letter. Typically, she'd enclosed a large, dramatic, fabric poppy. I wound it around the top of Poppy's incubator. I was pleased with the effect. Not eclipsing the precious occupant within but, nevertheless, showing that this was her home, and she was loved.

It was my husband who held her first. I have the photograph. He's wearing an enormous grin and all you can see is a bundle wrapped in a blanket with a whole load of tubes sticking out. After about ten nerve-racking minutes with my eyes glued to the monitors – I jumped every time he moved – it was my turn.

I knew I should do it but I was very nervous. What if she died in my arms? I sat in the chair and they passed her over slowly and carefully. She was cradled in my arms, swaddled tightly.

'I'll leave you for a few minutes,' said the nurse and, before I could stop her, she walked off.

The minutes ticked by. Poppy's oxygen levels dropped slightly, the alarm started to sound, but there was no one around.

'Do you think you should get someone?' I asked my husband.

'No, it's OK.'

'Please, just get someone.'

He came back with the nurse, who didn't seem the slightest bit concerned – she increased Poppy's oxygen and everything settled down again. But that was it – I wanted them to put her back.

*

Over the next few days Poppy came out of her 'box' every afternoon. And I got a little more confident each time. When the alarms went off, I learnt to stay calm, whisper in her ear and she stabilised.

One afternoon, I was the only parent around and all the babies were having a good day. The atmosphere was relaxed, the spring sunshine streaming in through the windows.

'Now's a good time to do some cuddling. What do you think?' asked the nurse.

'Yes, that would be lovely,' I said, and I actually meant it this time.

I settled into a chair and she opened Poppy's incubator. Before I knew what was going on, she had got Poppy out, undressed her, undone my buttons, slipped her down my shirt and buttoned it all up again. She then put a blanket over the two of us so we were cosy.

'I almost feel broody looking at Helen there, like that.' The nurses laughed.

It felt amazing – this warm, cuddly, wriggly thing down my shirt, with the smell of new baby wafting past my nose. I supported her little bottom with one hand and gently stroked her back with the other. I couldn't stop kissing the top of her tufty head. The radio was playing gently in the background and I sang along to the tunes. I felt the most complete sense of peace.

When things get really bad, I think back to that moment. Just at that moment I was truly happy.

Three weeks later we got the phone call we had always dreaded. It was 10.30 p.m. and I had been home for a week.

We were in the bedroom getting ready for bed. The phone rang and my heart fell to the pit of my stomach. I think at that moment we both knew.

'We just thought we should tell you that we've had to put Poppy back on the ventilator. She's OK but she needs a bit of extra help breathing. You don't need to come in – we just didn't want you to get a shock in the morning.'

'I think we'll come in anyway,' my husband said.

I felt sick. I pulled my clothes back on. Most of me was working on autopilot, but there was also a bit of my head working very fast and the question going round it was, 'Are you going to be up to this?'

I don't remember the drive to the hospital – what I do remember is the horror when we got there. Poppy was in a terrible state. She looked grey and shrunken and she was writhing in agony, a real look of terror in her eyes; she was trying to pull out her tubes.

'She's going to kill herself,' I thought. This tiny baby was so strong, it took all the nurses just to hold her down. No other baby was getting any attention that night.

A young Asian doctor was in charge. His English was not good but we didn't need a translator to feel his panic. The nurses were shouting at him to do something as Poppy's oxygen levels crashed and the chorus of alarms deafened the room.

My husband faced the doctor. 'You obviously haven't got a clue what you are doing. So you are going to get on that phone and find someone who does. I'm not suggesting, I'm telling you. I expect a consultant to arrive within the next fifteen minutes, because I am not going to stand here and watch while my daughter loses her life because you don't know what you are doing.'

And that is exactly what he did.

I was in the corridor in time to glimpse the consultant arriving. Dragged all the way from another hospital in the early hours of the morning, he was grim-faced.

There was a look of relief from everyone as he marched into the ward. I stayed outside, peeping through the window as he rolled up his sleeves and got down to business, hands straight in the incubator twiddling the dials of Poppy's machines, giving injections and barking commands that sent the nurses scuttling to and fro.

I retreated to the visitors' room and lay down on the sofa listening to the alarms from Poppy's monitors. They were getting less frequent, and then I realised they had stopped altogether.

'She's either dead or she's alive,' I said to myself.

My husband walked into the room. 'It's OK. They've stabilised her,' he said. 'And he's pretty sure it's meningitis.'

Then we were sitting side by side, and my husband held my hand as an exhausted consultant faced us.

'Thank you. You saved our daughter's life,' my husband said.

He looked traumatised and shook his head. 'Just listen to what I've got to say first. I've had a call from the lab. It's definitely meningitis.'

'That's brilliant,' I cried. He stared at me. 'Well, surely if you know what's causing it, then you can give her the right antibiotics?' I said.

'Not at all. Meningitis is just a word we use to describe an infection in the brain. That infection can be caused by any number of bacteria and until we know which one, we won't know the right antibiotic to use. We've put her on a general antibiotic to stop her getting any worse, but we won't know if we can even treat it until we've identified it. Meanwhile, it's already been rampaging around doing damage for hours. Every time she struggled she was having a fit. How many times did she do that? Once? Twice?'

'Dozens of times,' my husband said grimly.

'Exactly. And every time she had a fit, another bit of her brain was damaged.'

I stared at him in disbelief.

'The only way I saved her life tonight was injecting her with Rohypnol. You've not heard of it? Perhaps its other name, "the date rape drug", will mean more to you. She was fitting so badly we had to paralyse her. She's not stabilised, she's paralysed.'

At that moment I couldn't take on board the full implication of what we had just been told. All I could think was at least Poppy was out of immediate danger.

We were shown to a room on the floor above, where you go to sleep if your baby is either really ill, or dead. We didn't even take our clothes off but fell into a fitful sleep holding each other close. Whatever the morning held, we were still a family. We had survived the night.

*

I had vivid dreams in which Poppy died, over and over again. I can still remember a couple of them – we were on a fairground ride, Poppy's booth shot off and I had to watch, helpless, as she was crushed to death. In another I drove off a cliff – I managed to swim to safety, but had to watch, clinging to a rock, as Poppy drowned. It was as if my mind was trying out every different scenario and, no matter which way I played it, the end was always the same – Poppy died. But those fevered nightmares must have served a purpose, because I woke up feeling stronger. Grim, but determined to face whatever the day held in store.

In the morning Poppy was still alive, as I knew she would be. She seemed to be sleeping peacefully, although I realised this was probably just the drugs. I slipped out to phone Mum. It was a beautiful May morning, the sun coming up in a clear blue sky.

I sat on the pavement outside the hospital. Every so often an excited dad would come out to phone grandparents, or a car would come tearing in and an enormous lady would struggle out, helped by a partner clutching an overnight bag.

I saw the irony, but I couldn't feel it.

'Hello. How is our darling Poppy today?'

I remembered: the last time I spoke to Mum it had all been good news.

'Mum, she's not very well. She's got meningitis.'

'Oh.' I heard her intake of breath.

Mum had just started getting excited about Poppy. She'd started talking about the future. We'd had a few of those little conversations that mothers and daughters have when you have a new baby.

Without thinking I said, 'Mum, please can you come up? I think I'm going to need you.'

'Of course. I was just thinking how I might get up there. Don't worry, I'll find a way.'

Five minutes later she rang me back. 'Uncle Nigel is going to bring me. Don't worry, I'll find you wherever you are. Give Poppy a kiss from me.'

No matter how old you get, sometimes you do just need your mum.

Back up in the ward, the doctors were gathering for the morning round. The paediatrician, Dr Martin, had already managed to speak to my husband.

'I've been given a brief summary of what happened last night. Look, I'd like you and Helen to be there for the morning meeting. I think it's important you hear what we've got to say. Is Helen going to be OK? I hear she was a bit shaky in the night.'

'Helen? Oh, don't worry about her. She'll be fine. She's tougher than she looks. Nails.'

In the years that followed those words were to come back and haunt me. But actually I had rallied and I was now prowling around the unit feeling angry and dangerous.

A group of doctors of all levels were gathered around Poppy's incubator. It seemed a bit disrespectful to be standing having a conversation in front of her when she was lying there busily fighting for her life. Obviously a premature baby can't understand what we say – or can they? My instincts told me it was wrong.

Dr Martin demanded a complete report of the night's events. In the end she concluded that Poppy had contracted an infection. Because of those hours between the abruption and her being delivered, she had been bleeding and there was a small clot, causing a blockage in her brain. Her spinal fluid was sticky, which meant the infection had lodged in her brain and she now had meningitis. But they wouldn't know what sort of meningitis and how severe until the results had come back from the lab. She ended by saying: 'Once we have pinned down exactly which bacteria it is causing this, then we can talk about how we might treat it.'

Early in the afternoon, I was sitting with Poppy and Mum. The registrar came in with a piece of paper in his hands. He seemed in real distress.

'We've identified the bacteria that has infected Poppy. It's a gamma delta.'

'Well, that's good, surely? That they've identified it—?'

'No, I'm sorry. If the bacteria had been something else maybe she would have a chance, but it's the very worst bacteria there is. We need special drugs which we haven't got. We're ringing around the local hospitals at the moment and there may well be some, but Poppy's only chance is to have them injected straight into her brain – you're looking at six operations in the next week, if she survives at all. And then even if we manage to cure the infection, we can't reverse the damage it has already inflicted on her brain.'

Before I could think, the words came out of my mouth: 'Don't keep her alive just for the sake of it. Don't you dare keep her alive just because you can.'

At that moment I felt it with every core of my being. Visions of pulling out ventilator plugs flashed through my head.

The poor doctor looked haggard. 'I'm glad you brought it up, because we need to talk. When your husband comes back we should have a meeting with Dr Martin. I'm going to give her the news now.'

He walked out. I turned round to my mum.

'Mum? I hope we can stop this. It's madness. I think that's what he meant, didn't he? We don't have to go on with this?'

'I'm sure that's what he meant,' she said. And then she added: 'You know, whatever you decide, I'm right behind you. I know you will know the right thing to do.' I felt the bond and the wall of strength between us. I so needed it at that moment.

I was not surprised that Mum was behind me, but I was not at all sure my husband would be.

I found him and all in a rush told him what the doctor had said and that I did not want to continue treatment. It was madness and wrong and I wanted Poppy to be allowed to die in peace. Of course it was a decision for both of us, but I really hoped he felt the same way.

It occurred to me that even though we had been together so long, I had no idea what he might think: we had such radically different views of the universe. This had never been a problem – we used to tease each other and have friendly disagreements over too many drinks in the pub. Now I saw it might matter very much indeed.

He surprised me with his calmness. 'Let's hear what Dr Martin has to say. I'm not saying you're not right but I want to hear some statistics before I can come even close to making a decision.'

I was relieved. And of course he was right: we shouldn't make a decision until we had heard everything the doctors had to say.

As we went back into the unit there was a motorcycle courier standing at the desk delivering a bag of medicine. The registrar walked past. 'It's Poppy's medicine. We found it at a nearby hospital, they've sent it straight over.'

'You haven't started treating her, have you?' I cried out. 'Please don't.'

Everyone turned to look at me. Even I was alarmed at the sound of desperation in my voice.

'No, we haven't. Don't worry, we're not going to do anything until we've had a chance to discuss all the options.' He squeezed my arm.

We were ushered into the visitors' room. Dr Martin gave us a calm, clear, bordering on the brutal, breakdown of the situation. In her opinion Poppy's chances of surviving the treatment were only around 10 per cent. Even if she did survive, she would be mentally and physically damaged. To what extent, it was impossible to say but in her opinion it was likely she would have cerebral palsy, probably quite severely. She confirmed that the treatment was very invasive, operating on the brain many times.

She said because of the severity of Poppy's condition and the prognosis for her future, we, as Poppy's parents, could choose not to go ahead with the treatment. Of course this would mean she would die. She apologised for putting us in this position, but ultimately only we, her parents, could make this choice. She stressed that whatever we decided all the staff in the unit would be behind us.

I said that I felt very strongly I did not want Poppy's treatment to be continued.

'And you?' Dr Martin asked, turning to my husband.

I looked at him, saying a silent prayer.

'If there is any chance at all that Poppy could survive this treatment and go on to live with a decent quality of life, then of course we must go ahead with the treatment. But from what you've said it sounds like there is no chance. Am I right?'

Dr Martin nodded her head.

'Then I agree with Helen. I don't want her to be treated.'

I think they looked relieved. I'm sure the registrar was. Dr Martin was good at giving nothing away, but I had the feeling she agreed too.

'In that case I think you should take a couple of hours to really think carefully. You can still change your mind. Ring your family. There may be people you want to see Poppy before she passes away. Is there anything else you'd like to ask or need to say?'

'Yes, thank you for giving us this opportunity,' I said. 'Thank you so much.'

They looked at me as if I was slightly unhinged. Maybe at that moment I was.

'Believe me, if there was any chance that Poppy might come out of this with any quality of life we would not have had this conversation,' Dr Martin said, and strode out of the room.

With Poppy still heavily sedated, we left Mum sitting with her and my husband and I went outside to talk. We walked around the streets at the back of the hospital. The sun was hot. We passed an ice cream van and found ourselves in the park. All around us there were children playing on the grass. It all seemed so cruel. We lay on the grass, my husband face down, sobbing. I held him. 'It's going to be OK. It's going to be OK,' I said.

'It's not OK. Poppy's going to die.'

'But we've still got each other. We still have the life that we had before. If we can just get through this afternoon, I don't know how, but somehow we are just going to have to be strong. We have got to do this for her.'

Everything I said to my husband I meant, although deep down I knew it couldn't be that simple. But, relative to what we knew we were going to have to face over the next few hours, the years ahead didn't seem so bad. It was beyond comprehension what we were about to do and witness.

By the time we got back to the hospital I was desperate to see Poppy. I went over to her incubator. She opened her eyes wide and stared at me, wide awake. I took her hand and she squeezed my finger really tight. Yes, Poppy looked grey, yes, she had lost so much weight, but she seemed very much with us. I felt sick to the pit of my stomach.

They wheeled Poppy into a side room; our favourite nurse was already in there. As the registrar took my husband and me into the room he said, 'Poppy is very ill. She'll slip away very quickly.'

Poppy was taken off the ventilator. Suddenly, I could see her face again, and I felt the bitter irony that now that she was most ill, this was the least medical intervention she had ever had – just one small line feeding her painkillers.

I sat in a chair and they handed her to me, wrapped in a blanket. I cradled Poppy in my right arm but it didn't seem comfortable. I should have held her upright, close on my chest. It seems so cold, so impersonal now.

My husband sat with his arm around me and we waited for Poppy to die. We sang to her and talked to her and stroked her. I remember saying, with tears streaming down my face, 'Poppy, come back soon, come back,' and the nurse, crying too, gave me a strange look.

And Poppy just carried on breathing.

'Sometimes they need permission to go,' the registrar said. He stroked her forehead and said, 'It's OK, Poppy, you can go now.'

I said the same. It made no difference. My little girl didn't want to go anywhere.

The nurse and the registrar left, and we were on our own. Eventually, Poppy's breathing became less regular and she began to struggle. She stopped breathing and we looked at each other as if to say, 'This is it' and then she took another a deep breath, and we jumped. She was fighting all the way and I wondered whether it was too late to change my mind and whether my instinct was wrong and that Poppy was supposed to live and I was committing an act of murder.

And it also went through my mind that for all my brave words to my husband earlier, that actually our love might be dying along with Poppy. I wondered how we could ever come back from this.

And then she took one huge breath and didn't take another.

We held our breath.

And then she took yet another huge gulp of air.

My husband ran out of the room and straight into the ward, shouting, 'Help! You've got to come and help us. She's still alive. She won't die.'

The other parents, sitting with their babies, looked at him in horror.

The registrar came back in and with tears streaming down his cheeks he upped the level of morphine straight into her line and into her blood. 'I have never known such a strong baby. It may not look like it but she is very, very sick. You have got to believe me,' he said.

And then, within seconds, Poppy had gone.

People have asked me about the agony of the decision, but there was no decision really. I had no choice. I would have gone around pulling out the plugs myself if I hadn't been given the option.

Years later, I met a woman who had also had to take this decision about her premature baby girl. 'I knew it was time for her to go,' she said. 'Oh, yes. A mother always knows, doesn't she?'

*

A very clear picture came into my head that day. There was a beautiful yellow butterfly in a white, sterile room with only a tiny window. She was flying around, banging her wings against the wall, but for one brief moment I had the opportunity to open the window and let the butterfly fly free into the blue sky. If I didn't take that chance, Poppy would have been trapped in that room for ever. Just try and stop me. I would have fought tooth and nail, even against my husband. It was as if that day I had a sudden insight into the workings of the universe. And so I let the person die that I loved the most.

But that certainty didn't stop me feeling guilty. Poppy's final hour, where she didn't want to leave, was like Charlie Junior's tear for Clara. A mother knows best – or does she? It haunted me and it haunted my relationship with my husband. Years later, I asked him how he could have betrayed me after everything we had been through together; for me, Poppy's life and death bound us closer. I felt if I treated him badly I would be letting her down. I could never leave him because he was the only other person who had known her. But he had just shrugged. 'I felt completely the opposite. Because Poppy died, the universe owed me.'

It was a seminal moment for me.

So, yes, knowing how difficult it is to watch your child suffer and die and then to carry on and somehow pick up your life with everybody pretending that everything's all right now, when it's not at all, causes huge damage. For me, I found it difficult to love again. Something in you dies, with your child. And then you lose something more in the coping. I seemed to gain strength but lose softness. I found it hard to really feel love for anyone, most of all myself. My heart goes out to Clara and the series of real traumas she went through. How is it possible ever to be happy after that?

Having lunch with my mum and second cousin, Jean, that phrase cropped up again, this time uttered by Jean: 'Of course she never got over it. And him the only boy.'

To which my mum nodded in agreement.

But what did that mean: 'Never got over it'?

It also prompted another question. Driving home, I turned to Mum and asked, 'Do you think I've ever got over Poppy's death?'

There was a long silence. I could see Mum choosing her words very carefully. 'Funnily enough, I was thinking that too. And I think you have, but it took a long time and it was hard. There was something about you having Daisy which seemed to make a difference.'

I knew what she meant. Daisy was the fourth child I gave birth to. In common with other mothers who have lost children, I was always a child missing. When I had one child, Amber, I felt I should have two; when I had Scarlett and therefore two children, I felt I should have three. But when I had Daisy, I felt as if I was only ever meant to have three children. I can't explain it, except Daisy was a complete surprise. A little miracle, a gift. It was how I felt the universe had given back.

Of course, it was while I was pregnant with Daisy that my relationship with my husband abruptly deteriorated, as if something healed and something broke all at the same time.

Everyone asked whether I hoping to have a boy. But when I had the scan and once again I was told I was having a girl, I was overjoyed, as I had been with all my girls. I felt blessed.

She was angelic, beautiful and happy, very comfortable in her own skin – as she still is. We had the Daisy we were always supposed to have.

Of course I am not the same person I was before I had Poppy, and I wouldn't want to be, but I do think that I have somehow managed to reclaim a bit of myself: the softer, funnier, more vulnerable bits. And I definitely feel love now – huge, overwhelming sometimes – for my daughters, and for other people too.

Which brings me to Mr D. I don't talk about Poppy much; I know it upsets him. But, one day, after we had been knocking around together for quite some time, I felt compelled to start telling him a bit more. I got to the part where I saw Poppy's face for the first time, and Mr D hung his head and looked very emotional.

'This is really difficult for you, isn't it?' I said.

He sighed and nodded.

'OK, I'll stop.' But then I said, 'But you know, Poppy is a really important part of me. She's an exotic piece of patchwork right at the centre of the quilt of my existence.'

At which classic piece of 'Swainy' hyperbole he couldn't help but smile. '"Exotic piece of patchwork in your quilt of existence", eh?'

'Well, yes. She is part of my warp and weft, woven right into my psyche. I have had four daughters. She is real. It happened. Her existence changed me. Without Poppy I wouldn't be who I am now.' And then I said, slightly hesitatingly: 'I just wonder, if you can't handle this bit of my experience, is there a bit of me you can't handle or accept too?'

And Mr D thought and nodded and he kissed me, and I felt us draw a little bit closer. And I went on to tell him some more, and he listened, even though I could see it was really difficult. But later on that evening, when we had moved on to all sorts of lighter, fluffier topics, we found ourselves reminiscing about the first night I went back to his flat, the night we went to that old ancestral haunt, the Gladstone. And I told him for the first time how, after he went to sleep, I was wide awake, lying next to him, super-aware that our bodies were touching, and I had been filled with literal, physical waves of emotion flowing through my body, so powerful they were almost unbearable. It wasn't lust, it was like anticipation, like going over the top of a rollercoaster. I had felt extremely alive and glad to be alive. And I had known something significant had happened and was about to happen.

Which brought me back to the question I posed my mum – have I ever really got over Poppy's death? Talking to Mr D, I realised that there was the answer: that first night we spent together was just one of many moments I've had – not just with Mr D but with all sorts of people, especially my children and sometimes on my own – where

I've felt truly happy and, yes, glad to be alive. And I think however Poppy is woven into my fabric, her existence no longer stops me from experiencing profound moments of love, joy and happiness.

Which is a roundabout way of saying I have or, at least, I have *enough*.

But what of Clara? Her loss was never mentioned – no support, no therapy, no opportunity to while away time scribbling out her grief, too busy just trying to make a living? Trapped with her grief, with nowhere for it to go but to lie inside, toxic, for a lifetime?

Then there's the guilt. It never quite goes away. I went to see the film *Philomena*. It's the true story of a woman who, as a young unmarried teenager in Ireland, got pregnant and was forced to give up her son for adoption. With the help of a journalist, she travelled to the States to find him. Apologies now if I'm about to spoil the film for anyone who has never watched it, but for me the most profound moment came when the journalist had to tell Philomena that he had found her son, but he was dead. The first thing she says is: 'But I will never have the chance to tell him I'm sorry.'

I know exactly how she feels.

Did Clara just want to say sorry to Charlie Junior, like Philomena, like me? A deep, eternal desire for repentance and absolution. The first duty of a mother is to ensure her child's survival and if they die, we have profoundly failed.

And then another pressing question – did Clara feel that losing Charlie Junior meant she lost Charlie Senior as well? I think I know the answer to that one too – or is that just my stuff? I'm beginning to get her story and mine mixed up. It all feels too familiar …

# CHAPTER SIX
# The Albatross

Clara was waiting on the platform of Marlow station. At her feet was a large suitcase, by her side, her eldest daughter. She was wringing the fingers of her gloves with impatience. Where was the train? She didn't dare look at Alice's face. Suddenly there was a distant rumble. People wandered to the edge of the platform and peered along the tracks. First came traces of smoke above the treetops, then a whistle, and finally the familiar chug of the engine.

'Here it is,' Clara said under her breath.

She felt Alice grab her hand. 'Oh, Mum, I'm gonna miss you.'

Clara couldn't say anything. She just squeezed the hand.

And then the noisy, smoky engine pulled in. There was the slamming of doors, people jumping out, people jumping in. Alice grabbed her suitcase and stumbled.

Clara took it out of her hands and pushed her towards an open door. 'Get in. I'll pass it to you. Quick.'

Clara had been running through this moment in her head and it wasn't turning out how she had imagined. Too panicky, too quick. But at least Alice was in a compartment. Clara hauled the suitcase up after her and shoved it in.

Alice just stood, staring at her.

'Come on, close the door then.'

Alice slammed the door, and then leaned out of the window. Suddenly she looked young, younger than her sixteen years.

Clara had gone to a lot of trouble to make her a new outfit. Its main feature was a blue-grey, long coat that complemented her fair complexion and periwinkle Swain eyes. The coat was nipped in with a belt to show off her neat waist, and covered a full skirt that was fashionably short, coming to her mid-calves. Alice was also wearing a new soft felt hat that was almost the same blue. It was perched jauntily on the side of her head. Her auburn waves completed the look. But what caught Clara's eye was the way she was clutching the open window with hands wearing brand new white gloves. Clara's grocery shop, now open on the high street, had bought those kid gloves and she felt a moment's pride. Alice looked beautiful, but so young, like a child dressing up in adult's clothes, playing pretend. Too young to be leaving her family, travelling all the way to distant relations who had never even condescended to meet Clara. It felt wrong.

A whistle blew, and the train started to creep off with a slow chug, and then another, and another, faster.

'Are you going to be all right, Mum?' Alice shouted as the distance between them grew.

So Alice was as worried about Clara as Clara was about Alice. It was the wrong way round, against the natural order of things.

''Course I am!' Clara shouted back, trying not to look upset.

The train started to move off faster.

'Bye, Mum. Love you!' Alice shouted.

Clara waved and nodded. She realised one of her hands was clasped over her mouth. Then she pulled herself together. It couldn't be helping Alice. She should walk away. Like Lot's wife – if she turned to look back at her daughters left in Sodom and Gomorrah, she'd end up as a pillar of salt and that wouldn't help anybody.

So Clara walked determinedly out of the station. Inside the pain was physical – grief, like losing her father, like losing her son, all over again. Sometimes you have to let go of the people you love. Clara knew this was best for Alice. So did Alice.

In the end there hadn't really been a choice.

*

It had all come from a rather unexpected source. Charlie Swain Senior had been estranged from his family ever since they had sent him down to London in disgrace. He had received a letter to say his father had died, years before, but after that, nothing. Then, out of the blue, another letter arrived on their doormat.

Katie picked it up and ran into the kitchen. 'Who's this for, Mum?'

Clara took it from her and peered at it closely. 'It's for your dad.'

'Who's it from?'

Clara studied the handwriting. She didn't recognise it. 'I don't know, Nose Ointment.' Then she looked at the postmark: Luton. That was interesting.

When Charlie came home for his lunch, the first thing she did was to hand it to him. 'Letter for you.'

Charlie looked surprised. He recognised the handwriting straight away. 'It's my mother.' He sat down and opened it.

Clara watched his face closely. 'Bad news?'

'No … well, yes and no.' He was taking his time reading what looked like only a few lines.

'So?'

'My aunt, Mary Ann, has died. Mother wants to know if I can come to the funeral.'

'Oh. That's a bit sudden, isn't it? What do you think that's about, then?'

'Well, there's only one way to find out, isn't there?'

'So you're going?'

Charlie stared at Clara. She didn't like it when he looked at her like that. Hostile.

'Yes. Yes, I am. It's about time I saw my family.'

'And I'm not invited.'

'No, you're not.'

'And that's all right?'

'Yes. I don't see why not. It's a family occasion.'

There was a very obvious answer that Clara could make to that. She thought about it and then decided to let it go. She was working hard on picking her battles, otherwise their home would make the Western Front seem like a mere scrap in the playground.

'I'll take one of the girls with me.'

'Oh, yeah? Why?'

'It will be good for them to meet my family.'

'Well, I don't think it will be good for Dora to do another funeral.'

It was over two years since Charlie Junior died, but Dora was still having nightmares.

'No, I was thinking of Katie.'

'Katie?'

'Yes.'

'Why?'

'She's the prettiest.'

It was true, Katie did have neat little features: a tipped-up nose and pretty, rosebud mouth. Bertha was seen as a bit pale, ginger and skinny. But Charlie saying this out loud sent a massive, visceral wave of protectiveness towards her other daughters through Clara.

'What are you like?'

'What do you mean?'

But he wasn't going to find out because at that moment Charlie became aware of his twin daughters standing quietly in the corner, watching. Grace was standing behind them.

'Katie, I'm taking you to see your aunts and your family. What do you think of that?' He stood up and swept a rather surprised Katie in his arms.

Bertha stood back and looked up at her mum. 'What about me? Am I going?'

'No. You're staying here to help me,' Clara said quickly.

Bertha kept quiet but was mortally offended.

She wasn't the only one. Later that night, in the bed the sisters all shared, there was talk.

'Why's Dad taking you, Bossy Boots?' Alice asked, poking Katie.

'Because I'm the best.'

'Rubbish.'

'It's because he thinks she's the prettiest. But he doesn't know you like we do,' Grace said, sniffing.

'You're only jealous.'

'Yeah, you're pretty now but that's 'cos you're five. Wait and see. You're gonna be a right heffalump by the time you're ten,' Grace said, poking her again.

Katie leapt up and tried to wallop her big sister, but instead managed to crush Dora's leg.

'Ow! Watch it, idiot!'

At which point Bertha started to wail.

'What's wrong with you?' Grace asked.

'Well, I'm five too, and Dad's not taking me.'

'Oh, baby … who wants to go anyway? Better off staying here with us.' Alice had a soft spot for the little quiet one.

'Yeah. Just think – a dead body being lowered slowly into the ground, everyone in black, crying, veils covering their faces, and the ghost of dead Great-Aunt Mary Ann looking down on you, watching … Urggghhh! I wouldn't go, no way. You're better off here.' Dora pulled Bertha close and flung the covers over both their heads.

Alice and Grace giggled. Dora's melodrama could be quite useful sometimes.

'Shut up, all of you. I ain't afraid of no dead body,' Katie said gamely.

'We'll see,' Dora mumbled from under the covers prophetically. Then they all went quiet as they remembered their brother.

By the time Charlie and Katie set off for Luton, Bertha's quiet envy had reached boiling point. The final straw was having to watch her sister being dressed by their mother by the kitchen fire during breakfast.

Clara helped Katie step into a brand new black silk dress with lots of frothy petticoats and a huge sash. Katie was wriggling and complaining: 'Oh, Mum, it hurts. It's too tight.'

'Shhhh! It's not too tight.'

Bertha suddenly snapped: 'Shut up!' She picked up her bowl of porridge and threw it across the kitchen, where it landed on the wall right next to the mark where Clara had thrown the iron ladle a few years before.

There was silence, everyone shocked.

Katie's trip gave Bertha evidence of what she had felt ever since she could remember – that she was the spare, unwanted child. Even worse, a girl. She used to say, 'I was the bottom of the barrel.' This feeling was the key to how Nanna moved through the world.

Take Nanna's name – Bertha. Names say something profound about how our parents see us – their hopes and dreams, and what we mean to them. The name Clara and Charlie chose for Nanna set the tone for how she saw herself. Clara loved the name Katie: it was a family name, and so it was given to her as the firstborn twin. But the baby no one knew was coming – well, while she could think of plenty of boys' names, there were no girls' names left in Clara's head or heart. So she plucked a name out of the ether. As it happened 'Bertha' turned out to be a rather unfortunate choice because, just a few years later, 'Big Bertha' was the nickname the army gave to any large German gun. Nanna was teased mercilessly at school. And she thought Bertha sounded ugly. Later on, she would change her name to Betty.

Meanwhile, she had an enduring love for the name Katie. When I was expecting Poppy, she kept on saying, 'Why don't you call her Katie?' And then again, when I was pregnant with Amber: 'I think Katie's a lovely name.' Well, yes, it's a nice name, but there were others I preferred. Even my mum urged me to consider Katie. Why? What were they trying to resolve with this gesture? One thing I did know was that

I wanted my baby to have no part in this. I wanted a fresh slate and a clean page for her. I wouldn't saddle my baby with the baggage of four generations of female ancestors. But then, who was I kidding? If only it was just about giving them a new name.

Anyway it was odd, Nanna's relationship with her twin. She loved her, and yet competed with her. It was the Carnation milk anecdote. Nanna never quite got over the fact that her mother, unable to breastfeed them both, had chosen to feed Katie. Clara said it was because Katie was the weaker of the two, but Bertha wasn't convinced, and still simmered with resentment. She sometimes wickedly put Katie down, and yet sort of wanted to be her, but was glad she wasn't. Genuinely mixed and mixed up. Having a prettier, more confident, more loved twin, whom Bertha herself loved to bits and indeed leant on, made it all a bit complicated.

Nanna hid this sense of being unwanted, but her actions were telling. Despite being self-effacing she was adept at drawing attention to herself. For example, her clothes. Mum tells how Nanna made herself the most lurid check coat during the Second World War – bright red and green, large plaid. It clashed with her red hair but heads turned and comments were made on every outing. Nanna had her ways of stating her existence: I am here! I exist! In my bright plaid coat which clashes with my hair, you *will* take notice of me!

Yes, Nanna was most put out not to have been chosen to go to Great-Aunt Mary Ann's funeral. However, in this instance, she definitely had the last laugh.

Great-Aunt Mary Ann had been the landlady of the Royal Hotel public house in Luton. Now her body was lying in state in the upstairs of the Royal and, according to the tradition of the time, was receiving visitors before it was buried.

When Charlie arrived with Katie, the female Swains were rather abrupt. Sitting in the private dining room above the bar – Great-Aunt

Mary Ann residing in the front room – they were all having afternoon tea. It was quite intimidating. There was his mother, Caroline, looking considerably older and stouter, and a selection of aunts and uncles and cousins, all in black.

'We didn't expect you to bring a child with you,' were Charlie's mother's first words, after twenty years.

'This is Katie. Go on, say hello to your grandmother.'

It wasn't as if Katie wasn't used to mourning. She still remembered the house after Charlie Junior died – the windows closed, the clock stopped and all of them in black. But there was so much *more* mourning in this huge pub – the blinds were closed so the room was in semi-darkness; the large mirror had a cloth over it (in case the spirit of Great-Aunt Mary Ann got caught in it); and the aunts were all wearing heavy veils and black gloves, tea cups delicately poised.

Her father nudged her forwards.

'Good afternoon, Grandmother.' She found herself curtseying.

Charlie smiled proudly but his cousin Sarah just said: 'I haven't got anywhere to put her, you know. We have a room for you, but otherwise the hotel is full.'

'Well, she'll just have to draw up a chair in the front room and spend the night with your aunt, may she rest in peace,' Caroline said. 'Is that all right?'

Charlie didn't think it was all right at all, but all he could do was nod.

Katie didn't like the sound of the 'may she rest in peace' but knew better than to ask.

When it came to bedtime Katie was ushered into the front room and shown a chair right next to the open coffin of her great-aunt. And there she spent a long night, surrounded by spluttering candles, next to the body of her dead relative – coins on her eyes, a bandage tied round her chin, and cotton wool in her mouth.

*

Of course the first question Clara asked Charlie when he arrived back – with a rather pale and subdued Katie – was why the black sheep had been taken back into the fold.

'I've no idea. No one said anything to me, not about nothing.' But then Charlie had to put his boot in: 'Except the usual, "Oh, fancy all girls – no son."' Clara looked away. He said it like it was her fault. A lot of the time it did feel like her fault. 'No – perhaps this is it. Remember I told you that my aunt Charlotte is married to a hat maker?'

Clara nodded.

'Well, this William she's married to is doing pretty well. He's got his own business and they need to take on some more girls. Anyway, they've asked if Alice would like to work for them.'

Clara had to sit down.

'Think about it – it's a great opportunity. She can't help you out in the shop for ever, not with Grace too.'

'I know,' she said.

It was difficult to argue with Charlie. With the war coming to an end, men were pouring back from France looking for work. With 40 per cent of soldiers unemployed, jobs were scarce. Since she had left school two years before, Alice had been helping Clara in her shop. It was a happy arrangement. But now Grace had left school too, and there wasn't enough work for them both, and the family could do with one less mouth to feed.

One of the few industries that was still an exclusively women's preserve was hat making. The wages were uncommonly high – so high that Luton had a reputation for slovenly houses and lazy men: the women being too busy to scrub their floors, and earning so much that the men didn't bother to work. There was competition for their skills, too, so a small company like William's had a high turnover of young women – good workers were often poached by one of the big factories with the promise of higher wages. But a young lady relative would be more likely to stay.

Alice also had a sewing pedigree: one of Clara's sisters was seamstress to the royal family, while Charlie's brother Sidney was the official tailor to Wormwood Scrubs prison (a fact which always conjures up images of grey boiler suits with arrows on them). Added to this, Alice had started picking up sewing skills when her mother ran Darn It!.

Most importantly, Alice would be learning a trade.

As Clara had explained to Alice, it was a great opportunity.

But Alice had just looked at her mum askance. 'You promised you would never send me away, EVER.'

Clara was silent. In the end all she could say was, 'It won't be for ever. I'll find a way to bring you back. You'll see.'

Alice had flung her arms around her mum's neck. They had never been parted and Clara was only too aware how much they had been through together.

So, in the autumn of 1918, Clara waved goodbye to Alice on the platform of Marlow station.

She wouldn't see her again for a year.


Charlie Swain was not a bad man. He had feelings. In fact, in some ways he had too many feelings.

On the journey back from France, he had known that the main problem he had just then was in finding a credible story for why he was home after little more than a year fighting for Queen and country, pretty much as fit as he had left, with the war raging fiercely and men needed at the Front more than ever. But it turned out that that was the easy part.

Charlie suspected that not everyone believed his tale of gas canisters rolling under trucks – especially his wife – but no one openly challenged him. The brewery gave him back his job, and he was given a hero's welcome in the pub.

It was Charlie's conscience that was the problem: it didn't take him long to realise that his white lie was going to mess with his head. He had been looking forward to getting away from the shells on the French roads; however, he hadn't counted on the lethal emotional grenades that would explode when he got back home.

When Charlie got back to the brewery most of the men had gone, their places taken by older men, and women. It's not that he minded the new intake, but they made him feel uncomfortable. Why was he there when they weren't? Was he no more use than an old man, or a *woman*? Unfortunately, the army had given an unequivocal answer to that one.

He'd only been back a couple of weeks and was engrossed in mending a broken pump, when Bill came over. 'Here, Charlie – have you heard the news? Young Johnny Price is coming back.'

'Eh?'

'Yeah. He's back home and they say he's starting any day now.'

Charlie was confused. 'But I thought he'd lost a leg?'

'Well, he has, but he's got a wooden one and he's pretty nifty on it.'

Charlie realised Bill was waiting for a reaction. 'That's great,' he said, and started working on the pump again with great vigour.

Charlie tried not to think about it but when, a couple of days later, he walked around the corner and bumped straight into Johnny, he found himself staring at the wooden leg. It was as if a spell had been cast on his eyes, forcing him to confront something really unpalatable. He walked straight past Johnny, ignoring him. From then on he went to great lengths to avoid the young man. If he walked into the pub and caught sight of Johnny – usually surrounded by admirers and being bought drinks – Charlie would walk out. In the end, he even stopped going to his local and found a new watering hole.

But Johnny was not the only war-wounded hero in Marlow: they were everywhere. As Charlie walked along Marlow High Street, a familiar figure would pass him missing an arm, or in a wheelchair. At the end of their row of cottages there was Johnny Gardner who had been gassed and come back not just struggling to breathe, but mentally unhinged. Charlie dreaded walking past his house because he could often be sitting in a chair outside the front door, his face hollowed out and ghastly, as if he were constantly seeing ghosts. Every time Charlie saw him, he felt as if someone had just walked over his own grave.

There was no respite at home, either, with the girls enthusiastically knitting socks for soldiers. It was the moment when the five-year-old twins learnt to knit. Those evenings spent competitively creating footwear turned my nanna into a champion of the knitting needle. I used to watch her working away, busy chatting, the sound of the needles clicking, not bothering to look at what she was producing, as if the needles were an extension of her arm. Fascinated, I asked her to teach me, and I am now a champion knitter too. But Charlie felt like they were mocking him. As the sisters excitedly compared their efforts, he would shout at them to shut up.

Clara noticed but kept her thoughts to herself. Again she was picking her battles.

One day, however, she broke her silence. A regular customer didn't turn up for her eggs, but a neighbour came in her place.

'Have you heard?' the neighbour said. 'Terrible news. You know Fred, her youngest? Well, he's been killed.'

'Oh, no.'

'Yes. She was scanning the newspaper and there was his name in the list of the dead. Killed by a shell. Terrible. The letter came not long after.'

'Poor thing.'

'She's taken it hard, of course. He was her favourite and she begged him not to go.'

Clara nodded. She felt the mother's pain there.

When Charlie came home, Clara told him.

'And why are you telling me this?'

'Because I thought you'd be interested.'

'Why would I be interested in someone else's son dying?'

Clara stared at him, not knowing what to say. He moved towards her threateningly. 'Are you deliberately trying to punish me?'

'Punish you?'

'You don't understand, do you?'

'Understand what?'

Charlie teetered on the brink of telling her, but something stopped him. He felt as though if he let it out, the genie would never go back into the bottle. He changed tack. 'My son never got the chance to serve his country, die a hero's death.'

'Well, at least he died here in his home, with me.'

'That's a good thing? There's no honour in Charlie's death. It's shameful. That Fred boy is a hero. He will never be forgotten. How many people have mourned Charlie?'

'But so many have died! And you can't expect people to mourn Charlie. He never went out. I don't know about you, but I think about him every day, all the time. And I'm his mother and that's all that matters. He's here,' she said, her voice rising, her finger jabbing at her chest, 'in my heart. Bloody engraved there, everything he went through, for ever, whether I like it or not.'

'Well, I wish I'd died a hero's death.'

Clara looked at him, suspiciously. 'Really? And why's that?'

'Why do you think?'

'I really don't know.'

Charlie hesitated, then walked out of the house and down the road to the pub.

That wasn't the end of the rows. Charlie came home later, more drunk, spending more of their housekeeping money in the pub. Clara would wait up for him, sitting by the fire on her own. Sometimes she would just stare into it, thinking hard. There was a gap in her middle: it started as hurt, blossomed into fury and before she knew it, there would be a cauldron of rage waiting to explode when Charlie got home. On those nights, with the noise of shouting ringing in their ears, the little girls in the bed upstairs were so frightened that they would pull the covers over their heads and the bed would shake.

Some of the sisters said that on those nights, they thought Charlie was violent to Clara.

Charlie said strange things during these arguments, like: 'You blame me for our son's death.'

To which Clara replied: 'No, if anything I blame myself for his death. What I do blame you for is drowning yourself in drink. For not realising how precious your living family is and not looking after them.'

'If I did that then I really would be admitting I killed him.'

'How do you work that one out, then?'

But he didn't have an answer.

This confused Clara. In the end, one day, she said, 'I think you blame yourself for Charlie's death.'

Clara may as well have hit him, because now she *had* let the genie out of the bottle. Charlie felt that it couldn't have been just a coincidence that Charlie Junior had died within a couple of months of him returning home, having drunk too much and with a rucksack full of watches stolen from dead English soldiers. He felt the universe had punished him for his war crimes. But of course he couldn't admit this to Clara, because his war record had to remain a secret. And then there was the fact that Charlie had treated his son as if he had died, and talked as if he had died – and then he had gone and died. For that he could never forgive himself.

Of course, he might have been able to if he'd known Charlie Junior had contracted Pott's disease long before he started misbehaving at the Front. It is just one of the many tragedies in my great-grandparents' difficult relationship.

There were moments, however, when things looked up.

The morning after one of those stormy nights, Charlie woke up with an idea and said to Clara, 'Why don't you open a shop? I've some money saved from the Front.'

'You didn't tell me! I've been struggling all these months. What money, anyway? Where did you get it?'

'It doesn't matter. Do you want it or not?'

Clara did want it. With food still in short supply, prices had gone up and the market for any produce, particularly home-grown, was very lucrative. Clara took Charlie at his word and the next day took out a lease on a shop in the market square, opposite the church. 'Swain's Grocers' was in business. But while it helped their financial position, it did little to ease Charlie's state of mind. He lost his job at the brewery for deserting his post and being under the influence. A spell as a car mechanic ended the same way. And then somehow he managed to get hired as the keeper of Marlow's lock. It was a good job and a lovely house came with it, right next to the weir. For once there seemed to be enough space for all of them. Charlie didn't think his inability to swim would be a problem. Which it shouldn't have been, except he could not stop drinking. It was hard to operate the winch when you were half cut, especially if you kept nipping off to the pub next door whenever the coast was clear. With Alice gone, Grace helping in the shop and Dora being too nervous, the twins were now sent off with the wheelbarrow to collect their father from the pub when a barge was waiting. It didn't look good for the keeper to arrive lounging in a barrow. In fact my nanna used to ruefully reminisce about it.

Charlie's secret – the albatross around his neck – was getting heavier. It was becoming difficult to exist.


Years ago, I heard a piece of music which I think is the closest I've come to what the torture of a guilty conscience might sound like. It was a dark winter's evening close to the end of the year. I was once again in the chapel of St John's College, Cambridge. This time I wasn't performing, only listening. I was heartbroken. I had temporarily split up from the man who was to become my husband and was lost, falling through the void. I did what I do when I'm in that place, and went to commune with my maker, whoever He/She/It might be.

The chapel was cold and shadowy, lit only by the candles on the choir stalls. I crept into one of the pews behind the choir, wrapped my coat more tightly around me and slunk down, wanting to remain alone in melancholy reverie.

I was undisturbed until the choir filed in and started to sing an anthem that was unlike anything I'd heard before: a rich deep, deep bass voice calling out: '*O vos omnes.*'

I sat up. They were singing in Latin, but I understood the words. They were the lamentations usually sung in the week leading up to Easter – always my favourite time of year for sacred music, I like my tunes miserable:

> *O all you who walk by on the road, pay attention and see,*
> *if there be any sorrow like my sorrow.*
> *Pay attention, all people, and look at my sorrow,*
> *If there be any sorrow like my sorrow.*

Unaccompanied, the clashing chords twisted and turned and went down and then twisted again and went down further – it was dark, and I loved it. On top, the clear boy trebles were repeatedly swallowed up by the deep, sinister bass, and then remerged again over the top, pleading, '*O vos omnes.*' But help wasn't to hand, and down the music went again, clashing in minor. My senses shivered. Who on earth had written something so chilling?

Afterwards I tripped across the road to the pub where I knew I'd find the answer: there was the choir propping up the bar.

'What were you singing?' I asked Tim the bass.

'Did you like it?'

'It was fabulous. See? Goosebumps!' I pushed up my sleeve and held out my arm.

Tim was a good bloke. He laughed. 'Let me buy you a drink. And how are you?' he asked. He knew about the break-up.

I was determined to save face: I gave him a practised grin and brought the subject back to the music. 'So, who wrote it?'

'Who do you think?'

'No idea. That's why I'm asking.' He raised his glass to me and in return I said, 'I think it's either very early or very late.'

'Interesting. Everyone agrees he was certainly way ahead of his time. A musical Hieronymus Bosch.'

'Oh, early then. Wow! ... So?'

'It's Gesualdo.'

'Who's Gesualdo?'

'You've never heard of him?'

'Nope.'

'Oh, well. You might find his life story even more exciting than his music.'

'I knew it. He must have had something truly dreadful happen to him to write such spooky music.'

'Well, not so much what happened to him as what he *did*. He caught his wife in bed with her lover and murdered them both. I think he cut off the lover's knob and stuck it in his mouth.'

'Blimey!'

'Yes. The good thing is that after that, he went on to write the most weird and wonderful music.'

I finished my pint and strode off to the college library to look up Gesualdo. I was not disappointed. Formerly a composer of mediocre love ballads in fifteenth-century Naples, after murdering his beautiful wife and her young aristocratic lover, he escaped to his castle in the wilds of Puglia and locked himself in a room and wrote increasingly desperate religious music. He remarried and then murdered his son. He then commissioned a mural on the roof of his Great Hall (which still exists), where he is shown receiving forgiveness from God while his first wife and her lover are burning in the flames of hell. It didn't relieve Gesualdo's torment, however, because he went on to don a hair shirt and hire twelve monks to whip him three times a day. In the end, the wounds from these whippings went septic and he died.

It seems a guilty conscience can indeed be fatal.

Gesualdo was obviously not a very nice man. But was it him, or what *happened* to him? Did the shock of the deceit send him into a violent spiral from which it was impossible to recover? Of course Charlie didn't murder Clara – he only cut down her washing line. He didn't turn to flagellating monks – he tried to find absolution in the bottom of a beer glass. In the end, neither worked.

Shakespeare was perceptive when he wrote *Macbeth* – a guilty secret doesn't bring a couple together but drives them apart. I know this. It happened to me too.

We both felt guilty about the part we played in our daughter's birth and death. It was guilt that involved and implicated each other, and we couldn't look at each other. Partners in an unforgiveable crime. The fault line grew into an unbridgeable fissure in our marriage.

And when he disappeared, those long nights waiting for him to come home, never answering his phone, like my great-grandmother sitting by the fire in the silence with the children sleeping upstairs, I would tackle him when he finally crashed in. But he turned it back on me: I was too demanding, I didn't understand his job, it was his lengthy absences that enabled me to live in the style to which I was accustomed. And I took it and blamed myself for asking too much. And I trusted him and now I feel stupid. But is it wrong to trust the person you love?

The years I tried to reach out and repair our marriage. Now I know it was impossible, because he was carrying a secret, another family, and the secret was a barrier to us ever meeting authentically. The thing is, knowledge is power and because he never told me what was really happening, I had no choice. He kept me (probably inadvertently) jailed in a gilded cage. As soon as I knew the truth, I had a choice and it was an enormous relief. I had the permission and power to kick open the door, which I did.

Someone once described marriage as being like a house: once secrets are not shared within the house or, worse, taken outside to others, it is no longer secure. The windows are open, the door unlocked, burglars get in.

With a toxic cocktail of guilt and secrets, we had no chance, and by the time the tangled web of his other relationships was exposed, the damage of those years of lying was too great for us ever to meet again. I tried for over a year but trust had gone, and with it respect and love. He couldn't look at me because when he looked into my eyes he saw what he'd done. I was the inconvenient truth. Tragedy, stupidity and waste, and a family broken apart. Like taking a glass; no, actually something heavier – a china vase – and throwing it at the ground with such force that it smashes to smithereens, sharp splinters everywhere.

I feel like I'm being melodramatic, but am I? Because what words are there to describe the pain and messiness of the break-up of a long relationship and the family unit?

# CHAPTER SEVEN
# If A Job's
# Worth Doing ...

Charlie didn't mean to fall in the river in March 1919. It was a beautiful night, cold but clear. He was meandering home along the towpath from the pub, watching the moonlight ruffling the river. The rushing sound of the water tumbling over the weir filled his senses. And with all this nature going on, he must have wandered from the path straight into the river.

It was exactly as they said. His life flashed past him in slow motion, starting from the day before and then winding back – past every birthday, every Christmas, every birth, death – good and bad, there was no mercy. And just as they said, Charlie did bob up to the surface three times, and then when he went back down under for the third time he knew he wouldn't be coming back up again and he was filled with a sense of peace. It was exquisite – the shock of the cold water, numbing his pain and washing him clean. Charlie had been running really hard and now he'd escaped. A bit like when the fourth pint hit his senses, washing away the bad stuff. But compared to drowning, alcohol was just a temporary fix. Suddenly Charlie realised this was the real thing, there was a way out.

But just as Charlie got close enough to touch his nirvana, he saw a face peering through the surface of the water and an arm reaching down and grabbing him by the scruff of the neck, hauling him back to earth whether he liked it or not.

Mr Wilkinson, a local town councillor, couldn't understand why Charlie was not more grateful to him for having saved his life. As Charlie lay on his back, his body struggling for breath, while his mind was cursing, Mr Wilkinson said, 'Good thing I was walking past. I heard a splash. And there you were. I reckon I got here just in time.'

Charlie just coughed and stared back at him. Mr Wilkinson helped him to his feet and supported him the short distance back to the lock keeper's house. Charlie didn't look at him, didn't say goodbye as he walked in and shut the door in his face. Not one word of thanks. The next day Mr Wilkinson reported him to the authorities for being drunk.

Charlie was hauled before a committee and told that he had lost his job. In shock and terror, he had to have a drink and went straight to the pub. When he was finally chucked out and had to stagger home and tell his wife that he had been sacked again, Clara greeted the news with surprising calm. All those nights sat alone by the fire, waiting, had not been wasted. Because Clara had been making plans. There came an evening when, for no discernible reason in particular, Clara suddenly saw her situation in a whole new light. In short, she decided to take control of her own and her daughters' destinies. For the first time she saw that she had a choice. And as soon as she realised that, everything felt better. Outwardly nothing had changed, but inwardly there had been a revolution. And when Charlie staggered in and told her he had been sacked, she was ready for him.

Clara stated her position clearly so there could be no misunderstanding: 'I've written to my sister Rosie. Remember her? She's the one in East London. She says there's a job going at the Seabrooke's Brewery in Grays. It's simple, Charlie. You can either move with us to Essex or we go without you anyway. Your choice.'

Charlie, stunned, just nodded.

'You're coming with us, then?'

Charlie nodded again. Actually a fresh start, an escape, was a rather compelling idea. 'Thank you,' was all he could say.

Clara looked at him, puzzled. 'You're totally sozzled, aren't you?'

'I may have had a drop of the old jag juice.'

'More like a barrel.'

He stared at her. His eyes always lost their sharp, fresh blue after his second pint. After his third they switched to a rheumy, glassy, vacant look, as if the shutters had come down.

Clara decided to carry on while she was on a roll. 'I also want Alice back from Luton.'

Charlie stumbled backwards slightly. 'Why do you want to do that?'

'I've got plans for her.'

'Well, William Russon's got plans for her. She's doing well. He's not going to want to lose her, not after he's trained her up.'

'She can do better.'

'How do you know? It's a good job. What's the family going to think?'

'They can go to old Harry.' Clara pointed her finger at him and jabbed him in the chest. 'Listen to me, Charlie Swain – if you don't write to your sister, I will.'

Charlie knew when the game was up, so he took the path of least resistance and just nodded.

But Clara still needed one more thing for her plan to work – money. She knew that her shop in the high street hadn't used up all of Charlie's secret stash as, at breakfast most days, he'd look up from his racing paper and cheerfully ask: 'Hands up who's my favourite girl today?'

At which all of the sisters would sit up and put their hands in the air, and then, rummaging in his pockets, he'd say to the one who got there first (usually Katie): 'Right, favourite girl, you can go and put this on Prince Dreamer at the 3.45 at Kempton.'

And Clara would watch, narrow-eyed, as the chosen daughter would dutifully trot off to the bookies to put on a bet for her dad.

Clara had searched everywhere, but she couldn't find his pot of gold. Little did she know that Charlie had hidden the money from his war time 'souvenirs' in the outdoor lavatory cistern, while the loot he hadn't managed to sell – which, years later, Dennis would pour out of a BHS bag – he had buried in the allotment underneath the roots of the apple tree.

So Clara carried on. 'And I want all the money you've got stashed away. I won't ask where you got it or where you've been hiding it, I just want it.'

'What money?'

'Don't give me that. Don't even try. I know you've got it. I've seen you putting your hands in your pockets for the gee-gees.'

There was silence. Then Charlie just sighed and said, 'What for?'

'To make us more money, before you gamble it all away.'

Charlie looked at his wife, swaying slightly, weighing up his options. Ordinarily he would have responded with a 'Get Lost!' but Clara had bided her time and waited for a moment when he was supremely vulnerable. Charlie was distracted by an image of walking into the house and there being no one there – a cold, dark kitchen without a fire, a bedroom with no little girls piled on top of each other, arms and legs tangled up and hanging out everywhere, like puppies. He had lost one child already, and that hurt enough. Never to see the rest of them again – well, he felt physically sick.

'I can't live without you,' was all he said.

Clara nodded. She had somehow, finally, seized control of the household and their destiny. It was so easy that she wondered why she hadn't done it before.

Within days the Swain family had packed up their belongings and travelled from the quiet, prosperous banks of the river at Marlow, east into London, and almost out the other side. Within a couple of weeks, and with a bit of finessing, Charlie had managed to get himself the chief engineering job at the Seabrooke Brewery in Grays. And then within a couple of months Alice arrived back from her year in Luton, to much rejoicing from everyone, not least her mother.

The Swain family immediately felt at home. They were still on the Thames, but it was completely different to its Marlow incarnation: it was not a tamed, bucolic playpen for anglers; it was open sea and choppy waves. No men in boaters wooing their maidens in rowing boats, but large barges and ships going into the Port of London, and fishing boats going backwards and forwards to the North Sea.

Grays was next to the big docks at Tilbury. There were also chalk quarries, brickworks and, of course, the brewery. The people reflected the difference too – there was no West Country burr to their voice. They were estuary, rougher and tougher and generally poorer. Clara no longer felt like an imposter.

With the extra money Clara had managed to wrench from Charlie, they rented a large house on the corner of the main road to London. Clara had chosen it specially, because its front room was a shop. It was the largest retail space that Clara had ever had, and she was determined to sell everything.

Ways of preserving food and its transportation had undergone a revolution. Clara was able to fill her shelves with all sorts of new products that were terribly exciting to the 1920s housewife: tins of peas, beans, ham, meat loaf, pilchards, peaches, pears and apples. Then there was tea, powdered custard, Oxo cubes, Horlicks, Marmite and, the latest craze, which came from France – packets of crisps complete with blue twists of salt.

There were big jars of sweets: mints, Black Jacks, sugar mice, sherbet, liquorice allsorts, toffees, lollypops and the sinister 'unwanted babies', which we now know as Jelly Babies – all of which the girls helped themselves to when Clara wasn't looking. Clara also made cakes and pastries, while Katie and Bertha were given the task of making lemonade. The shop was colourful and filled with the smell of fruit and vegetables.

Although Clara was a private woman, she was astute enough to realise the social aspect of shopping – it was one of the few opportunities housewives had to meet and chat. So Clara put a 'resting chair' in the corner, where the local gossips could hold court and draw people into the shop.

As Clara's shop prospered, Charlie acted as if he was proud of her. In the pub he would boast, 'My wife, she's a regular Mrs Selfridge, she is,' or 'Watch out for my missus – she's giving Liptons a run for their money,' but underneath the bravado, he was a bit uncomfortable.

One night, wandering home from the pub and feeling hungry, Charlie had a flash of inspiration: he would turn his beloved shed into a fish and chip shop.

At no time in British history did we eat more fish and chips: most families ate their dinner from the folds of old newspapers at least once a week. And in the days before health and safety inspectors, anyone could set up a shop in their backyard. Charlie reckoned he could open his shop three or four nights a week after work.

The sisters watched as Charlie spent a weekend banging, sawing and going in and out of the haven that was his shed. Finally, a canister of gas and a big chip pan went in. Then Charlie produced a sack of potatoes and set the twins peeling, Dora mashing peas and Grace mixing batter. That evening, the Swain family sat around the kitchen table and tasted the first fruits of Charlie's chippy.

Even Clara managed a smile. 'Blimey, Charlie, this ain't 'alf good!'

'Yes, Dad, scrummy,' the girls agreed.

However, the attempt was short-lived. Unfortunately, Grays was very well served for pubs; indeed, it had the reputation for having more pubs per head than any other town in the country. For the first couple of weeks Charlie managed to resist their lure, but then a Friday evening came along, and he'd had a hard day at work, and it was his mate's birthday … Charlie started heating up the chip pan and calculated he had time for a pint. He swung over the fence and popped over to the pub across the road, where they were all celebrating. He was just going to have one ... but then he kind of forgot and the next thing he knew Grace had run into the bar, shouting: 'Dad, come quickly! Ya shed's burning down!'

Immediately there was a stampede of merry men across the road, rolling up their sleeves ready to do battle with the flames. Unfortunately, they were disappointed – Charlie's shed was already a smouldering wreck.

Charlie put on a brave face and accepted his mates' jokes, but he was subdued for the next few days. He avoided his family and friends and spent his time out in the yard clearing up the mess and building himself a new shed.

Charlie decided to take the attitude that everything happens for a reason, and the reason his shed burnt down was that he hadn't aimed high enough. Much to Clara's extreme scepticism, less than a month later Charlie had rented a shop down the road and opened a more substantial fast-food enterprise.

For the first few months Charlie's new chippy was a success: on Friday nights there were queues stretching out of the shop, around the corner and down the street. Clara was surprised when Charlie even started to give her extra money. But, after a while, those queues started to dwindle – they stopped reaching around the corner, and then finally Charlie realised the queue never even left the shop.

He couldn't understand why: no one had anything but praise for the quality of his batter.

In the end he had to shut the shop, which was a shame because Charlie was actually a victim of his own generosity. The reason people stopped coming in the shop was because they'd realised that, at the end of the evening, whatever food was left Charlie used to give to the poor and hungry that were hanging around his back door. Word got around and people soon decided not to go in the front, but just wait a little longer and get a free meal around the back.

Charlie decided retail was not for him, and from then on stuck to engineering.

Charlie and his daughters thought Clara's plan was just to open a bigger shop but, not for the first time, they underestimated her. Six months after they moved to Grays, with the family gathered around the kitchen table, eating supper, Clara made an announcement: 'You're all going to have piano lessons.'

There was a stunned silence. Then Grace piped up: 'Don't we need a piano?'

'We do, Gracie, we do. Which is why I have bought one.'

'What?' Charlie put down his knife and fork and stared at his wife.

'Yes. The shop is making good money and I've saved up and I've bought one. It arrives next week.' And then she muttered, 'How many cigarette cases and pocket watches does a man need, anyway?'

The girls looked confused, but Charlie blushed bright red and stared down at his plate. Clara must have found his hidden treasure chest of 'souvenirs'.

'You'll all start with the piano, but if there's anything else you want to learn you can do that too.'

The girls looked at each other.

'Do you think I could learn to sing?' Alice asked tentatively.

Her mother nodded. 'I think you should definitely learn to sing.'

Alice had a wonderful soprano voice. She annoyed her sisters by breaking into old music hall songs at every opportunity, for example, 'Where Did You Get That Hat?' when Bertha tried out a new creation; 'If You Were The Only Girl In The World' when Grace walked past a boy she rather liked the look of (or 'A Little Of What You Fancy' if she was feeling particularly cheeky and their mother wasn't around); and 'Down The Road, Away Went Polly' every time Dora picked up enough courage to leave the house. 'I Do Like To Be Beside The Seaside' was reserved for their Sunday promenades along Grays beach.

Meanwhile, Bertha fancied becoming accomplished at something a little more sophisticated: 'I'd like to play the violin,' she piped up.

The sisters rolled their eyes, and snorts of hilarity filled the room as the giggling infection started to spread.

Bertha blushed, but Clara banged on the table. 'Stop it, all of you. If Bertha wants to play the violin, she can play the violin. Can't she?'

She shot a threatening look at Charlie. But he had drunk a relatively respectable three pints and was feeling warm and sentimental towards his littlest, quietest daughter. ''Course you can, my darlin'.'

'But where's she going get a violin from?' Grace giggled.

'I think I know someone who might just have one,' Charlie replied, unexpectedly.

'Really?' Clara asked.

'Trust me!' he said, and everyone rolled their eyes again.

However, true to his word, a week later Charlie came back from the pub with a violin. It came without a case, however, and while Charlie didn't think this would matter, as Bertha had to catch a bus across town to get to her lesson, she found it rather did.

Nervously, she mentioned this to her mother and then, when nothing was forthcoming, she dared to ask her father.

'What's wrong with just carrying it?' he asked.

'People look at me and I'm really scared I'm going to drop it or knock it on something. An old man on the bus last week stopped me and said I really shouldn't be carrying it around like that and did I know how much it was worth—?'

'Well, I guess he's got a point. All right, my dumpling, I'll tell you what – I'll make you a case,' and he ruffled her red hair, which she'd spent quite a long time straightening.

Bertha forced a smile. She had no doubt he would make her a case, but whether it was a case she would actually want to carry around – that was another matter.

That weekend Charlie retired to his shed, and noises of banging and sawing floated around the yard. Katie and Bertha crept anxiously down the path and peeped in through the window. They couldn't see anything – there was too much grime. At one point Charlie emerged and went off down the street whistling. The girls tried the door of the shed, but he'd locked it. Their father came back a few hours later with a can of varnish and the smell of the pub about him.

But it wasn't long before he emerged with his creation.

'Bertha, come and look at this!' he shouted.

They all ran into the yard. In Charlie's arms was what looked like a baby's coffin.

'Oh, my Lord!' Clara clapped her hand over her mouth.

'What?'

'You gave me quite a turn,' and then Clara started to giggle and then the others all joined in too. All except Bertha.

'What's the matter?' asked Charlie, confused.

'It looks like something you'd bury!' Grace said, laughing.

'Cheeky besom – any more of that lip and I'll swing it at yer head,' he said.

The girls stifled their laughter, but Bertha turned and ran up to the bedroom and buried herself under the covers. She knew she was going to have to carry that violin case the length of Grays for a very long time, and if her sisters all thought it looked like a coffin, everyone else would too.

Which is exactly what happened. In fact, the whole episode was so upsetting it turned into one of those anecdotes which Nanna not only relayed to me many times, but is still repeated by members of the extended family: 'Did you hear about the time Charlie made your Nanna a violin case that looked like a coffin?' Yes, yes …

The girls' other forays into the musical world were more successful.

Everyone was relieved when Alice's singing teacher introduced some more sophisticated songs into her repertoire, such as the songs of Cole Porter, Ira Gershwin and Noël Coward. 'I Wanna Be Loved By You' was a particular favourite, and 'Let's Misbehave' – she would grab any passing member of the family and serenade them, spinning them around.

Meanwhile, the piano gave them something fun to do in the evenings; it even persuaded Charlie to stay home. Alice would usually sing, and one of the other girls play; Bertha would attempt to join in with the violin, and they would perform music hall songs. Clara would sit in the corner and watch with a rare, beatific smile on her face. On nights like those she felt as if she had pulled it off. Every time someone said to her, 'All girls?' or, 'A house full of women! Your poor husband!' Clara would reply, 'Yes, we are blessed.' She felt a fierce protectiveness and determination that they did not have to be a second best. And the way she put this into action was to make them the very best she could. This meant nice clothes, nice manners and music lessons. Playing the piano and singing were the accomplishments of middle-class girls. It was one of the ways they were set apart, a cut above, but Clara saw no reason why, if they had the means, her girls shouldn't have these too.

But the music lessons were just the window dressing of Clara's ambitions for her daughters. As the shop was doing well, the girls wondered why, whenever they dared to ask for anything: money for soap, a new hat, some new shoes, their mother would tell them to get creative with what they already had. Which meant they became brilliant seamstresses, but left the girls agreeing that their mother was a bit of an old Scrooge. Grace did a brilliant impersonation of her mother's catch phrase: 'You've got to cut your coat according to your cloth.' Clara's other catch phrase was, 'If a job's worth doing, it's worth doing well.' It's been carried down the generations – only the other day I found myself using it on my daughters and felt a ghostly echo run down my spine.

It was all a bit unfair really, because Clara was quite generous by nature. She gave my twin second cousins both an expensive pedigree giant poodle for their twenty-first birthdays.

Clara was being frugal for a reason. Every night when the girls had gone to bed (and away from the prying eyes of Charlie), she would sit in the kitchen and count her shop takings. Luckily Charlie's job at the brewery paid nearly all of the housekeeping costs, so Clara was able to squirrel away her profits in an old tin in her knicker drawer – keeping them away from Charlie's acquisitive hands – until one day, when she did an audit, and she realised there was some missing. Charlie had found her stash and had been using it to pay his gambling debts.

Of course, today, Clara would just have opened a bank account, but in the 1920s women didn't have bank accounts – there weren't even joint accounts. Clara's only option would have been to give the money to Charlie to put in an account, which would have been like turkeys voting for Christmas. And so a game of hide and seek began. The money would be safe for a while, and then a pound or so would go missing, and Clara would have to rack her brains for a new hiding place. She never tackled Charlie directly about the missing money, and neither did he say anything, both colluding not to have the row.

Clara got pretty inventive with her hiding places and, one night, after she had counted her takings, she realised that she had finally reached her target. It had taken two years.

The next day she called the girls together and announced: 'The shop has been doing well and I know you've been wondering what I've been doing with the money. Well, now I can tell you – I've been saving up to send you all to secretarial college.'

There was an astonished silence.

'I'm going to get you trained as shorthand typists.'

Grace piped up first with, 'Blimey!' and then Alice flung her arms around her mum. 'That's brilliant, Mum! Lordy, lordy! Thank you.'

'I'm going to be a secretary. La-di-dah!' Grace said, spinning around, grabbing Dora and making her do a little dance.

Clara found herself getting quite emotional.

'Alice, Gracie, Dora – I've enrolled you already and you start next month, as soon as Dora finishes school. Katie and Bertha, you can start in a couple of years when you're old enough.'

The girls carried on all squealing with delight, except for Bertha, who was very quiet. They all turned and looked at her.

She said shakily, 'But, Mum, I thought I was going to stay on at school.'

'What?'

'Well, Mrs Simpson says I'm good at English and if I keep on going like I am maybe I could go to grammar school and university, and then teach English.'

'Bertha!' They all exclaimed in horror.

'What's she doing, putting ideas like that in your head? Who do you think you are, Lady Muck?'

'No, Mum, of course not. It's just I'm good. I think I can do it. I really do. She says she's coming to see you.'

'No, she jolly well isn't! I've got half a mind to go and see *her*, putting ideas like that into your head.'

Everyone was quiet. Clara and Bertha stared at each other and then Bertha tried again: 'I don't want to be a typist, I want to learn English.'

'You will do what you're told. You ungrateful—' and, quick as a flash, a *thwack* rang around the room as Clara slapped Bertha right on the cheek.

There was a collective intake of breath from the sisters as Bertha, open-mouthed, put her hand on her stinging cheek. There was a pause as no one dared move or quite knew what to do next. Then Bertha turned and, trying to muster some dignity, walked out of the room.

'I'll burn all those books of yours if you're not careful!' Clara shouted after her.

Alice squeezed her mum's arm. 'She don't mean it, Mum. It's just gonna take a bit of time for her to get used to the idea. We're grateful, aren't we?'

They all nodded and Katie piped up, 'I'll say!'

Later on, the girls discussed Bertha's behaviour.

'She's got a nerve, speaking to Mum like that,' Grace said.

'Ha! The little mousey that roars,' Alice agreed.

It had been quite a brave thing to do. Nearly all working-class girls left school at fourteen, and a daughter was considered the property of her parents until she married. While she was generally able to chose her own husband, she had little choice over her job. Not an arranged marriage but an arranged career. And a career that generally had to end when they married.

Bertha knew this, but she was not giving up. She didn't speak for a whole week. At night in the communal bed, she slept on the edge, back turned away from Dora and Katie, the sheet pulled over her head. The room assumed an awkward silence.

Grace was dying to have it out with her: 'Mum's right – who does she think she is? Does she think she's better than us or something? Poor Mum.'

'Leave her alone,' Alice said, 'You getting all hot and bothered isn't going to help. She's little. She'll come round when she sees us going into the city and earning good money every day. Bet ya!'

In the end, when Clara had had a good week to calm down, she decided to talk to Bertha. She told the girls to stay out of the kitchen and she summoned Bertha in.

'Look, I know you like your books. And I'm proud of you being so clever. When I was little I liked my books too. But then I had to give them up. I didn't have time to read no more and I still don't. I had to earn a living. And while we are a lot better off now, we're not so much better off that we have time to read and don't have to work to keep ourselves.'

'But I can be a teacher and look after myself!'

'No, you can't, Bertha. Look at me. Teaching is not for people like us, it's for ladies who are top drawer. Who can afford it.'

'But if you can send us to college—?'

'That's different, that's only one year. I can't afford to pay for you to sit at your books for years. And how could I do it for you, especially you the littlest, and not the rest? It's not going to happen.'

Bertha knew it wasn't but tears were streaming down her face.

Clara tried again: 'Look, I don't want you to end up like me, slaving in a shop all your life. I want something different, a better future for you girls. This is a way out.'

Bertha finally shrugged her shoulders and nodded. Clara put her arms around her and they made up. It was the last time Bertha's teaching ambitions were mentioned.

And Alice was right. Bertha watched her big sisters going off to college and coming back all polished, excited, with new, glamorous friends. And when they started their jobs – dashing off for the train in the morning in smart clothes, coming home with confidence and money – she saw the point. When people asked her what her sisters were doing, Bertha enjoyed telling them about their jobs in the city – they were always impressed. None of her sister's school friends had stayed on past fourteen or fifteen. They had gone to work in the local factories or shops, or gone into service. Bertha soon found she was excited that she would be doing something more prestigious too.

# CHAPTER EIGHT
# The Veneer

It was late April 1928, and the 8.05 a.m. train to London, Fenchurch Street, was due to arrive at any minute. The Swain girls, however, still hadn't appeared.

The commuters at Grays station kept looking at the large clock that hung above the platform. The sisters' timing was unpredictable, but the manner of their entrance was consistent and could be summed up in one word: dramatic. The five girls, with their reddish hair and way-out clothes, would storm onto the main concourse, filling up the space with exuberance and excitement, like leaves whirling around in an autumn gale.

For the citizens of Grays, the Swain sisters were a daily distraction from the monotony of the commute, with one question always in their minds: what on earth would they be wearing today?

Like most girls of their age and class, the sisters made their own clothes, and they were rather good at it. Weekly ladies' magazines would have patterns of the latest fashions from Paris – the *Pictorial Review* was their favourite – and the girls would pour over it, cutting out designs that took their fancy.

With all of them on London wages, the Swain sisters had the money to buy quite luxurious fabrics, and in the evenings the sewing machine they shared was never silent, although it was the source of much arguing. The main culprits were Dora and Bertha, who were particularly into their fashions, although as Dora only tended to wear navy or black – bright red lipstick was the only colour that was allowed to disturb her vision – the sisters couldn't understand why she was bothering.

'It doesn't look any different from the last one you made,' Bertha would complain.

To which Dora would retort: 'What you don't understand is class and style,' which never failed to wind up Bertha, not least because the littlest sister had her own ideas about what constituted chic.

Bertha's wild taste in colour had been apparent from a young age. For the whole of the 1927–1928 season she lived in her 'technicolour dreamcoat'. A forerunner of the Second World War red and green plaid, her late-twenties coat was in the wraparound style that was fashionable at the time, and was constructed from large blocks of vivid velvets – oranges, reds and purples – that clashed rather effectively with her bright red hair. It was finished off with a sable collar that Bertha had funded from her first few weeks' pay, working at the BBC.

What her sisters didn't know was that their mother had let Bertha off from paying her full contribution to the housekeeping as a secret treat for bagging such a splendid job!

Eventually, the sisters arrived. Bertha's coat had been left at home. Spring was lingering at the threshold, and the sisters were wearing either long cardigans or jackets over their silk shirts and pleated skirts – Alice's was scandalously short, only just hitting the knee. This look was completed with a range of accessories: scarves, beads and corsages of fabric flowers. They were still all wearing their cloche hats and gloves and, according to the fashion of the time, their faces were powdered, with rouged cheeks, kohl-shadowed eyes and cupid bow lips. (Nanna persisted in reapplying her lipstick and powder right up until her eighty-ninth year. She would reach into her handbag, bring out her compact, and then start reapplying whatever she felt was lacking. It didn't matter where she was or who was looking.)

Alice and Grace walked onto the platform, arm in arm and giggling; Katie trotted in after them; and then, following close behind, came Bertha, gliding. She had what can only be described as a 'distinctive' gait – the movement of her legs was barely perceptible, but her hips made up for it, swinging gently side to side like a boat rocked by a gentle ocean. Her left hand was poised, outstretched as if permanently checking to see if it was raining, and her smart crocodile handbag hung on her right arm, which was folded neatly across her waist. Bertha had spent many hours in the bedroom practising this effortless sashay. She would walk backwards and forwards with a book on her head, turning every so often to gaze at the effect in the mirror, much to the merriment and accompanying voiceover from Grace: 'And here we have her Royal Shyness, Princess Bertha of Essex, glorious in her very loveliness.'

And then Alice would join in, singing a popular love song in the manner of Gertrude Lawrence, such as 'Someone To Watch Over Me' or, when she ran out of inspiration, simply the National Anthem with adjusted words: 'God bless our gracious B' – until Bertha would either dissolve into giggles, which sent the book tumbling, or grab the book from her head and throw it at one of them.

Dora, as ever, was having to run to catch up. Grace turned round and shouted at her: 'Get a wiggle on, Swainy!'

'Swainy' was the name that Dora's admirers on the Grays to Fenchurch run had christened her, much to the amusement of her sisters.

As Dora trotted along the length of the platform, the train came level and then overtook her and came to a halt. The girls bounced up the steps into a carriage, and Grace hauled Dora in after them. She lowered her voice and whispered to her, 'You spend far too long faffing with your hair, you do! You'll get your wages docked again if you're late. How will you get to the fair then?'

Dora wrestled her arm out of her sister's grasp.

'Oh, shut up! I don't want to go to the fair, anyway.'

'Ohhhh, get you! Did you hear that, Alice? Dora doesn't want to go to the fair.'

'Why ever not?' Alice asked.

'None of your beeswax,' Dora snapped.

Alice and Grace rolled their eyes, pushed the tips of their noses up with their fingers and mouthed 'Bluenose' to each other, and then giggled. If Bertha was the princess of the family, then Dora was the queen.

But the girls did have something to be proud of. They had all found themselves jobs in prestigious establishments in London: Alice was working in the typing pool of a bank in the City, Grace was secretary to the boss of a famous hat company, Dora was a secretary in a patent office in Lincoln's Inn, Katie worked as the secretary to an editor at the *Daily Express* in Fleet Street, and all of Bertha's Christmases had come at once when she had got the job in the typing pool of the newsroom at the fledgling BBC.

Being a shorthand typist was glamorous in the 1920s. Women were only allowed into offices with the invention of typewriters and shorthand at the end of the 1800s. They were seen as more physiologically suited to typing and scribbling than men – a case of nimble fingers. Increasingly, clerical work got the reputation as being for sissies and so men withdrew and job opportunities opened up for women. Demand for these skills grew rapidly. At first it was only middle-class, grammar-school or university-educated women who could hope to get such a position (however mundane the job really was), but by the time the First World War had finished there were a few working-class girls entering into the hallowed sphere of the office. However, it was just a few. Secretarial college was expensive, and most people did not have the money to send one of their daughters to college, never mind five. And it wasn't really working-class girls who went into offices – by the time they left college, they had been turned into polished, middle-class ladies.

It only took a week of Alice, Grace and Dora trotting off with great excitement to Pitman's College in London for the change to be noticeable. As they sat down to their meal on Friday night, Charlie was struck by the way all three of them were sitting up straight as pins. This was extraordinary, as Dora's stoop had been so bad as a child that Charlie had made her a back brace. 'One bent child is enough,' he had muttered under his breath as he strapped in a complaining Dora. Now they were all seated, hair neat, hands clean and folded on their laps, silently and patiently waiting for their supper.

Charlie asked: 'Why do you look like a line of lampposts?'

Katie and Bertha giggled and Clara turned round from the stove and looked. He was right – they were seated beautifully.

'It's Miss Faber. She makes us walk backwards and forwards with the *Encyclopaedia Britannica* on our heads and if we drop it, she hits us with a ruler,' Grace said.

The clerical colleges were really finishing schools with typing skills attached. The young ladies learnt how to answer the telephone properly, the right manners, deportment and how to dress appropriately. Miss Faber had eschewed marriage and dedicated her life to turning out a generation of accomplished, well-mannered and presentable young ladies who would quietly, efficiently and, most importantly, elegantly, run the nation's offices.

Alice was haunted by a bruising encounter during an early shorthand lesson. Her attention had wandered to the thought of her trip to the cinema the night before with a certain boy ... that is, until Miss Faber barked a question at her.

'Miss Swain!'

Alice jumped. 'What, miss?'

'What? *What?* Kitchen maids say "what".'

There was laughter around the class.

'What does a young lady say?'

Alice felt herself overwhelmed with embarrassment. 'Pardon?'

'Pardon? Pardon? You belong on the stage of the music hall, Miss Swain, rather than in an office.'

Alice tended to agree, but kept quiet.

'No, young ladies either say, "Excuse me, could you repeat that?" or, occasionally, if the relationship with the person you are in conversation with is less formal, it might be appropriate to say a simple "Sorry?" So, shall we start again?'

'Yes, Miss Faber. Um … excuse me, please could you repeat that?'

'Yes, Miss Swain.' Miss Faber turned to address the room. 'Remember, you will be mixing with authority, the top echelons of whatever establishment you are employed by, and as such you will be close to power. You will have a personal relationship with men at the very top. They have wives at home, but you will be their wife in the office – in fact, you will be spending more time with them than their own spouse. If you don't please him, if he doesn't feel comfortable with you, he will cast you off for a better model. Therefore, to protect your position, you must speak like his wife, you must look and act as if you are at her level, even if you are not. Otherwise, you will find yourself back scrubbing the floor of a tradesman's kitchen.' And she turned and looked pointedly at Alice. 'It is the veneer.'

And then the lesson resumed, much to Alice's relief.

If Miss Faber's first impression of the Swain girls was one of alarm, they soon grew to be her favourite pupils. Their competitiveness with each other meant they picked up shorthand quickly and were top of the class for the number of words per minute that they could type. She liked the style of their red hair and unusual yet elegant clothes. She saw a great future for them.

But Miss Faber wasn't the only enduring influence on the sisters. For the first time, they mingled with real middle-class girls. And, like chameleons, they learnt to imitate their ways. My Nanna made friends with a young rich Jewish girl from Hampstead called Hetty, and for years she would arrive at Bertha's house with exotic presents for my mum and her brothers.

Clara watched with pride as her little cockney caterpillars turned into upmarket butterflies. Armed with top marks, excellent references and the best telephone manners, the sisters were able to go straight into the top rank of clerical jobs.

Like most things in Britain in the 1920s, there was a strict pecking order. There were the girls who went straight from school and learnt typewriting on the job. A cut above those were the girls proficient in typewriting and copying, who could be found in the better class of typing pools and businesses. And right at the top were the secretaries – those were girls with superior secondary and commercial qualifications, who worked as secretaries for one person. They had a very personal relationship with the boss, and were respected and courted as they held access to him. Power by proxy. They also answered his telephone and organised his diary. They were indeed the wife in the office.

It was Clara's plan, come to fruition. Ten years before, when she had sat by the fire in Marlow waiting for Charlie to come home, this was exactly what she had dreamt of – to have all five of her girls in office jobs, all working in town, all with a chance of moving up and out of the hand-to-mouth existence she had grown up in. Of course, just a few decades later, Clara might have reached higher for her girls – grammar school and university and a leap into the middle class – but before the Second World War this really was as good as it got. And it was certainly a better life than her own. For many women, just to see their daughters step up the social ladder was a great achievement they would take pride in: it was enough.

But it was exactly at this moment of triumph that things started to become unstuck. In fact, that day late in April 1928, when the girls strode onto the station, was actually the last day when Clara appeared to have pulled it off – broken the spell, if you like – because, the next day was the day of Grays fair. And the day that Alice agreed to elope with Joseph Davidson. The wicked fairy had barged back into the christening and the whole fragile illusion that the spell had been broken was shattered by a wager made in front of the Mighty Striker.

# CHAPTER NINE
# Flappers!

Alice first saw Joseph dancing on a table in the ballroom of the Queen's Hotel in Grays. He was wearing a rather distinctive orange bow tie. He was tall and thin, wobbling like a drunken giraffe, his limbs unfeasibly long and lanky. He caught her looking at him and grinned, his wavy hair flopping into his eyes as his arms flew wildly over his head. He was kicking so hard it looked as if he was going to fly off the table at any moment.

Alice was to ponder it later, that first locking of their eyes. She felt like she knew him. And she felt a sense of responsibility – she needed to get him off the table, or at least slow him down, before he did himself a mischief.

Things had got rather out of hand. The revellers had launched streamers over the top of the extravagant chandeliers, and balloons were being kicked around with abandon. Alice suspected that the band had drunk too much as well, as their playing had become frenetic. She took a breath from her high-kicking Charleston and gazed at the sweating players and the way they manhandled their instruments as if trying to snap them in two. Their clothes were awry and their faces glistening with drops of sweat, which plopped down onto their music. The bacchanalian troop seemed appropriate for the stage. It was festooned and framed by golden cherubs and vine leaves, like a Roaring Twenties' hallucinogenic trip. The business of getting dressed up and going into a grand hall, pounding with live music, packed with a few hundred young people, had got them all over-excited. And what with it being New Year's Eve as well, the party tipped into a frenzy.

But now Alice's attention was focused on the young man with the orange tie, and getting to him before he fell off the table. She pushed her way through cavorting bodies. The swinging arms and legs posed quite a hazard, but she batted them away. And then, just as she was feet away, the inevitable happened: Joseph Davidson kicked his legs too hard and came flying off – straight into Alice's arms.

'Wooooo … crikey!' he said, breathless. 'I'm sorry. Are you all right?'

'I'm all right, yes,' she replied. 'But are *you* all right?'

And then, as both of them struggled to catch their breath, they started to laugh.

'I think I need a breath of fresh air,' he said.

'Me too.'

Joseph raised a single eyebrow at Alice's forwardness as she raised a metaphorical eyebrow at her own forwardness too. And then she laughed again. 'How do you do that?'

'What?'

'That thing with your eyebrow.'

'Years of being surprised by young ladies.'

'I see.' Alice stopped smiling.

He realised he'd said the wrong thing. He took her arm. 'But none as pretty as you. It would be an absolute pleasure to escort you.'

Alice hesitated and studied his face. It quite hurt her neck, he was so tall. But she saw only good humour, and the unease evaporated.

'Thank you,' she replied, and took his arm. They started to pick their way through the dancers to the door.

'Actually, it should be me thanking you. You saved me from a rather nasty tumble there. Thank you.'

'It's my pleasure, I think.'

'Well, let me make sure it is.'

And they stopped and looked at each other, and then he bent down and placed a kiss on her lips. All around them the room was moving and the music pounding, but Alice was only aware of the warmth of his breath and the sensation of his lips on her lips. She felt the pressure of his hands on her waist and the smell of him, so unlike the feminine world she inhabited. He was like a foreign creature. Their faces parted and he looked at her, studying her face.

'You have eyes like a pussy cat.'

Alice laughed.

'And you have a tongue like the devil.'

And then they both laughed and she totally forgot about Grace, whom she was supposed to be chaperoning – and who was supposed to be chaperoning her – as she let herself be led outside.

Meanwhile, Grace had totally forgotten about Alice. She was gazing at the band too, but they had a greater hold on her attention because her boyfriend, Bill, was the piano player. This had the disadvantage that she either had to dance with Alice, or sit out the dances like a rejected wallflower, which she wasn't. Young men couldn't help but notice Grace's cheeky look and the way she danced with a joie de vivre that seemed to guarantee a good time. But Grace politely declined all offers. She knew from experience that Bill's intense preoccupation with his piano was deceptive. If she started dancing with another man, he would look up, glower, and at the end of the song jump down from the stage and assert his territorial rights. In fact, Grace never danced with another man again – something she was to ponder at leisure in the decades to come. But tonight she was still living in a state of enchantment. Bill gave Grace the same passion and concentration that he gave to his piano.

'I love you more than I love the songs of George Gershwin,' he said.

And she replied with a smile: 'And I love you more than I love dancing the Charleston.'

And then he said with a look of utter seriousness: 'Ah, yes, but nobody could love Gershwin as much as I do.' And he would bend down and kiss her on the lips.

And on this New Year's Eve, on the stroke of midnight, as the room erupted into a mass of cheers and embraces, Bill leapt down from the stage, pushed his way over, grabbed Grace and kissed her passionately in front of everybody. Except nobody was looking – they were all too busy kissing someone else. That is until the trumpet player came over shouting, 'Come on, Bill, put her down. "Auld Lang Syne"!'

Bill whipped off his tie, tied one end around his wrist and another around Grace's. Grace objected: 'Bill Smith, what are you doing? Stop it right now!'

But he just grinned and said, 'No one is going to separate me from you. Not now, not ever,' and he set off, pulling her up through the crowds, Grace struggling to keep up and nearly falling flat on her face. She kept protesting, 'Bill, watch out! Stop!' but he ploughed on – very much a man on a mission.

When they reached the stage he executed a complicated and rather ungainly manoeuvre, pretty much hauling a slightly hysterical Gracie up onto it – at one point she was lying flat on her front like a beached whale and wondered what on earth Miss Faber would say – then he hauled her up and dragged her over to the piano. With his arms wrapped around Grace and one wrist still tied to hers, Bill then proceeded to play 'Auld Lang Syne' faultlessly. Grace was laughing so much she thought she would do herself some serious damage.

It was only when the song ended and Bill had well and truly kissed her, and she had come back up for air, that Grace looked around to see if Alice had witnessed the exhibition. But she couldn't see her big sister anywhere. The room was crowded, but Alice's strawberry hair usually stood out, not to mention the bright pink silk dress she'd insisted on wearing.

'Can you see Alice?'

Bill scanned the room. It was beginning to empty as the exhausted youngsters began to go home to their mums and comfy beds.

'No. Last I saw, she was dancing with you over at the back.'

'I didn't see where she went. One minute she was there, the next she was gone.'

'Well, let's go and see if we can find her,' he said, and took the opportunity to steal another quick kiss.

They wandered around the hall, still tied at the wrist until Grace started to get panicky, muttering under her breath, 'Mum only let us go on condition we didn't lose sight of each other. She's going to kill me.'

'She won't have gone far. She's probably just off with some bloke somewhere.'

'That's exactly what I'm worried about.'

Grace was thinking of Alice's previous form. Despite being rather shy, Alice always seemed to be surrounded by suitors.

'Those young rascals gather around our Alice like bees to the sweetest honeypot,' Charlie used to say proudly to Clara. But she would give him a worried look. Because that was the problem – Alice was the sweetest Scarlet Sister, always wanting to please, which was good if it was her mother making demands, but potentially ruinous if it was a young man.

She would watch her two eldest daughters getting ready to go out on a Saturday night, with a lack of corsetry to hold them in, their arms bare, skirts short – and the cosmetics … 'What do you look like? A right pair of dollymops! You'll get the neighbours talking,' she would say, shaking her head.

Grace would carry on applying her bright pink lipstick and say nonchalantly: 'Who cares?'

'*I* care and you should care. You don't want to get the reputation for being that sort of girl.'

'What sort is that, then?' Grace paused and cast a coy look at her mother.

'The sort of girl my mum would have locked up in her room and thrown away the key.'

'Are you going to lock us up, then?'

And there was Clara's dilemma. She loved to see her girls experiencing a freedom that she had never had – and very few women had ever had. The dislocation of the First World War had opened the cage, the young lady birds had flown, and many of them could not be put back in. They had worked in larger numbers and earned more money. They had opportunities for activities like the cinema and dances. Sometimes they were unchaperoned. Their skirts had become shorter due to a lack of material during the war and, when it ended, many women fought the pressure to bring hemlines back down, seeing it as a matter of personal freedom.

Watching her girls get ready on a Saturday night filled Clara with pride, but she worried for them, and their reputations too. It was uncharted territory and she couldn't see how it was going to end. As they walked out of the door and cheerily pecked her on the cheek, she felt anxious. She always waited by the fire until they came home.

Clara was not alone in her worries. The blue-stocking feminists of the Victorian era watched askance as women used their hard-won freedom not to go into politics, but to attend dances. Money from these new jobs was spent on cosmetics to make themselves more attractive to men. Sylvia Pankhurst disparaged, 'the emancipation of today which displays itself mostly in cigarettes and shorts ... painted lips and nails and ... absurdities of dress which betoken the slave-women's sex appeal rather than the free woman's intelligent companionship.'

Those early feminists made an unholy alliance with reactionary men. Doctors condemned high heels on the grounds that wearers would displace their wombs, and when the first dance hall opened in Hammersmith a clergyman said 'the morals of a pigsty would be more respectable in comparison'. When the Charleston came over from the United States, the *Daily Mail* denounced it as 'reminiscent only of Negro Orgies'. It would be the sisters' favourite dance.

Of course this argument rumbles on today. As women, we're still doing it: a mixed message, a confusion. I watch my teenage daughter riling against the Church of England for not taking women bishops, declaring her intention to become a journalist and campaign for women's rights, while going off to school every day with highlighted hair, mascara and ludicrously short skirts. She then announced she was going to be a cheerleader, spending her time cavorting on the touchline in skimpy clothes, supporting the boys at her school rugby matches.

'Is this what women threw themselves under horses for? All those women who went on hunger strike so we could get the vote and equal rights?' I said. 'Can't you do something useful, like write for the school newspaper?'

'Only geeks do that,' came the reply. 'At least I'm keeping fit.'

It seems we can't help ourselves, and of course I'm as guilty of this ambivalence as she is, along with plenty of others in my generation.

Back in the 1920s the young women in short skirts, smoking, dancing and hanging around with young men were denounced as 'flappers'. But did they care? As Alice and Grace danced the night away, flinging their limbs around with a wild freedom, they had a sense of elation – for the first time in their lives they were really having fun. How could anything that felt so right, be wrong?

Back in the dance hall, Grace was still worrying about her sister and her ability to attract unsuitable men: 'I don't know how she does it.'

'It's the eyes,' Bill said. 'Mischief. The quiet ones are always the worst,' he added. Grace shot him a look. He laughed and squeezed her hand. 'Let's take a look outside. I bet she's up to mischief in a dark corner.'

They hurried into the street, and it didn't take them long to spot the pink dress enveloped in the arms of a tall man.

'Alice Swain, what are you doing?' asked an exasperated Grace.

The couple quickly broke apart and the man turned around.

'Joseph Davidson!' Bill said. 'Well, I never!'

'Hello, Bill. Let me introduce you,' Joseph said.

'No need, I know Alice.'

'She's my sister,' Grace added.

'And this is my girlfriend, Grace,' Bill said.

Joseph and Bill were classmates from primary school so the happy foursome chatted until the clock on the town hall struck one and the sisters realised they were supposed to be home.

'Quick!'

Grace, still attached to Bill by his tie, grabbed Alice's hand and started to run down the road, the three of them making a ridiculous picture and laughing so hard that Alice tripped and her shoe went flying.

'Who do you think you are, flaming Cinderella?' Joseph said, running after them and picking up her shoe. He bent down and carefully placed it on Alice's dainty, stockinged toes.

'Does that make you Prince Charming, then?' Grace said archly.

'I'd like to be,' Joseph said. Still bending on one knee, he took Alice's hand. 'Alice Swain, would you do me the honour of coming to the pictures tomorrow night?'

Alice blushed right to the roots of her strawberry-blonde hair and said, somewhat to everyone's surprise, 'Only if I can chose the film.'

'I don't care what we see as long as I'm with you,' Joseph replied, still holding her hand.

At which Grace rolled her eyes at Bill and grabbed Alice's hand. 'Come on, you! Enough of this charmer. If we don't get back soon, none of us will be going to any movie or anywhere ever again. Mother'll have us chained to her knickers for ever.'

'Grace!'

But she just laughed and started pulling Alice down the street again.

Finally in bed, surrounded by their sleeping sisters, Alice and Grace lay with their limbs aching, voices hoarse, and heads buzzing from too much excitement. Grace propped herself up and stared down at her big sister. Alice was looking dreamily at the ceiling, with one hand behind her head, her fine hair framing her face like a saint's halo in a medieval fresco.

Grace whispered, 'What's your New Year's resolution then, saucebox?'

And without hesitation Alice replied, 'To marry Joseph Davidson.'

Grace leapt up. 'What? Are you serious?'

'Totally. Tonight I met the man I'm going to marry. It's Destiny.'

'Destiny? I'll tell you what it is – it's nuts! Have you been on the old jag juice?'

'No, my dear. I just know what I know. The future has been revealed to me tonight.'

'Ha!' Gracie snorted too loudly and a little sister stirred. 'How do you know?'

'I just do. Believe me, when you meet the man you are going to marry, you just know.'

Grace was slightly affronted. 'Why don't I feel that about Bill, then?'

'Because you are not going to marry him. Whereas I am going to marry Joseph Davidson. And I am going to marry him before the year is out, you'll see.'

'I'll hold you to that.'

'Do that. In fact, what do you bet me?'

Grace giggled. Unlike her father, Alice may have eschewed the delights of alcohol, but she had inherited his love of a wager. She spiced up her daily life with a constant string of flutters.

'OK, Mrs Davidson-to-be, I bet you I marry Bill Smith before you marry Joseph Davidson, and whoever loses has to catch the bouquet at the wedding.'

'Done!'

They shook on it, nestled down and finally went to sleep.

The next night a rather weary Alice met Joseph Davidson outside the Empire cinema in Grays. Going to the pictures was the sisters' most popular pastime after dancing. With no televisions, and cinemas offering a respectable way to escape their parents, most young ladies went to the cinema at least twice a week, particularly if they were working.

With their London wages, the Swain sisters had no problems finding the means to indulge. Of course, they liked the romantic movies best, particularly if they were sitting in the back of the cinema with their suitor of the moment. Chaperones were pretty helpless in this environment, and cinemas soon earned the nickname of 'petting pantries'. Which is why Alice had told her mother that she was meeting Edith, a rather upmarket friend she'd met at Miss Faber's, of whom Clara totally approved.

As Alice rounded the corner, the person actually waiting for her was rather taller, thinner and more dashing. She felt all jittery and nearly had to turn around and walk round the block to collect herself.

However, Joseph spotted her before she had the chance. 'Hello, beautiful,' he said, and she smiled shyly back at him. 'So, what are we going to see today?'

'*A Woman of Affairs*.'

'Oh, really? How intriguing!' He did that thing with his eyebrow again – the left one shot right up his forehead. 'I can see you're going to be constantly surprising me.'

Still smiling, Alice blushed. Joseph grinned back at her, but his eyes were quite intense. Like looking at the sun, she couldn't hold his gaze for long and had to look away. Joseph bent down and kissed the top of her head. 'Come on, then. I don't want to miss any of this woman's affairs.'

Settled at the back of the cinema, in the warm darkness, Joseph and Alice held hands. *A Woman of Affairs* was everything Alice had hoped for: it starred Greto Garbo and was intensely passionate and wonderfully doom-laden. Diana (Greta Garbo) is in love with Nevs (John Gilbert) but her parents don't approve, and Nevs is sent to Egypt. It ends with Diana driving her car into the tree in front of which she and Nevs had declared their love and eternal fidelity. So it wasn't cheery, but it did offer lots of opportunities for Joseph to take Alice's hand, and gently stroke her palm with his thumb. And when it got really sad and she started to cry, he offered her his handkerchief and carefully and seriously wiped away her tears, and then left his comforting arm around her shoulders. But, most of all, it gave Joseph the opportunity to say to Alice at the end: 'Nothing must ever get between you and me and our love. See, it only ends badly.'

At which Alice spooked Joseph, leaving him wondering what he'd got himself into by saying, with slightly too much passion: 'I promise you, Joseph, nothing ever, ever will.'

From then on, Alice and Joseph could always be found together. Friday nights they snuggled at the pictures, Saturday nights they danced – although Alice wouldn't allow him any more table-top exhibitions – and Sunday afternoons they met on the 'monkey parade'. This was the traditional promenade where groups of young women, dressed in their Sunday finest, would walk through the municipal park and along the seafront, observed by groups of young men. The groups mingled, flirting took place, and couples split off from the crowd. It was open and public and semi-respectable. However, Alice was not in a group – she was very much glued to Joseph Davidson's arm. They had so much fun together – Grays had a boating lake parallel to the seafront and on a fine Sunday afternoon, Joseph would take her out and row her into the middle and refuse to take her back to the shore unless she kissed him. He was a rubbish rower. His long, skinny arms seemed to be incapable of moving at the same time, so they would go round in circles for a bit, Alice practically rolling around on the bottom of the boat laughing, and then she would grab the oars and do it herself.

On one occasion, she wrestled the oars from him and started singing in her pretty soprano voice, 'What Shall We Do With The Drunken Sailor?'

Joseph listened, entranced, and when she had finished he said, 'You are not like anyone I have ever met before. That's why I like you.' And then he stood up and started serenading her with 'Run, Rabbit, Run', in a loud but execrable voice.

Now they were causing a scene. People were staring. Particularly when Joseph flung open his arms and tried to kneel down on one knee and what with his centre of gravity being so high above the water and not being great at balancing anyway, he wobbled; and then his arms flung back wildly and he fell backwards, straight into the lake.

'Crikey!' Alice had no idea whether he could swim or not, and all of a sudden she had a vision of her father, Charlie, falling into Marlow lock and sinking three times. 'Help!' she shouted.

But there was no need – times had changed, lidos were springing up around the country, not least in Grays, and Joseph had grown up perfecting his breaststroke. But if drowning wasn't a problem, hauling his long, suited frame back into the boat was. Alice held an oar out to him, and dragged him to the side of the boat. He tried to haul himself over the side, with Alice helping and getting soaked. Then she got the Swain giggles – the more she tried to haul him in, and the boat tipped perilously to one side, the more she laughed hysterically.

Eventually he was trying not to laugh too. 'Alice, stop! Just get a grip. One, two, three … come on! Put your back into it …'

In the end they gave up and Joseph swam to the edge and got out, to the delight of the crowd, who clapped as he hauled himself out of the water. Someone provided a towel.

Alice rowed herself back to the shore, also to claps from the crowd. And as she got out, Joseph dashed over, picked her up in his arms and kissed her – getting her soaked again – to the accompaniment of more cheers.

And that should have been that – just a crazy little mishap on a sunny spring day, to be remembered and recounted with merriment in years to come. However, as sometimes happens, it sparked off a rather serious chain of unintended consequences.

A couple of days later the local busybody, Mrs Barlow, was sitting in the 'resting chair' of Clara's shop and bursting with a bit of mischief.

'So, Mrs Swain, has your Alice dried off yet?'

Clara was serving Mrs House and trying to concentrate on measuring out some sugar. 'I'm sorry, Mrs Barlow. I'll be with you in a minute.'

'No, I was just saying … that little mishap of Alice's beau on Sunday.'

Clara stopped her measuring. She wasn't aware of any beau, never mind a mishap.

'Oh, did you not hear?' asked Mrs Barlow innocently. She turned to Mrs House. 'Your Jessie was over at the boating lake on Sunday, wasn't she?' she asked.

'Oh, yes! It was quite a palaver by all accounts. Lucky that Joseph Davidson can swim and there was no harm done.'

'Except for a ruined suit. And pride.'

'Oh, no. Jessie said they were laughing all the way, and Joseph did a little bow at the end and Alice flung her arms around him, even though he was soaking wet.'

'Well, I never! Quite a one isn't she, your Alice?'

Of course Clara still had no idea what they were talking about, but she was not going to give them the satisfaction of letting on. Instead, she said, 'Alice is indeed special and sunny-natured and always looks on the bright side. And I'm sure she had no problem expressing her joy that this gentleman was safe and sound. Now, is there anything else I can help you with, Mrs House? Because I have to shut up shop in the next few minutes.'

'Right, well, I'll be off then,' Mrs Barlow said, getting up, satisfied that her work was complete.

That evening, when Alice got home from work, her mother was waiting. Alice didn't even have time to take off her hat.

'What on earth have you been up to?'

'Nothing.'

'That's not what I've heard.'

'What have you heard?'

'Sunday afternoon. The boating lake. With a sopping beau.'

At this point, the sisters who were gathered round the kitchen table started to giggle.

'Ah, that.'

'Yes, *that*. When did you think you were going to tell me about it?'

'Well, there's nothing to tell, Mum. Just a little accident. I didn't fall in. No one was hurt.'

'And the beau?'

'What beau?'

'Don't give me that! If the Mrs Barlows of this world know you've got a beau, then surely your mother has got a right to know.'

'Well, I didn't tell you because there's nothing to tell. I haven't been walking out with him for long, and it's nothing serious.'

At which point Grace snorted and Alice shot her a look.

'Who is he?'

'You don't know him.'

'Well, why don't aquaint me then? Let's start with his name.' Clara's habitual control was slipping. She was beginning to sound menacing.

'Joseph Davidson.'

'Why haven't we been introduced?'

'No reason. As I said, we've only just started seeing each other.'

'In which case, there'll be no reason why you can't bring him to tea on Saturday, will there?'

Alice could think of many reasons not to bring Joseph to tea – not least because he was a bus driver and a Roman Catholic. Alice may have come under the influence of a nun at primary school, but the Swain family were profoundly Church of England. However, she had been somewhat outmanoeuvred by her mother. 'No, Mother. Indeed. I shall ask him to call at five o'clock, shall I?'

'Yes, you do that. I look forward to meeting him.' And Clara strode out of the kitchen, satisfied.

'Lordy, lordy, Alice, what are you going to do?' Grace whispered.

Alice shrugged. 'What can I do? She's going to have to meet him some time. And she's going to have to lump it. I tell you – I'm marrying him whether she likes it or not. It's Destiny.' And with that she turned on her heel and followed her mother out of the room, her sisters watching, open-mouthed.

No more was said until Saturday afternoon arrived and with it Joseph Davidson, knocking on the front door with a loud rap.

Alice had been lurking in the hall and ran forward and flung the door open quickly so that, before anyone could see, she could give him a kiss on the lips and then bury her head in his shoulder, inhaling his smell with deep breaths. 'I've missed you so bad.'

Not for the first time Joseph was taken aback by her fervour.

'I've missed you too, sweetheart,' he said, and she looked up at him and smiled.

Grace came bounding out into the hall and beckoned with a flourish. 'Come on,' she said, in a dramatic whisper, 'Mother's waiting.'

Alice grabbed Joseph's hand and pulled him into the back room that served as their parlour Laid out on a table was a fine spread of dainty cakes, pastries and sandwiches, which Clara had taken some time out of her busy day to prepare. She was determined to show this Joseph what an upmarket family the Swains were.

However, Clara immediately wondered why she had bothered. She was not impressed. Not impressed at all. He walked in and she couldn't help but say, 'My, you are tall!'

At which all the girls (none of them having wanted to miss the show) chorused, 'Mother!'

Joseph didn't handle it well. Instead of smiling and thanking her and putting her at ease, he looked embarrassed.

There was an awkward silence, until Alice made an attempt to start again by saying, 'Mum, this is Joseph Davidson.'

'Obviously. Pleased to meet you, Joseph Davidson. I'm Mrs Swain.' Clara got up from her chair and went to shake his hand. He took it but his handshake felt limp and sweaty. Clara never trusted a man with a limp handshake. It's another piece of Swain advice that has been handed down to me, as well as never trust a man whose eyebrows meet in the middle or a man who carries a purse. She also didn't trust a man who couldn't look her in the eye, and she didn't understand why he didn't return her gaze – he was either rude or shifty or both. He just stood there looking like a fish out of water. 'Or maybe an eel,' Clara thought. 'He's that long and skinny.'

'Sit down then,' she said, her annoyance beginning to show.

Alice grabbed Joseph's hand, sat down on the sofa and pulled him down next to her.

'Would you like a cup of tea?' Clara was already pouring his cup.

'No, thank you. I don't drink tea.'

'What?'

'No, I'd rather have a glass of water, if you don't mind. Thanks.'

'Oh, I know what you'd rather have.'

Charlie, who had been silently sitting in the corner, leapt to his feet. 'How about a glass of the old giggle water?'

Joseph looked uncomfortable. 'No, thank you. I don't drink.'

Which rather stopped Charlie in his tracks. And while this should have endeared him to Clara, all it did was to make him look stranger.

'Katie, go and get this young man a glass of water,' she snapped.

'And get me a beer too,' Charlie added.

All the girls shot him a look.

'Now, surely you'll have a piece of cake?' Clara said.

'Just a sandwich, please.'

There was an uncomfortable silence as Clara filled his plate, her lips pursed. As she picked out the best of her dainty cucumber triangles, out of the corner of her eye she could see Alice clinging to Joseph and looking all moonfaced. 'Goofy-in-love' was the phrase that ran through her mind and she was so irritated she tipped over Joseph's plate, which brought on another chorus of 'Mother!' and some hurried clearing-up.

When calm had been restored, Clara jumped straight in with the question that was on everyone's mind. 'So, I don't believe Alice has told us. What exactly do you do?'

'I'm a bus driver.'

'Oh!'

'Yes. The Grays to London line.'

This piece of information helped Charlie to recover from the shock of having a teetotal man in his house, and he leapt into action. 'Must be great getting behind the wheel of those big engines. I've done quite a bit of car mechanics myself. In fact, I drove trucks in the war.'

'Really, what kind?' For the first time, Joseph perked up too.

'Yes, Charlie, tell us about it. Alice's father is remarkably quiet about his wartime experiences,' Clara bristled. It was typical for Charlie to be so easily won over.

Charlie suddenly remembered all the danger that lurked in talking about his army career. He changed the subject quickly. 'So, how did you get into that?'

'My dad's a bus driver. Same line.'

Clara snorted. The girls all looked at her.

'And your mother?'

'Well, Mum's always been very busy, what with there being fourteen of us.'

'Fourteen?' Clara couldn't hide her shock.

'Yes. Twelve boys and two girls. But she does take in washing and she helps out a lot at the church.'

This was getting worse. Taking in other people's dirty laundry was the last resort of the very poor, and something that even the Crisp family in Southwark had never had to do. There was nothing Clara could say to that so she asked, 'Oh, and what church is that?'

'The Church of St Thomas of Canterbury in East Thurrock Road.'

There was a stunned silence.

'But that's the Roman Catholic church, isn't it?' she asked.

'Yes. We're Catholic.'

Alice felt a kind of panic sweep over her. Within the first few minutes absolutely all the skeletons in Joseph's marriage-potential cupboard had tumbled out, while all of the good things about him – his fun, kindness and charm – had remained firmly hidden. She looked at him. He didn't seem himself at all. He had gone a kind of pale grey and there was sweat on his brow. She looked in desperation over at Grace but all she got was a sympathetic frown back.

Suddenly, Joseph slumped forwards.

'Oh my God!' Clara cried. 'Katie, where are you with that glass of water?'

'Bring the beer as well!' Charlie shouted.

Alice leapt up and laid Joseph out along the length of the sofa. In fact, they all jumped up and gathered round him.

Joseph's eyes were rolling. He looked like death and was all clammy.

'Crikey, he's having a turn,' Grace said. 'Loosen his collar.' She started fiddling with his neck.

'Leave it out – I'll do it!' Alice pushed her out of the way.

Katie rushed in with the glass of water and the glass of beer.

'What on earth—?' she started.

'Quick, give him a sip,' Clara said.

Katie panicked and flung the glass at him instead, soaking his face.

'Katie!' they all shouted.

'You idiot!' Alice said, and punched her in frustration.

'Ow! I don't know, he looks like he's dead,' Katie howled.

Luckily, the accidental shower seemed to have something of a Lazarus effect upon Joseph – he shook his head a bit, his eyes stopped rolling and he looked around, slightly confused.

'Here, give him some of this.' Charlie grabbed the beer from Katie's other hand and poured a little down Joseph's throat.

He choked and then seemed to remember where he was.

'Are you all right, Jo?' Alice peered anxiously at his face.

'Yes, yes, sorry. I don't know what happened. Perhaps I can have a little bit of your cake?'

'I think you should, young man. Looks to me like you don't eat enough,' Clara said, and produced a piece of her best Victoria sponge.

As he sat up and started eating, Alice said, 'Oh, Jo, you gave me such a turn! I thought you'd dropped off yer perch.'

'Yes, you came over a bit queer, son,' Charlie said. 'I'd start drinking more beer if I were you. It's nutritious.'

At which point, Bertha and Katie started to giggle.

Joseph, still looking a bit grey, nibbled at his cake while everyone watched, and then he said, 'I'm feeling a bit poorly. I think I'd better go home.'

Clara looked at the magnificent spread she'd made and said pointedly, 'Well, that's a bit of a shame.'

Joseph got up and took his leave. Everyone followed him out of the room except for Dora and Grace. Dora sat in the corner, ominously quiet.

'Well?' Grace asked.

'Someone just walked over a grave,' she said.

'Oh, Dora, belt up! Don't you think we've had enough drama today?' Grace said, and walked out of the room in disgust.

Alice knew what her mother was going to say. Fortunately, Clara kept it short. 'He's not good enough for you,' she said. 'I don't ever want him to cross the threshold of this house again.'

But Alice didn't stop seeing him. She just was careful to be discreet, and Grace provided alibis. Of course the parental disapproval heightened the excitement. Alice felt like she really was Greta Garbo in *A woman of Affairs* – the good girl of the family was for once being extremely bad. And the moment when her badness tipped from being a relatively innocent rebellion to something more serious was the May Day carnival.

Every year the people of Grays celebrated the coming of summer with a party. Pagan tradition collided with a modern steam fair and everybody turned up. It started in the recreation ground with the crowning of the May queen. A local beauty would be dressed in a papier mâché crown and a velvet robe trimmed with fur. Clara was most put out that none of her girls, not even Katie, had been chosen for this honour, noting with disgust that the May queens were always blonde. For years she had been forced to watch little girls parading down the high street in their pastel-coloured dresses festooned with garlands of flowers and headdresses. In the end she was so disgusted she boycotted the carnival altogether.

This suited the sisters perfectly. They had free rein to get up to whatever mischief took their fancy, especially as their father would be spending the whole day in the pub. Alice, Joseph, Grace and Bill mingled in the high street watching the procession – lots of decorated wagons filled with over-excited citizens dressed in bizarre outfits. There was the obligatory Boudicea and her army of warrior daughters; blacked-up minstrels; Robin Hood and his Merry Men; with the Morris dancers bringing up the rear. There was cheering, flag waving and a band.

In the press of the crowd Alice and Joseph held hands. Alice was aware of his tall frame pressing against her body and felt as if she was about to faint with the desire to hold him and kiss him and never stop. In fact, a few times Joseph did manage to kiss her, but Grace pinched her arm and hissed, 'Stop necking, you idiot!'

In the end Alice got fed up and whispered to Joseph, 'Come on, let's get away from the old fire extinguisher.'

'We're off to the fair!' she shouted and pulled Joseph away before her sister could stop her.

The fair would look a bit tame these days, but for the people of Grays in 1928 it was like Disneyland. As well as the traditional attractions of the coconut shy, shooting range and hook-a-duck, steam power had produced rides like the Gallopers and swing boats. Grace and Joseph darted around like children in a sweet shop. He made her laugh by missing the target in the shooting range and doing a ridiculous dance in the hall of mirrors – his body was strange enough without the help of a distorted mirror. As they whirled round on the Gallopers he shouted, 'I love you' and she shouted back, 'I love you too,' and in the dark tunnel of the ghost train he whispered it in her ear more seriously and added the words 'for ever' and held her tight against him. In her head Alice found herself adding the words, 'Til death us do part' and felt a little shiver.

They came out of the ghost train and blinked in the sunlight, then Joseph said, 'Come on, let me show you how strong my love is.'

He pulled her over to the Mighty Striker, where a crowd had gathered to watch the butcher swing the mallet, and try and fail to get the arrow to shoot all the way up the pole and hit the bell. It was obviously quite hard.

Joseph turned to Alice. 'Do you fancy having a bet on this? I bet you I can hit the bell.'

Alice laughed. 'Oh, Jo! Do you really want to lose? If Muscles the butcher can't do it, I don't rate your chances, do you? But if you insist. So, what's the prize?'

Here, Joseph went all serious and seemed to struggle for words. He started a few times, stopped and then finally managed to spit out: 'If I hit the bell, you have to marry me.'

'You're joking!'

This time Joseph said it with more confidence. 'No, I'm serious. I've never been more serious about anything in my life. Marry me if I hit the bell.'

And Alice found herself saying in slight desperation, 'But Jo, you'll never hit it!'

At which Joseph Davidson grinned and replied, 'Just you watch me!' He took off his jacket, handed it to Alice, and pushed his way to the front, saying, 'Excuse me, ladies and gentleman, apologies, but there's a life-changing wager at stake.'

The crowd in their festive good humour laughed at the lanky boy, and cleared a path for him. Joseph paid his penny, rolled up his sleeves and grabbed the hammer. Alice watched with the most disabling butterflies as he practised his swing with a flourish, braced himself and then brought the hammer down with a resounding thud. There was an intake of breath as the arrow shot up and hovered three-quarters of the way up the pole.

'You're gonna have to try harder than that, beanpole!' someone shouted.

'I'll eat my entire collection of sausages if you manage to hit that bleedin' bell,' the butcher said, laughing.

'You'll do that anyway!' someone else shouted.

There were laughs all round.

'Oh, Mary Mother of God, just get on with it!' Alice thought. And then she started to pray. 'Please, please, please, dear Lord, can he hit the bell.'

'You've got three goes, you know, mate, so two more,' the fair man reminded him.

'Yes, sir, I know. That was just a warm-up,' Joseph said.

He pushed his floppy hair out of his eyes. With legs apart he rocked backwards and forwards, bounced the mallet as if he was about to serve at tennis, raised it in the air and brought it down with a huge grunt. The arrow shot up, past the three-quarter mark and looked like it might go the whole way.

Alice was transfixed. 'Go on, up, up, up!' she willed. But the arrow stopped just short of the bell. 'Ahhhhh,' the crowd sighed. 'Dammit!' Alice muttered under her breath, and the lady next to her shot her a look.

'This is your last chance,' the Mighty Striker man said.

This time there were no theatricals. With a look of the utmost concentration, Joseph took a huge swing and with a giant roar hit the hammer on the pedal. The arrow shot up like a rocket and hit the bell. It rang round the fairground.

'Oh my God!' Alice cried, and clapped her hand over her mouth. The lady next to her said, 'You need to watch your language, young lady!' but Alice took the wind out of her sails by giving her the most enormous hug and bursting into tears. Meanwhile, the butcher was trying to shake Joseph's hand, but he was already pushing his way through the crowd, as they slapped him on the back with a 'Well done!' and 'Champion!', trying to get to Alice.

He peeled her off the lady and picked her up and swung her round and then kissed her full on the lips. At which the crowd again did a collective 'Ahhhhhh' again.

Their embrace was finally broken when the fair man tapped Joseph on the shoulder: ''Ere, don't you want your prize money?'

'No, I've won the best prize of all,' was the reply. At which the crowd cheered and Alice kissed Joseph and then he turned and said, 'But I'll take it anyway.' And then there was laughter.

And that is how Joseph Davidson proposed to Alice Swain.

Joseph's victory over the Mighty Striker started a hurricane of secret activity in the lives of Alice and Grace. That evening, the girls were hiding behind their dad's shed for a late-night cigarette when Alice dropped her bombshell.

'You're getting that bouquet, Gracie.'

'What bouquet?'

'My wedding bouquet.'

'You're having me on!'

'No, he proposed today.'

'And you said yes?'

''Course I did. You haven't been listening, have you? It's Destiny …'

'Oh, but Alice, it'll kill Mum.'

'It ain't, because she ain't gonna know.'

'What do you mean? Oh, I really do think you've gone a bit barmy. It's been a hot day … Have you had too much sun on your head, or ginger beer, or has candy floss got into your brain? I dunno!'

'No, I haven't. Look, this whole wedding is going to be a secret and you're going to help me.'

'Oh, I am, am I?'

'Yes, you are.'

'And why would I do a daft thing like that?'

'Because you love me, and you know I love him. Look, do you like Jo?'

'You know I do.'

'Do you think he and I go well together?'

'Yep. You're both as mad as hatters. But isn't it worth just taking a little time, Alice? There'll be other men who are as mad as a hatter like you and maybe have the extra advantage of being acceptable to Mum as well.'

'Oh, stop it! Imagine if I said that about Bill. We're like swans – we've found each other and that's it … we mate for life.'

'Yeah, well, that's a myth, isn't it? Swans don't mate for life at all.'

'Don't they? Oh, Grace, look, you're not taking this seriously.'

'No, you're right, I'm not. And that's because it's a ridiculous idea.'

'It's not at all! You know as soon as I marry the bank will show me the door. If we keep it secret, I don't lose my job – in fact, I earn as much as possible and save it, and Jo will do the same. He can take on extra shifts and we wait until we have enough money so we can get our own place and show Mum and everyone that we're serious, and Jo's worth something.'

'But you can do that without being married. Why don't you just get engaged?'

'Because what's the point in waiting? We know we're meant for each other. This way we don't have to wait.'

'Well, you don't have to wait to do It.'

'Oh, stop it! It's not like that.'

Grace shot her sister a quizzical look, then grabbed the cigarette packet off her and lit another one.

Alice tried again: 'If you wanted to elope with Bill and asked for my help, what do you think I'd say?'

Grace took a long drag and blew the smoke towards the stars just visible in the early summer dusk. 'You'd help me.'

'Exactly.'

A pause. Then, 'All right, I'll think about it.'

And that's how the girls started a frenzy of preparations. Alice had always wanted to become a Roman Catholic and now she started secret conversion classes with the priest of St Thomas's church. Grace helped Alice make a dress and a veil and gave her alibis for her meetings with Joseph. There were several near-misses, not least when the local gossips reported back the drama of the Mighty Swinger to Clara.

Alice brushed it off: 'I was walking past and stopped to have a look. Half of Grays was watching, Mum.'

'And if you was just passing, why did he push his way through the crowd and give you a great smacker on the lips, then?'

'Who says?'

'Mrs House.'

'Oh, Mum, you know what she's like. It's all exaggeration with her. Stir, stir. She'd put two and two together and make a hundred, she would.'

'It'd better be a hundred and not four, my girl,' Clara said and stared intently, looking for any sign of duplicity.

But love had made Alice bold and she just stared right back.

More serious was when Alice left her wedding veil on the sewing machine and Bertha found it and took it into the kitchen.

'Oh, Mum, that's just my friend May, who's asked me to help her with her wedding veil.'

'Really? You didn't tell me. I've never heard of this May before.'

'Yes, I've told you about her.'

Alice caught Grace's eye and she leapt in to help her big sister: 'She has, Mum. We met her at Miss Faber's. You remember – she's marrying a man she met in the bank.'

'Good for her,' Clara said pointedly.

After that May became very useful, as she provided alibis for Alice's frequent disappearances. It wasn't that Clara wasn't suspicious, but with Grace backing her up, it was difficult for her to prove Alice wasn't telling the truth.

Grace, however, could see one major flaw in the plan. She didn't like to bring it up, but one day she couldn't help herself: 'What if you get pregnant?'

'Not going to happen.'

'What, you're not going to do It?'

'Don't be silly. No, trust me, I've taken care of it.'

'What do you mean, "taken care of it"?'

'That's for me to know and you to guess. I bet you your purple silk scarf I'm not pregnant by our first wedding anniversary.'

'No. No more bets, I believe you. But I'd wish you'd tell me how.'

'Little sister, when you are old enough to really know, I'll tell you, I promise …'

It was a real advantage that Alice worked in town: every day, she walked past a mobile women's health unit. In 1927 Dr Marie Stopes and her Society for Constructive Birth Control opened the first birth control caravan. It travelled around London giving out leaflets, advice and the cervical cap. Alice borrowed a ring from her mother's drawer and queued up. Posing as a married woman with an already too large family, it really was taken care of.

On 16 October 1928, just over ten months since they first met, and as Alice had predicted – before the year was out – she walked down the aisle of the church of St Thomas of Canterbury and became Joseph Davidson's wife. There were only two guests: Grace and Bill. Her dress had been made from a pattern cut out from the *Pictorial Review* and was a simple, sleeveless cream satin slip, with a drop waist and a yellow sash embroidered with tiny seed pearls. She carried a bunch of white roses that she'd bought from the flower stall in the market on her walk across the town to the church, her dress covered from gossips' eyes by her coat.

'Are you sure about this?' Grace asked as they rounded the corner and walked towards the church.

'Yes, I've never been so sure about anything in my life.' Which wasn't quite true: Alice was sick to the pit of her stomach.

When they reached the church, Alice looked up the aisle and saw Joseph waiting at the altar. Grace hurriedly opened the small suitcase she was carrying and got out the troublesome veil, while Alice took off her coat. With a few swift manoeuvres involving net and hair pins, Alice was transformed into a bride.

'Ready?' Grace asked.

Alice nodded and Grace suddenly kissed her sister and hugged her. 'You are just the bravest, best sister. I want you to know, whatever happens, whatever anyone says, I think you are amazing.'

That was the moment when Alice had to wipe away a few tears. Grace saw the way things were going and said, 'Come on, you. Let's get you married.'

She took Alice's left hand and walked down the aisle alongside her, in the place of their father, ready to give her away. When they reached the altar Joseph turned and looked at Alice and smiled. Suddenly her courage was restored.

The sun shone in through the windows, creating ladders up to heaven. It wasn't the big, fancy wedding Alice had dreamt of, but it felt much more special – sacred, even. A private, unbreakable commitment, with no people to get in the way of her vow to her Maker. When Joseph placed the simple gold band on her finger – purchased from the pawnbrokers on the high street – Alice felt elated. At the door of the church after they had walked back down the aisle together as man and wife, she kissed him with such a passion he lost his balance and nearly fell over. And then as Bill and Grace threw confetti over them, Alice passed over her bouquet to Grace.

'I won,' she said.

The foursome ran straight from the church to catch the ferry across the Thames Estuary for the honeymoon – a long weekend in Margate. Alice would never have been allowed to go away without Grace as her chaperone, and she had told Clara that they were going on a trip with their girlfriends from Miss Faber's.

Such weekend jaunts sent members of the older generation tutting, but they were not unusual for unmarried, working women in their twenties. Ever since the end of the First World War, trips to the seaside had become commonplace. Public transport made it easier and coastal resorts close to London developed fun diversions. There were also plenty of boarding houses, where a newly married couple and her sister and boyfriend could get lodging – as long as the sister and the boyfriend had separate rooms, which Grace and Bill did.

Margate was the sisters' favourite. There was the beach and bathing facilities, the grotto and sunken gardens, and its very own pier. I have photos of all the Swain girls over the years: on the beach in ridiculously revealing bathing costumes – surely it wasn't allowed then? – and walking happily along the seafront promenade with the pier behind. Grace looks quite the flapper in her cloche hat, coat open to show her drop-waisted slip and little dainty Mary Jane shoes. Bill wears his trilby hat cocked at a jaunty angle, a cigarette in his hand.

The biggest draw was the Dreamland Amusement Park. It had Britain's first ever roller-coaster ride: the mile-long 'scenic railway' which offered an amazing view of the seafront as the train ratcheted slowly up to the top and then plummeted down the steep track. It also had the

*Bill and Grace, with friends*

*Dora*

*Bertha and Grace*

first ever train disguised as a giant caterpillar, which whirled people round its track faster and faster until, just as it reached maximum speed, the passengers were plunged down into total darkness and a klaxon blasted in their ears. As they were flung back into bright daylight, their faces were hit by a jet of compressed air. It really was heady stuff for the 1920s. Of course there were also bars, cafes, restaurants, and a zoo with a lion that was so tame they encouraged parents to sit their babies on its back to have their photos taken.

The happy foursome took full advantage of all these delights. Not exactly the romantic idyll expected today, but still a lot of fun. Hands were held and kisses snatched. Grace couldn't help but notice that Alice and Joseph couldn't leave each other alone, which was interesting – everything going well, then. Bill also noticed the fizzing sparks between the new Mr and Mrs Davidson.

Grace couldn't wait to get home and quiz Alice for the gory details, although she didn't hold out much hope – Alice was annoyingly discreet when it came to things like that.

A giant Haunted Snail had taken Bill's eye. It was like a ghost train, except people had to walk through the insides. Entrance was via its mouth, which was set in a sinister, Cheshire-cat-like grin. He wouldn't rest until Grace had agreed to go in there with him. They walked into the huge mouth, holding hands and giggling. As they went further inside, it got darker. They were all on their own. They pushed their way through cobwebs, spectres jumping out of cupboards, spiders falling on their heads and ghoulish wails assaulting their ears. It was almost pitch-black. Suddenly, Bill grabbed Grace and kissed her so passionately that her feet came off the floor. She returned his kiss and then, remembering herself, pushed him off with a squeal.

But Bill got down on one knee and said, 'Grace, will you do me the honour of marrying me?'

And before she had time to think, the word was out of her mouth:
'No.'

'No? Are you serious?'

'Yes.'

'So it's yes.'

'No. It's a no.'

Bill was dumbfounded. 'Why?'

'I don't know, it's just not right. This snail … On their honeymoon …
It don't feel right.'

'Oh, what, so if I'd given you roses and an orchestra and a diamond,
you would have said yes?'

'I don't know. I'm sorry.'

And with that Grace ran out of the Haunted Snail past a bemused
Alice and Joseph, leaving Bill alone in the dark bowels of the snail, still
on his knee.

A tricky few hours followed, with Alice and Grace holed up in the
newly weds' bedroom, drinking cups of tea and crying, and Joseph and
Bill stationed in the pub, drinking. Messages were ferried backwards
and forwards.

Bill was furious. He felt he had been led on and made a fool of and
if they weren't getting engaged, then they were finished. It was one or
the other.

Alice and Joseph met halfway on the pier and swapped messages.

Joseph was insistent. 'We've got to get this sorted out by tonight,
because I'll die if we can't share a room tonight.'

Alice felt a lurch in her stomach that was very much like when she
had gone over the top of the scenic railway. 'Let me go and have another
word with her.'

Back in the room she asked the one question that mattered: 'Why
did you say no?'

'I don't know. It's just what came out. It had nothing to do with my brain, it was just down here,' Grace said, pointing at her stomach. 'But now I think I've made a terrible mistake. I keep thinking what it'll be like without him.'

'Well?'

'Empty, lonely. Especially now you've gone and got married.'

'I'm not leaving home yet!'

'No, but you will, soon. We can hardly go out dancing like we used to, can we? Who am I going to go out with now? And the thought of spending every evening at home … it would be like going backwards.'

'You'll find someone else.'

'But will I? Will I find anyone who makes me feel the way he does? I don't want to be one of those old spinsters, spending the rest of my life as the poor maiden aunt, on the shelf, typing up a man's letters and taking his phone calls while his wife makes a home and a family. I don't want people to look down on me – "Poor Grace, she did have a man once but he got away." I want a home of my own.'

'So?'

'So I just don't know.'

'But forget all that. Do you love him?'

'Yes, I do.'

'So?'

'I don't know. There's something not right and I can't put my finger on it.'

'Hmmmm. Well, you'd better put your finger on it soon, otherwise he really will be the one that got away.'

Silence.

'All right, I'll do it. Go back and tell him if he proposes again I'll say yes.'

'Oh, Grace, are you sure?'

'Yes. I mean, are you ever sure? Yes, yes, go on!'

'I think you can be sure.'

'Well, maybe that's just you. That's not me. Now go and tell him.'

So Alice went out with a new message.

An hour later Bill and Grace met on the promenade. Bill couldn't look Grace in the eye. With Margate Pier behind, Bill asked Grace to marry him again and this time she said yes. But it was a muted, angry proposal and a nervous acceptance.

They never talked about this awkward engagement, but it cast a shadow over the beginning of their life together.

As the four of them left to go home, Joseph took Bill aside. 'I want you to do something for me. If anything ever happens to me, can you give this to Alice?' He pressed a letter into Bill's hand.

'What's this for?'

'Don't read it. I can't explain. It's just in case.'

'In case of what? Blimey, mate, you're a bit gloomy!'

'No, not gloomy. Nothing is going to happen. But you never know, do you? Life's a funny thing. Can you give me your word? It's just for my peace of mind.'

'All right then. But cheer up, it may never happen.'

'No, it might never. Thanks, Bill, I knew I could count on you.'

And the four of them ran for the bus and went home.

# CHAPTER TEN
# A Funeral and Three Weddings

*Grace's wedding*

*Dora's wedding*

*Katie's wedding*

It's interesting which of the sisters' wedding photos have survived. There are quite a few of Grace looking remarkably joyful – in fact, everyone looked happy at that wedding. Grace is all Roaring Twenties in a drop-waisted short dress and a veil like Elizabeth Bowes-Lyon. There are lots of Katie looking simply stunning in gold lamé, with lilies: quite the thirties film star, but the most photos that survive are from Dora's wedding. It's a wedding on the brink of the 1940s with a full-length dress, again in gold – a brave departure for Dora from her customary black or navy – but the material is shot taffeta, with a tiny waist and elaborately curled hair in that forties style and again, like Katie, carrying a dramatic bunch of arum lilies. When I went to see Dora's daughters, the twins rushed upstairs and came down with the dress, still in perfect condition. I couldn't get over how modern it seemed – an evening dress I could still wear to a do today, except I'd never fit into it. I have a relatively small waist, but Dora's seems unfeasible, especially as she wasn't young for those days – twenty-eight when she finally married Spencer Sier.

In contrast there are no photos of my nanna, Bertha's wedding. Apparently she wore coffee-coloured lace and carried yellow chrysanthemums, the better to offset her bright red hair. There are also none of either of Alice's weddings.

It could just be a coincidence, but I think there's a reason why no one kept or perhaps even took photos at their weddings. I think it was because they were weddings that were not universally approved of. In fact, I'd go so far as to say that the number of wedding photos that survive are in direct proportion to how popular the marriages were with the family, particularly with Clara. Hence the large number of photographs of Dora and her grammar-school, bank-manager husband, and none of Bertha's marriage to the penniless, orphan carpenter, William Kendall – my grandfather.

Obviously there is a reason why there are no photographs of Alice marrying Joseph Davidson – the wedding was a secret, she practically eloped. But Alice did marry again, and there are no photographs of this wedding either. And I wonder whether it's because Clara's disapproval of Joseph Davidson disappeared into insignificance compared with the opprobrium she felt for Alice's second husband, Thomas Corbett. Clara could never understand why Alice ran off with Tom in such a hurry; why her favourite daughter, the one with whom she most identified, and for whom she had such high hopes, ran off to a mining village in the Welsh valleys and came back with a baby in her arms.

But then, as Clara didn't know about Alice's dash to the altar with Joseph Davidson, it would be rather mysterious.

Alice was to look back to that day in January 1929 and feel terrified that it was possible for her whole life to evaporate into thin air and not to have the slightest inkling. A wave of sheer existential dread would turn her stomach. She really tried to erase the memory of that day, but every so often it would leap out and leave her reeling.

For Alice it was just an ordinary day at the bank. It was hard work and long hours – she had to be at her desk by 8.30 a.m., in a long line of one of many long lines of ladies typing the letters of the bank employees – all men. They were shut in a windowless, hot room, segregated from the naturally lit, cooler offices on the more elevated floors of the bank. There was no prospect of promotion and, for most women, it was just a useful interlude between leaving school and becoming a wife. The job was prestigious and relatively lucrative, but the day-to-day reality was not glamorous.

The thought that sustained Alice was the money she was accumulating. Alice and Joseph had set themselves a target when they got engaged, and they reckoned that by the time they reached the anniversary of their engagement in May 1929, they would be ready to put down a deposit on a house, reveal their marriage to the outside world and try for a baby. Alice couldn't wait. She was nearly twenty-eight, and she had had enough of comments about 'being on the shelf'

– interestingly, not from her mother, who preferred her daughter to be working than married inappropriately; nor from her sisters; but from everyone else.

Those were the thoughts that were filling her head as she hurried back in the cold and dark from Grays station at 8 p.m. on 15 January 1929. As she trotted along, an arm shot out and grabbed her, nearly sending her slipping on the ice. Alice's first thought was that it was Joseph – sometimes he managed to come and meet her.

But when she wheeled round it was Bill Smith.

He looked dreadful.

'Hello, Bill. Gosh, you gave me a fright. Are you all right?'

'No, not really.'

She studied his face. 'What's the matter? Oh my God, has something happened? Is it Grace?'

'No, Grace is fine. I don't know how to tell you this, Alice. I'm sorry.'

'What?'

'It's Jo. He's dead.'

And this is where Alice's memory failed. She experienced little flashbacks for the rest of her life, seemingly unprompted – the feel of her head hitting the pavement as she fainted with shock, the look on Bill's face as he bent over her, the burning sensation of the whisky from his hip flask as he poured it on her tongue, the words 'heart attack', the terrible unearthly wail that must have come from her, and then the feel of the cool sheets as Grace tucked her into bed, and then blackness, sleep.

What Grace told her afterwards was that she stayed in bed for nearly a week with the covers over her head and the curtains closed. Grace told everyone that Alice had a migraine. The ladies of the Swain family, and indeed their descendants, including me, suffer periodically from disabling headaches, with wonky vision, flashing lights and sickness. The world becomes blurry and unreal, and the pain blots out anything else that might be going on. There have been times when I too have welcomed them.

On this occasion the family migraine bought Alice a bit of space. She slept. In fact, she hardly woke up. When she did come to, she thought it was an ordinary day and she got ready to leap out of bed, and then she realised she was alone in the room and why. And Alice felt like the pedal on the Mighty Striker, pummelled by the hammer of Joseph's death so that the alarm bells went off in her head and she had to shut down again, knocked unconscious by the sheer shock of what had happened. All her hopes for the future, which only she (and Grace and Bill) had known were gone.

An enormous, aching loneliness gripped her and her teeth started to chatter so that all she could do was close her eyes.

At some point she realised she had a letter and remembered Bill had given it to her, but seeing her name written in Joseph's hand just made her feel sick.

On the fifth day of Alice's hibernation, Grace came in and opened the curtains, and sat down beside her bed. 'I haven't said anything to Mum or to anyone else. I haven't let on about you and Jo. I don't know what you want to do, but I'm guessing it's best if no one ever does know.'

Alice stared at Grace and then nodded.

Grace took her hand and started stroking it. 'But it does mean you're going to have to get up. Not right now, but soon. Mother is murmuring and worrying about the bank. Anyway, the funeral is tomorrow, at St Thomas's. I'm going to go. Please can I take you?'

And Alice found herself nodding again.

'Good girl! We'll get you looking really nice. Dora's already offered to lend you one of her black dresses. I've told everyone we've been invited as Jo's friend, and to keep Bill company. Mum raised an eyebrow but she didn't say anything. I think everyone is feeling for poor Mrs Davidson.'

What Grace didn't say was that Clara had said, 'At least she still has eleven other sons,' which sent a stricken look around the family as they remembered Charlie Junior. She also said, 'Well, he didn't look well when he came here. Good thing Alice stopped walking out with him, otherwise where would she be now?'

At which Grace kept very quiet.

The funeral was quite an affair. Joseph had been popular and, of course, came from a large family. There was plenty of vocal grief at such a young and tragic death, which meant Alice could sit at the back of the church unobserved and lost in the crowd. As the coffin was carried in, she buried her head in Grace's shoulder and couldn't look up. She tried very hard not to think about the last time she had been in the church, getting married, but the priest's voice was echoing in her head. She could feel her wedding ring on a chain around her neck hidden beneath her dress, cold and heavy. Alice wrapped her scarf around her ears and Grace took her hand.

As the coffin was carried out she had to look away again.

'Are you all right to go to the cemetery?' Grace whispered.

Alice shook her head. Instead, she walked purposefully home, hardly able to breathe. People stepped sideways to let her pass: like the night she first saw Joseph and pushed through to stop him falling off the table, the normally placid Alice felt she might punch anyone who got in her way.

She flew into the house and ran up the stairs, closing the bedroom door with a bang. She grabbed the chair and put it under the door handle so there could be no sisterly interruptions.

Then she opened Joseph's letter.

*My dearest Alice,*

*I am writing this letter dreading that you will ever receive it. But my greater dread is that I am taken from you and I never will have had the chance to explain.*

*Please, please forgive me. I have not told you everything that you, as my darling wife, should know.*

*Just before that night when I met you, our New Year's Eve, the best night of my life, I received the worst news. I had been feeling ill for a long time and then I was told that I had diabetes – you will probably know it as the sugar sickness. I was told I didn't have long to live. I am incredibly grateful for your patience at my skinny body, my strange diet, my 'funny turns'. I still have no idea how you could fall in love with anyone so strange. There were so many times I nearly told you, but every time I couldn't. For that I hope you can forgive me, knowing that I will never be able to forgive myself.*

*I was so happy, you were so happy. I thought if I didn't say it, it wouldn't happen. Somehow our love could conquer it or perhaps the doctors had got it wrong, or they would find a cure, or perhaps I'd grow out of it, and I write this with the prayer that God will spare me, although if you are reading it I know He hasn't.*

*I took a gamble. That maybe by marrying but marrying in secret we could have it all – that if we managed to make it past a couple of years, I would probably live, but if I didn't then at least we didn't miss out on truly loving each other. I have tried to have my cake and eat it and I am sorry.*

*Please forgive me and know that I didn't tell you, not because I don't love you, but because I love you too much. I wanted you, I wanted you to be my wife and if I died, then at least we had had that. You have made me the happiest I have ever been and my life worth living, however short it turns out to be.*

*Please now forget me, live your life, marry again, be happy. It's all I want. Do it for me.*

*All my love, for ever.*

*Jo*

Suddenly everything made sense.

In the 1920s diabetes was a certain death sentence – most people died within a year of being diagnosed. In the meantime they were put on a starvation diet (which included no alcohol). It made them thin, sweaty and prone to blackouts. Organ failure and heart attacks were the eventual result of the body's inability to process sugar. A few years before Joseph's death, insulin had been discovered by a Canadian scientist and was beginning to be manufactured and given to patients. However, it wasn't yet widely used in Britain. Just a couple of years later, Joseph's life would have almost certainly been saved, and he would have lived a full and relatively normal life. He was absolutely right to hope that a cure might be found in time.

Alice sat on the bed in a stunned silence, hit by waves of conflicting emotions. She read and reread the letter. There was relief, because suddenly, yes, it did all make sense; anger and hurt that he hadn't told her – she absolutely would have married him anyway, how could he not have believed that? And then horror that he'd had to carry this secret all by himself. But then with it she felt his love, and then quickly the agony of losing this love.

In fact, the more she thought about it, the more Alice felt grateful that Joseph had spared her the worry, although of course instead she did get the most terrible shock. On the one hand their secret marriage meant that they had spent time apart when they could have been together, but on the other it had given their time together a real poignancy and intensity and sweetness.

In the end, the bit she dwelt on was that last sentence. With it, he'd given her the clue and permission for her next move and the way to carry on – no, he had actually ordered her to do it.

After an hour or so she brought the letter up to her face and sniffed it, and then kissed it and said out loud, 'Thank you.' Then she folded it up and put it away in her own secret place, in a room filled with the secret places of five sisters. And a few of their mother's too.

*

That night, as their three younger sisters slept, Alice told Grace in a whisper about the letter.

'So, what are you going to do?'

'I'm going to do what Jo told me. I'm going to start again.'

Grace looked at her big sister, impressed. And then Alice grabbed her hand and said urgently, 'But you've got to help me.'

Grace couldn't help but say, 'Oh, no! What now?'

'Don't ever, ever, mention Jo again.'

'What, never?'

'No, never. If I'm to do what he says, I need to forget. I need to pretend it never happened, and if I pretend hard enough maybe it will start to feel like it.'

Grace studied her sister's face. She could see she meant it.

'All right. I won't mention him again. But if you change your mind …'

'I won't.'

Grace nodded and they hugged.


Grace remained true to her word and never mentioned Joseph again. Her sisters and parents never knew, and neither did their children, and when Alice went on to marry and have children, they never knew that their mother had been married before, either.

It was only in the very last year of her life that Alice told her daughter-in-law about Joseph. Just the once, and not even her own daughter. And it was only after she died and her son Brian went into her attic and started to go through her things that he found Alice's and Joseph's marriage certificate.

I wonder why she told anyone at all. If you go through your whole life keeping a secret, why do you feel the need as you approach the end to tell the story, just the once? Speaking it out loud, hearing the words, having a witness … perhaps all these things make it true.

*

Two months later, when Grace and Bill's wedding went ahead as planned, Alice played the part of the dutiful bridesmaid. She was helped by the fact the wedding was so different to her own. There was no secrecy about Bill and Grace's engagement. Bill was the son of a school teacher, a clever boy who'd won a scholarship to the grammar school in Grays. When they got married, he was working as a clerk to the South Eastern Water Company and therefore technically lower-middle class, and acceptable to Clara. Moreover, unlike Joseph's first visit to the Swain house, Bill had charmed everyone with his ease and gregariousness, and his ability to play the piano. Clara always did put a high premium on musical ability as, in fact, they all did. It's something else I inherited and might be one of the spells that needs to be broken …

I look at the photos of Alice at Grace's wedding and wonder. She's standing between Katie and Bertha in her cloche hat, wearing her bridesmaid's dress and smiling. It must have taken every ounce

*Bertha, Alice and Katie*

of strength to pull off that day and I feel a wave of admiration. No one would ever know that, during the service, she had felt a wave of complete desperation. There was a pain in her heart that actually was just that – a real, physical pain. At one point she wondered whether she wasn't having a heart attack herself. But she held on and the way she did it was with the thought that she must do everything possible to find herself another husband. This was the only way to stop the unbearable feeling. Until that moment she had been hibernating – leaving work late, going to bed early, avoiding her friends and staying away from the dance hall. But at Grace and Bill's wedding she resolved that she would put on her dancing shoes the very next day and begin her campaign to get a new life.

And that's how she met Thomas Corbett. He was dreadfully good-looking: tall, slim, dark, with sharp blue eyes. A Welsh miner from the valleys who had come to London looking for work, he was currently a milkman. And then the important thing – he was a champion Charleston dancer. He didn't say much but he danced beautifully, and when Alice danced with him it was possible to forget. Alice was the opposite of the girl in the red shoes. In the fairy tale the girl can't take off the shoes and is condemned to dance for infinity. It's a terrible, exhausting fate. But Alice didn't see it this way. As long as she kept dancing, she was happy. As soon as she took the shoes off, the pain would start again. So when Tom asked her to marry him six months later, the answer seemed obvious. This way she could dance for ever.

Of course, it wasn't at all obvious to her mother. Alice was under no illusion that if Joseph had been unacceptable, there was no hope for Tom. But she was determined that this time there was to be no secrecy. She arranged for Tom to come round for tea with her parents.

They sat on the sofa together holding hands, facing Clara and Charlie, with Clara looking daggers at Tom all the while, and then finally Alice found the courage to say: 'Mum, we've got something to tell you. Haven't we, Tom?'

Tom looked defiantly back at Clara. 'Yes, we have.'

'Tom has asked me to marry him and I have said yes.'

Clara was aghast. 'What, *him*?'

'Mother!'

'Are you mad? Are you going to give up your job to settle for him?'

'What do you mean "him"?' Tom's eyes were flashing.

Alice desperately tried to defuse the situation: 'Do you mind not speaking about Tom like that.'

'I'll speak how I find.'

'Oh, yes? And what do you find?' Tom said.

'I see a man who's come to London to see what he can get. And you see a good thing in my daughter. Much better than what you'd get back home. And Alice is too nice to see through you. But I've got your number. And I'm telling you, you are not marrying my daughter, not over my dead body.'

'Mum, I love him.'

'Rubbish! You love his blue eyes and his smooth talking. That won't last, my girl. Once he's got you, all that will stop. Mark my words, it'll be a life of misery and drudgery, at his beck and call.'

She turned to Tom. 'How dare you? How dare you take her away from a good job and a good future? What have you got to offer her? A ride on your milk float?'

Tom was clever enough to stay quiet and let Alice do the work.

'He loves me.'

Clara snorted.

'Look, Mum, I don't want anything else. I don't want the job in the bank. I want a husband and a family and I want that with Tom.'

'Well, you can't.'

'Mum, I'm twenty-nine. I can, and I'm going to.'

Clara turned to the silent Charlie. 'Are you just going to sit back and let this happen?'

'It seems there's nothing I can do about it.' He got up with tears in his eyes and went over and put his hand on Alice's shoulder and said, 'I'm sorry, love.' Casting a mournful look at Tom, he walked out of the room.

Clara had been frustrated many times in her life: if she'd had the iron ladle, now was the moment it would have got thrown, but today there was nothing to hand. She found herself playing the only card she had left: 'Well, you're not getting my blessing. If you marry him, I don't ever want to see you again.'

There was a dreadful silence in the room and then Tom spoke. 'Come on, Alice, pack your bag. I don't think there's any point in us staying here.'

And Alice, the good girl, the general, who as far as Clara knew was the only one of her daughters who did what she was told, got up in tears and went upstairs, packed her bag and left for Wales that night.

Almost two years to the day after Joseph died Alice remarried, and a year after that she had her first baby, Charlie and Clara's first grandchild, Jean.

Clara never forgave Tom Corbett for this elopement. Often it's easier for parents to blame someone else – usually their child's partner – for their actions, rather than accept their child's behaviour and decisions as their own. As we are all tempted to do when someone close to us, child, partner, parent, whoever, behaves in a way we find difficult to accept, denial slips in: it wasn't them, of course, it was that dreadful … (fill in the blank).

Clara never spoke to Tom directly again, which was awkward later on when she found herself living with him. There was a ban on his name and a sense of disapproval, unspoken but felt, not just by the sisters, but by their children too.

I sat in the back row of a conference on inherited trauma and struggled to stop myself weeping. All the time Clara and her ten years of endless work were in my mind. Actually, there were all sorts of family members in my mind, not least myself. But Clara's efforts to escape the family curse were particularly clear and targeted and heroic.

The distinguished psychoanalyst giving his paper described a traumatic event in a family as having the effect of stopping the clock. Unless the trauma is faced and worked through, the family is condemned thereafter to experience reruns. Time stutters. You move forward a little and then whoops, you are back where you started: Sisyphus endlessly condemned to push his rock up the hill only to have it roll straight back down again or, perhaps a more contemporary way of describing it, an eternal *Groundhog Day*.

With her ten-year plan, Clara seemed to have started the clock again, but it was just an illusion. She had addressed the material welfare of the family, but the emotional damage was untouched and left to fester. The family grief – which one, it's difficult to say – had already had an impact on Clara's daughters, which no amount of shorthand qualifications could reverse: Alexander's disgrace and early death in the workhouse? The terrible fate of Charlie Junior? The secret shame of Charlie Senior's war career and subsequent descent into alcoholism? Any one of them would do it. The family legacy of trauma. Because trauma acts to distort the mirror of the psyche, so that you can no longer see things as they really are. You chose people and paths that are not healthy for you.

And this is exactly what happened when Alice kissed Tom Corbett and agreed to run away with him, thereby setting in motion the boulder running back down the hill and the spell continuing into the next generation.

What Clara didn't know then was that Alice's wasn't the only secret being carried at Grace's wedding – the twins had been off having their own adventures.

My Nanna, Bertha, looks particularly happy in the photo. And this is because she was thinking of her own future wedding, and what she

*The scout dance where my grandparents met. William is on the far left; Bertha is fifth from the left on the second row.*

liked about Grace's and what she didn't like and how she could make hers better, because what no one else knew, but Bertha did, was that she was already secretly engaged to William Kendall.

Bertha was only fourteen when she first set eyes on William. He was the first boyfriend she ever had and, as far as we know, the only boyfriend she ever had.

Clara and Charlie were rather liberal parents. It was hard to be strict when the father of the house had so few rules for himself: on the rare occasions he tried to rein them in a bit, he got short shrift. So, from a relatively young age the high-spirited girls, all except for Dora, were out and about courting.

Dances organised by churches and organisations like The Boys' Brigade were very popular, as they were a more respectable alternative to the large dance halls. But however holy the umbrella over the occasion, everyone knew they were still a means for young women to meet young men. And while Bertha, at the age of fourteen, couldn't have skipped off to the Queen's Hotel without scandalising the neighbourhood, she could go to a Scout dance and walk out with her reputation intact.

Bertha lapped up an occasion and never missed a party. I loved to watch her working a room. She seemed to have been born with an innate charm. She was never loud, she never pushed herself forward. She didn't need to. People flocked to her and were enchanted by her. It's a talent and an enormous asset in life – to be liked and sought out. She was sweet, but there was just enough wickedness, wit and humour – the twinkle in her eyes – to stop her from being sickly. And she was a good listener. In reality she was a terrible gossip and loved the dramas of others, perhaps as a way of escaping her own. People found themselves telling her all sorts of things they probably shouldn't, and they were rewarded with a listening ear, a nugget of wisdom and then a naughty aside.

I took an early boyfriend to stay with her one summer holiday. We had a riot. She turned a blind eye to our student antics as we rampaged across the south coast where she lived, drinking, kissing, dancing to an eccentric combination of music at top volume during the day, and rolling around her living room floor at night. She taught us how to play bridge as we played footsie under the table.

In the end he had to go home. As we put him on the train, Nanna said with that twinkle in her eye: 'Well, J—. It's been a pleasure. Please come and stay again soon … preferably with the same girl.'

I look at my littlest daughter, Daisy, and wonder whether if you are the youngest in a big family you develop a special charm, because you have to.

Those dances were the playpen for the class act Bertha was to become. First came the excitement of preparation: she would spend the days before gossiping with her sisters about who was going, what they would be wearing and fretting about her own outfit. Her beautiful hair would be prepared the night before, tied up in rags to produce flaming pre-Raphaelite waves. On the day she would spend over an hour changing and rechanging her outfit so the sisters' bedroom floor would be strewn with assorted dresses and accessories, which she would then fail to put away (being the messiest of the sisters) and drive them all potty. This was not helped by the fact she had the run of all the sisters' wardrobes. There were inevitable rows as the sisters tried to get themselves ready around the maelstrom of Bertha's party preparations: tops were never put on the face creams and the kohl pencil would get trodden into the debris.

As Bertha had only just started at Miss Faber's this was one of her first dances, and therefore she was learning by a process of trial and error. For now she was very much reliant on her sisters' advice.

'What do you think?' she asked, holding up a pea-green satin shift.

'Soup,' said Dora.

'I wasn't asking you.'

'Hmmmm. Think this would be better for you,' Grace said, holding up a bright pink satin dress, the same dress, in fact, that Alice had worn to the New Year's Eve dance in the Queen's Hotel. I was going to call it the lucky dress, but in retrospect that's probably not quite right, and unlucky dress is not quite right either. Perhaps it should be known as the Dress of Destiny.

Bertha took her big sister's advice and wore the pink satin shift, and this was what first caught the eye of my grandfather, William Kendall.

With her red hair and red lipstick clashing with her pink satin shift, Bertha couldn't help but make heads turn. William watched this colourful creature sashay gracefully across the dance floor. She did not look like your average Essex girl and she, in the sweetest way possible, knew it. She'd only been at college a few months, but Miss Faber was pushing against an open door with Bertha. She was drinking up lessons on how to be a lady as if they were one of her baby bottles of Carnation milk.

It took William the whole evening to find the nerve to approach her; in fact, he didn't know quite how he was going to do it. In the end,

Bertha helped. She had spotted him too, leaning up against the wall at the back, on his own but looking entirely comfortable that way. She took the fact he was not larking about with the other young men as a sign of class and maturity.

William *did* look intense and serious. 'Still waters run deep,' was the phrase that came into her head, while the fact that Bertha happened to be reading *Jane Eyre* at the time and was obsessed with Rochester probably has more to do with my arrival on the planet than anything else. William was not tall but, like Rochester, he was dark. Not just dark hair, but that dark skin which only has to have a sniff of sun to brown up like toast on the fire. And he did love the sun.

An unsubstantiated rumour exists that William was the result of an affair between his mother and an Egyptian whom she met on a long train journey on the Cape to Cairo railway – she gave birth to William within months of arriving back at Tilbury Docks, while his father was still toiling away as an engineer at the bottom of the tracks in South Africa.

I would tease my mum. 'Of course he was Egyptian.'

'But he had blue eyes,' Mum would say.

'Ah, yes, but they were very dark blue and lots of Egyptians have dark blue eyes.'

'Do they?'

'Yes. Look at Omar Sharif.'

'He's got brown eyes.'

'No, he hasn't.' Actually I didn't have a clue, but I was enjoying myself. 'And you know Grandpa's hair never went grey? Well, that's an Arab thing.'

'Is it?'

'Yes.'

'But Omar Sharif has white hair.'

'No, he doesn't.'

'Doesn't he? Helen!'

I was giggling, but it has to be said Grandpa did look pretty exotic, and he certainly was his happiest ever rampaging across the Egyptian desert in a tank during the Second World War, which doesn't seem to have been the majority view of that experience.

But perhaps the most exciting thing for Bertha was the fact he never took his dark, brooding eyes off her. And Bertha was aware of that all evening. She had to stop herself from looking over at him: she could feel his eyes burning into her back. 'Come on, come over,' she started to scream in frustration in her head as she danced past him, looking in the eyes of yet another local boy, and yet at the same time, using every opportunity to catch William's eye and give the coy 'Come hither' yet chaste smile she'd been practising in the mirror.

By the time the evening was winding down, she was getting a bit irritated. She even wondered whether she would just have to invent an excuse and go over herself. Of course the fact he hadn't bothered with any other girl made Bertha feel all the more special – something that was a rarity in her life.

And then, just like that, William suddenly stood up from the wall, strode over and offered his hand. 'William Kendall.'

'Hello, William.'

'I wondered whether I might walk you home?'

'Well, thank you, but there's no need. I've come with my sisters.'

She gestured at Katie and Grace being chatted up by a group of lads, although she didn't really have to point them out – with their hair and bright clothes there was no one else she could have been related to.

Then Bertha cursed herself for making such a tactical error, because of course his face immediately fell and he said: 'Oh. All right then.'

So she said quickly, with that twinkle in her eye: 'No need to walk me home, but it would be a pleasure to have your company nonetheless, William. Thank you.'

William didn't know quite what to do next – she was a bit bolder than he had imagined. And she reinforced this impression when the next thing she said was, 'Let's go then, shall we?'

They started to walk out of the church hall and down the road. To break the silence Bertha piped up: 'Yes, I'd better be getting back, as my mother will be waiting up. I don't suppose you have that problem?'

Bertha said it innocently as a little conversation opener, the sort of manoeuvre she was learning at Miss Faber's, but she got more than she bargained for.

'No, I don't,' he said. And it just slipped out of his mouth. 'She's dead.'

It was a horrible, tumbleweed moment and William was surprised how affected Bertha seemed.

'Oh, I'm so sorry,' she said and tears started in her eyes. 'You poor, poor thing!' She took his hand. 'So, what do you do? Who looks after you? Has your father remarried or do you have a sister?'

'No, I'm an orphan.'

Bertha stopped in her tracks. *Jane Eyre* once more popped into her mind.

'So how have you grown up?' she asked.

At this William smiled. 'In the same way you did. Luckily, you don't stop growing when you lose your parents, otherwise I'd be even shorter than I am now.'

'Yes, of course … that came out all wrong. Not that you are short at all. I think you're the perfect height.'

Once again William was taken aback. Now it was Bertha's turn to blush, and to save her embarrassment William found himself talking quickly: 'My mother died of TB when I was a baby so I didn't really ever know her, but then my father died of dysentery a year later.'

'Oh, goodness, you poor thing! So where did you go?'

'Well, my grandmother looked after me, but then she died when I was five.'

The scale of William's tragedy was really beginning to feel too much.

'And so where did you go then?'

'I went to live with my old uncle. He's brought me up. Well, really his housekeeper, Mrs Beesom, has done most of the looking after.'

'Does he not have a wife?'

'No, she died. But he's a kind man. And he's a master carpenter. He runs a school for young boys to learn carpentry down at the docks, and he's teaching me. In some ways I'm quite lucky.'

Bertha wasn't sure that was the word she'd use, but this time she kept quiet. 'So you have an uncle. What other family do you have?'

'That's it.'

'No brothers or sisters?'

'No. My sister Margaret died last year of TB, too.'

Finally Bertha was speechless. They walked the rest of the way home in silence, but she had taken his hand and held it tightly all the way home.

As they reached her house, William turned to her: 'Can I see you again?'

She nodded. 'Yes, yes, I'd like that.'

'Good.' And he turned and walked back down the street, just stopping the once to look round, and see Bertha pausing at the front door, watching him. They smiled and waved at each other and William carried on walking slowly home.

That night in the confessional that was their shared bed, Katie quizzed her sister: 'So, what's with the handsome dark stranger, Bertie?'

'William Kendall to you.'

'And?'

'And he's not like anyone I've ever met before.'

At this all the sisters perked up and there was a chorus of, 'Ooooooooh!'

'She's going to marry him, you know,' Dora said to Grace.

'Oh, stop it! You with your predictions. Haven't we had enough of those?'

But, actually, as she was about Charlie Junior and Joseph Davidson, once again Dora was spot-on.

*Katie, Bertha and Bill*

From the moment they met, Bertha and William were inseparable. I have a photo of them at a picnic. My grandfather does look incredibly dark and handsome. He has a raffish grin on his face and is sitting on a grassy bank in the sunshine with his arms wrapped around Bertha, who is smiling, happy, in a pretty floral summer dress. In the background, sitting some way off, is her twin sister Katie, who is also giving a cheeky grin. If she's supposed to be chaperoning them then she doesn't look as if she's doing a very good job because they are pretty well wrapped up in each other.

My great-grandparents had several issues with William, one of which was his predilection for manhandling my nanna in public. 'He used to pinch her bottom when he went round to visit,' Mum said. 'Apparently Charlie took great offence.'

I can't imagine Charlie taking out his gun, as he wasn't exactly a tower of moral fortitude himself, but obviously public displays of affection still crossed a line in the 1930s. However, one advantage of being the youngest in the family is that your older siblings cut a path for you – certainly Bertha's relationship developed in the slipstream of Alice's elopement with Tom Corbett. However much Clara and Charlie disapproved of William (and being a penniless, orphan carpenter didn't earn him any Brownie points) the shock of Alice walking out of their lives meant that Clara was not inclined to make any ultimatums.

So William was tolerated and Bertha carried on seeing him. What Bertha liked best was going round to his uncle's house. It was a gloomy house, filled with the dark furniture that he had inherited as the last survivor of the doomed Kendall dynasty. Old Uncle came from a different age, a true Victorian, never speaking unless necessary and uncomfortable around women. Absolute silence was required at mealtimes. William, however, had been a naturally quiet, well-behaved child, so had lived a surprisingly harmonious existence with Old Uncle, especially as they both shared a common interest – carpentry.

With air travel still in its infancy, most people travelled long distances by boat. The large, luxurious cruise liners would arrive from crossing the Atlantic and Old Uncle would go and make repairs. Often he would remove and 'acquire' bits of furniture that were being replaced. William went to live with Old Uncle when he was six years old, but from the first day he arrived, Old Uncle started teaching him his trade and it was not long before he and William, with intense concentration on their faces and in absolute silence, would spend their spare time lovingly restoring these pieces of furniture and selling them on. I still have the most extraordinary sprung rocking chair, which Old Uncle 'rescued' from an American cruise ship. It reminds me of the rocking chairs you see on porches in New England. Intricately carved and quite bouncy, it is extra-heavy so as not to roll around on the ocean waves. I bounced on it as a child and now my girls enjoy it – although I've replaced the old tapestry upholstery with lime-green velvet.

When William was older, Old Uncle took him onto the ships. As the principal port of London, Tilbury Docks was the final stop for many of the boats that crossed the Atlantic, or went to Australia. It was also the headquarters of the oldest cruise line in the world, P&O. It was the principal point of immigration into the country. William loved watching the liners come and go, people embarking and disembarking, with bands playing and streamers thrown, tearful goodbyes and joyful hellos. It made him think about his own parents, who had disembarked there from Africa, only to pass away soon after. He wondered about that and felt that inherited wonderlust biting at his heels. He fantasised about stowing away, starting a journey where he didn't know the end destination. He dreamed of sunshine and wide open, wild spaces, childhood fantasies that were to have consequences for his family later on.

It took everyone by surprise that Bertha fitted in so easily with this unusual domestic arrangement. Somehow sunny Bertha managed to break through to Old Uncle and make him smile. As they sat in silence around the table, Old Uncle couldn't help watching this elegant, colourful, young child, with her perfect manners and deportment. He was touched to see the sweet looks that passed between William and Bertha as they silently nibbled at Mrs Beesom's apple cake.

And then there was Mrs Beesom herself. She was a widow with a married daughter. A short round pudding of a lady, with her hair always scraped back in rows of plaits pinned around her head, there was never a hint of impropriety between herself and Old Uncle and yet everybody wondered. It wouldn't be the first time that this housekeeping arrangement was more wide-ranging than the job description implied. She rather took to Bertha and treated her like a lady when she came to visit, ushering her in, taking her coat, serving her the best cakes.

'What a lovely young lady she is! She's a keeper,' she would say to William, and ruffle his hair.

And there we have the key to their whole relationship.

'You're very special,' William would say to Bertha.

'Oh, really?' she said.

'You sound surprised.'

'Well, I've never felt special before ever. I've always felt like the bottom of the barrel.'

'You will never be the bottom of the barrel to me. You are the top of the barrel. Actually the whole barrel, the one and only barrel,' William said.

And so she married him.


Years later, when Nanna cried on Dora's shoulder and said how much she envied Dora her happy marriage and her love for her husband, she said that she had married William because she felt sorry for him and she wanted to have children. Indeed, she always referred to her marriage as 'The Quest to Have Children'. 'The gap creates desire,' so they say. Bertha didn't feel loved at home, so at the age of twenty she married William and built her own.

And this meant not only leaving her family but her job. At the time the BBC prided itself on being a modern organisation and that included equal promotion and pay for its women employees. However, with a few stellar exceptions, women were confined to the switchboard, typing pools and the cafeteria. Clara's hopes for Bertha at the BBC were never quite fulfilled. And then in the wake of the Depression, in 1932, the Corporation brought in the Marriage Bar that decreed that only those married women of special importance were entitled to stay. So when Bertha married William in December 1933, this was the end of her career. She never spoke about it again. In fact, none of us knew she had worked there until I got my first job at the BBC sixty years later as an assistant producer. She took me aside and said, 'I am so proud of you. And making programmes too. I never would have believed when I worked there that a woman, never mind a granddaughter of mine, could actually make programmes. You have done everything I ever wanted to do. I am so proud.'

But when I carried on working part-time after I had my eldest daughter, Amber, and I was explaining my complicated child-care arrangements, she surprised me by saying, 'Well, I have no idea why you want to go back to work, anyway. If I were you, I'd stay at home and bring up my child.'

'Perhaps there's a way I can do both.'

'Why do you want to do both? You're very lucky – you don't have to work, do you?'

She was right – I was in the fortunate position that my husband could support the family. It wasn't about the money.

'No, but Nanna, I've worked so hard to get where I am and I really enjoy it.'

'Well, I don't understand you.'

And I didn't understand her. So I articulated something that had been bothering me since Amber had been born. 'OK, put it this way – what is the point in having daughters, and educating them and encouraging them to go to university, and have careers, just for them to give it all up to have more daughters to do the same thing all over again? Surely along the way we can leave more of an imprint on the world, do something more than just pass on our genes.'

'Now you're being silly. It's not like that,' she said, ruffled.

Really? Because it felt like that. But I realised I was in danger of seeming disrespectful of my nanna's life, which I wasn't at all. So I changed the subject.

But the conversation bothered me. Nanna was fifty-seven years older than me and it wasn't until that moment that I realised how much had changed – and how unbridgeable the gap between her generation and mine was and still is.

Of course I don't see it quite like that now. Ten years later, somewhere between losing a child and losing a husband, and changing career and having three more children – actually, just doing a lot of life

– I've realised there are many ways to leave an imprint, most of which don't involve paid employment or genetically reproducing. Everyday interactions with each other, small kindnesses and big conversations … I think we leave more of an imprint on the earth and on each other than we could ever imagine. And in that Nanna was a good example.

# CHAPTER ELEVEN
# Mind the Gap

Research has shown that we are most vulnerable to fall in love when we have just suffered a trauma, particularly a broken relationship. It's a phenomenon commonly known as the 'rebound'. Our defences have been attacked and we are weak; our judgement is skewed because what we thought was so, turns out not to be so. We are looking through a mirror darkly and struggling to cope with loss and pain. What better than to project a happy ending on to whoever might pop up in the debris? We desperately want to make it true that things happen for a reason and are for the best in the long run. We fill the gap with someone else.

But does it work? Is it not pinning our hopes of recovery on another, rather than doing what we should be doing, which is healing ourselves? Sitting tight, licking our wounds, rebuilding our sense of who we are, fixing the mirror before we go out in the world again, so we make a judgement out of strength, rather than weakness. Being with someone because we want to rather than because we need to. Otherwise don't we risk jumping from frying pans into fires?

The story of the sisters is haunting me and casting a shadow over my relationship with Mr D. Because the fact that he came into my life when he did, in the way that he did, means that I still have not sat in the gap. My whiskers are dysfunctional. I just don't know. Are we good together or I am just making us good together? I spend those dark hours before dawn, sleep evading me, fretting that I am just repeating. Am I relying on him to rescue me, when really I should be doing the job myself?

When I'm in a good place, I am happy, really happy to be with him. It's easy. He makes me laugh, I make him laugh. We play. He teases me mercilessly. We have private jokes, layers upon layers of them building up from that first day we met, the bricks constructing our relationship. I say something, I anticipate the reply, but he still manages to surprise me. It's like music, establishing patterns, only to break them and then resolve them. This is our dance of attraction. The Greeks called it *ludus*, playful love. He calls it Ludicrous Love – he emails me the definition on a wet Monday morning: 'Ludicrous – or taking-the-mick love: where one partner shows his or her affection for the other by pretending to ridicule them or generally use them for comic effect while actually being incredibly proud of them.' I smile for the rest of the day.

I am not helped by the fact that Mr D is short for Mr Destiny. He was christened this by my girlfriends because of the way we met. My friend Tom had bought tickets for my husband and I to go and hear an Icelandic band called Sigur Rós with him and his wife, Aimee. We often did things as a foursome. Such was Tom's horror at eventual events, however, that he took away my husband's ticket and gave it to his friend, who was also going through a divorce. 'I hope you'll still come, Helen. I think you'll like him,' he said.

'OK, whatever,' I replied, and then forgot about it. The concert was months away. In the meantime I started dating on the internet.

About ten days before the concert I was contacted by a man named D. I showed his profile to my friend, Emma. 'What do you think?'

'Hmmm, all right. He says he's a journalist, so …'

I wrote back and that's when the banter started between us, and it became obvious we were going to meet. That is until he asked me what sort of music I liked and whether I'd heard of a weird Icelandic band called Sigur Rós because he was going to a concert next Friday. At which point I screamed and texted Aimee and said, 'Is this him?' and she said something rude which meant basically yes. So I emailed him back again:

'Dear D,

Not only have I heard of Sigur Rós but I'm going to that concert, and I'm going with you.'

After a whole day of waiting, I received this email back:

'I'm sorry for my tardy reply but I was a bit spooked. I only joined the site the day before and you were the first person I contacted. Do you think we should meet before we meet?'

So meet we did. And then we found out there were all sorts of coincidences, not least that we had worked in the same unit at the BBC for years, not at the same time, but with some of the same people. And then we went to see the weird Icelandic band and our next date, well, our first proper date really, was at that scene of my ancestral crimes: the Gladstone.

The thing is, whichever way round, we were destined to meet.

So it's a good story that gives my girlfriends goosebumps. But 'Mr Destiny' is a hard name to live up to. It's dangerous, because it's so powerful it could become a self-fulfilling prophecy.

In the year after my husband went, I had the best time. I fell in love after years of not being loved; I ran from the chaos of my home into the arms of a playmate; I found myself going to places and meeting people that I had never dreamt of.

We are lying on a bed facing each other, naked, eyes locked, smiling. Neither of us moves. Outside, below, the sound of busy, busy Rome – excitable Italians, scooters on cobblestones, bells ringing – a cacophony coming through the open windows with the light breeze and the sunshine of the hot afternoon. But here in our room, with only a large bed, white sheets, and us, all is calm and time has stopped. It is happiness.

That night we find the perfect bar except it's a private members club, but they beg us to join and now we have our own club in Rome. Later, as midnight turns into the early hours of the morning, a shadow joins us at our table. We talk about our wedding days and for the first time I realise just how sincerely and deeply he had loved before, and the complete devastation when having invested everything, it still went wrong. Where do you go from there? How do you ever commit again? It's one of the fundamental questions that hung over Mr D and me (and still does). So we share our pain, our messiness, the inevitable baggage. Because we have those moments too: when the laughter we share stops, and the tears of our experience with another enter the room.

I guess what I'm trying to say is Mr D was the silver lining. It felt as if the universe, having taken away, might have given back something better. Late into the night we lie in bed and construct the plots of increasingly ridiculous novels together, and I'm aware that in these plots we are sending each other messages. We even start writing them: he writes his version, I write mine. When we are apart we communicate by sending each other the next chapter:

'Did you do this with your other girlfriends?' I ask him. He's had a few.

'No.' He laughs. 'I can quite happily say I have never had conversations like this with anyone else, especially in bed at two o'clock in the morning.'

And I kiss him.

Early on in our relationship, I'm chattering on about a piece of Renaissance music I'm singing with the church choir. The cadences are thrilling, hearing my voice harmonise with the familiar voices around me, the purity of the ancient notes. It's exquisite to the point where it's nearly too much, almost sexual. He's not religious, he doesn't sing, he's even less in favour of organised religion, and I realise I'm probably sounding weird: 'Do you mind about all the odd stuff I do? You know, plainsong, cassocks and vicars and things?'

He thinks for a minute and then says in all seriousness, 'No, not at all. You're not like anyone I've ever met before. That's why I like you.' He smiles at me with those brown eyes, giving me that look again. And

I hear an ancestral echo that makes me shiver, as if someone from the other side has been whispering in his ear.

So we had our adult romantic relationship but I didn't think he would want to hang out with my children too. And then it turned out that he did – he taught my middle daughter how to make omelettes, and my little one how to skim stones, and my eldest a new way of looking at *Made in Chelsea* – a socialist revolutionary way. It was occasionally annoying when he colluded with them – he taught the little one how to kick a ball onto the roof of the house, but he did come over and cook me a Valentine's meal and made a special chocolate mousse just for me with a heart cut out of a strawberry on top, as the girls danced around his legs. Whenever he left they were bereft too, and it left me wondering what I had done.

I had brought a man into the house just for him to leave and break our hearts all over again.

Because there were other times when being with Mr D did not make me happy, when I felt as if all it was doing was pouring salt into the wound and making it too painful, when I sensed he was withholding, drawing away, when he didn't say the thing I was desperate for him to say – then I felt the gap, and started to fall down it. They were often really tiny, insignificant things, but they left me lying awake as he slept beside me, my back to him and tears streaming down my face.

I was abandoned all over again.

I felt the immensity of the wound I was carrying, which actually was nothing to do with him and everything to do with the man who came before. And on these occasions he didn't bring out the best in me – I became needy, resentful, trying to pull him towards me and in the process pushing him away. I felt my finger on the relationship self-destruct button. I became a person I didn't recognise and I didn't like, and it wasn't his fault – I was the monster of someone else's creation.

The problem is the gap – the loneliness, the need to be locked with another in order not to spin into space. This gap was so clear to me I was literally staring into the void. It's always been there. And I realised my inability to sit with it, to not have the confidence that I won't fall down it if I am not hanging on to someone else, has caused me to make really bad choices in the past. And I decided that, at the age of forty-three, I should face this gap head-on.

Someone pointed out that the only person who will never abandon me is myself. I need to be content with myself. Not just for me, but for my girls. They need to see it is possible to be happy on our own, without a man. Then the spell would truly be broken.

I decided I needed to walk away. It was time to force myself to be the heroine. It was time for me to part with the lovely Mr D.

# CHAPTER TWELVE
# Keeping Up Appearances

I asked Mum how things had changed when the war started: 'Well, dear, I suppose it was all about bananas.'

'Bananas?'

'Yes. You see before the war we had plenty. And then during the war we didn't see any. Not one, not for the whole of the war. And then we didn't even see any after the war. We expected everything to go back to how it was before, but it didn't, not straight away. I think it was quite a few months before we saw bananas again. And then, one day, there was a rumour going around that there was one grocer in Grays that had them and well … there was a stampede! We ran down there. Even your Nanna. Oh, it was so exciting. In fact, one boy down our road got so over-excited, he stuffed himself and died.'

'Died?'

'Yes, dear.'

'From bananas?'

'Yes.'

'Really?'

'Yes. Well, they've got potassium in, haven't they?'

'If you say so, Mum.'

I chuckled. She makes me laugh, my mum. But then I make her laugh too.

And then she told me the Tale of The Pear: 'It wasn't just bananas. We didn't have any fruit during the war. Well, only fruit we grew ourselves, and we had a pear tree in the garden. One year it had just one pear. We watched it grow and get ripe. It was there for months. Every morning we used to look out of the window and talk about it. Then, one day, when Mum was out, John couldn't wait any longer and said, "I'm going to have that pear." And he ran out and picked it and gobbled it straight up, just like that. Oooooh, he was awful! I couldn't believe it. Well, when Mum got home from work she noticed straight away and there was a scene. She shouted at us and grabbed the broom handle and chased us round and round the garden, waving the broom at us.'

I couldn't imagine Nanna wielding a broom. She'd never been cross with me, ever, even though I could think of a few times when I'd deserved it.

A memory of me climbing out of the bedroom window at midnight and dancing around her neighbour's garden in my nightie, frightening them badly – they'd thought there was a burglar and called the police ...

'Wasn't she going to share the pear?'

'No, it was a different world in those days.'

Which I guess is true. Interesting times perhaps bring out things in ourselves we never even knew existed.

But then Mum recalled something else which I think is equally telling – not so much about the experience of the war, but about how my nanna, Bertha, dealt with it. She went on more seriously: 'There wasn't really much food. I remember Mum telling John and me to go out and pick dandelions for our supper. We had to have greens with our dinner. You know the government was very strict and we did what we were told in those days, but Nanna couldn't get hold of any. Anyway, she was determined that if we were supposed to have greens, we were going to have greens. So we had to start in the back garden and then go down the road and have a go at the hedgerows. She told us not to make a song and dance about it. Try not to let the neighbours see. So that's what we did.'

I pondered my nanna trying desperately to keep the show on the road. Like the little Dutch boy with his finger in the dam, at first trying to keep everything the same, and then at least trying to keep the appearance that everything was the same, even if underneath it most certainly wasn't.

The problem was that, before the war came, it had all been going so well.

On the eve of the Second World War, in the spring of 1939, Bertha's daughter, my mum, Dianne, was two and a half years old. Her first memory is watching with curiosity as her father, William, made an air raid shelter at the bottom of the garden. Like a giant human rabbit, his great burrowing had resulted in a huge grassy mound piling up on the lawn, which was brilliant for climbing up and rolling down. This kept Dianne amused for some time (entertainment expectations were low in those days), but when this got boring she plucked up courage and tottered down the sloping passageway to the heavy wooden door that was the entrance to the shelter. 'Peepo!' William shouted, and a panel slid back to reveal three peep holes and a large, navy-blue eye looking out at her. Dianne squealed with delight. Then an arm came through another hole and fiddled with a lock and the door swung open.

'Come and have a look inside, snooky nose.' William grinned at his intrepid, pint-sized daughter.

Inside it was just like a burrow, reminding Dianne of Peter Rabbit's home in her favourite Beatrix Potter book. There were bunk beds on each side and a shelf at the end. It was rather cold and dark, but a lot more than most people had. To have your own custom-made shelter in Grays was quite a thing, but then their whole home was quite a thing too. That was the bonus of being the daughter of a master builder.

When William and Bertha married, William bought a large corner plot of land and promised to build Bertha a house as her wedding present. 'Just say what you want and I will build it,' he said. And he did. It was a bungalow, which might not seem that glamorous now, but in the 1930s bungalows were a new phenomenon and the height of fashion. It was designed in the Art Deco style, with a grand heavy front door that had stained glass windows, and marble pillars either side. It opened into a wide hall with shiny parquet flooring. Bertha had a statue of a nymph on a plinth in the middle. One day Dianne slipped on the shiny floor and crashed into it and in one of those awful slow-motion moments, had to watch as it slowly toppled over and smashed on the floor. Obviously this was not a house built for children, but for Bertha. The kitchen had beautiful black and white floor tiles and all the latest appliances: a gas oven, a sink with running water and a telephone. They had a bathroom with not just running water but gold taps.

Bertha's show home bungalow became quite a talking point among the sisters, and their private feelings must have trickled down to their children. In the sitting room there was a green velvet sofa and Bertha had made kidney-shaped green velvet cushions to match.

When Alice's children came to visit, her son Brian jumped on the sofa and to Dianne and John's horror grabbed one of these cushions, held it above his head and said with great Swain drama: 'Look! A big green dollop!'

Bertha's children were horrified. The word 'dollop' was used in the same way that the 'S' word is today, and not a word that ever passed John or Dianne's lips.

'Put it down. Shut up!' John said, sensitive about his mother's soft furnishings. He had picked up the slight edge that was felt towards Bertha's unexpected good luck.

The mumblings started when William took Bertha on a surprise honeymoon to the Isle of Wight. This may not sound that special, but in those days it was the equivalent of going to Bali.

'Who'd have thought it?' Alice said as Bertha and William drove off in William's car in a shower of confetti.

'Yes. No Margate for Bertha,' Grace said and then regretted it as a shadow passed over Alice's face.

Bertha was supposed to have married a penniless carpenter but, by 1939, William was not only a master builder, but had found himself a partner called Sparky, and set up his own building company. William had turned out to have greater potential than anyone realised, but the clues had been there from the beginning. He wasn't an orphan in the Dickensian, destitute sort of way – William's father had been a highly respected engineer, and had been hired to go to Africa and design one of the great railways of the world, the Cape to Cairo Railway. William's grandfather had been a teacher, and one of his uncles, an artist. William himself had won a scholarship to the local grammar school, but there was no money for his uniform and Old Uncle had been determined that William would follow him into carpentry.

Although he left school at fourteen, William was a great reader. He was a committed atheist, but the early death of everyone he loved left him in a permanent state of existential angst. He spent hours searching for the meaning of life – unsuccessfully, I think – in the histories of the world's great religions and the works of the famous philosophers.

Not staying on at school turned out to be a good move for William. The 1930s saw the biggest boom in house building in British history. Bertha married William in December 1933; in the next two years, nearly 600,000 new houses were built, most of these in London and the South-East, and most of them were houses for the prosperous working-classes: the bungalows and semi-detached houses that William specialised in. Money was cheap to borrow and there were few planning restrictions. The cost of materials and labour had fallen and the government had a policy of clearing the slums. Grays doubled in size, with semi-detached houses and bungalows stretching out along the roads out of town, many of which still exist and were built by William.

Very soon Bertha found herself the wife of a man of substance in the town. They had a beautiful white Lancaster car – the only one in Grays. On fine Sunday afternoons the new Mr and Mrs Kendall would take a spin with the roof down, Bertha's red hair escaping from her pink chiffon scarf so that there was no mistaking who the passenger was. And soon she had a baby to take with her.

Bertha gave birth to John in 1935. Boys were, of course, a premium in the Swain family and he had a big head full of wonderful Swain curls (only blond). The picture was complete when, two years later she had a little girl, Dianne (not such a bonny baby, though – tiny and bald). But it all seemed rather perfect, especially when she had the home to match.

And Bertha did her bit to maintain the image. She was very fond of making the children copies of her own clothes, so they could walk around together turning heads – her very own, stylishly groomed tribe. Of course, having a boy put a limit on how far she could run with this concept, but at least she made them all matching coats. Dianne,

*Bertha and John*

meanwhile, had more potential. One spring Bertha spent hours creating herself and Dianne matching dresses for the coming summer, with white Peter Pan collars, low-slung waists and box-pleat skirts. The first outing of the dresses was during a visit to Alice's.

The sisters had taken advantage of the holidays and fled from the bombing in London to stay in the Buckinghamshire hills with Alice, who had moved there a few years earlier. One hot afternoon they decided to walk from Alice's house in High Wycombe over the hills to the river at Marlow – a bit of a trip down memory lane. Of course, the sisters had always dressed competitively and now they included their children in their competitions, but on this occasion Bertha felt she had trumped all of them with her and Dianne's head-turning matching frocks.

'Golly, Bertha, did you make these?' Grace asked. 'You've put a lot of work into this pleating.'

'Pity she'll be grown out of it by next summer,' Katie chipped in.

Bertha knew with that comment that she'd scored a direct hit. But things didn't quite turn out as she'd planned.

It was a hot day and about halfway to Marlow the children started to complain; even the sisters started to feel a bit faint.

'What about we pop into the Crooked Billet?' Alice said.

'Yes, think of the poor children,' Grace replied, with a twinkle.

So they trooped into the pub garden, deposited the children, and came back with a few trays of orange juice, and gins and tonic. All was peace until there was a crunch, a squeal, and Dianne spewed her juice all over the table.

'Dianne! What are you doing?'

'Mum!' she screamed and spat out a whole load of blood.

'Look! She's bitten a great lump out of her glass!' John shouted.

A 'scene' commenced which involved lots of spitting, shouting, hankies, a hysterical Dianne and an even more hysterical Bertha, who kept shouting for an ambulance. That is, until it became clear that Dianne was not in mortal danger, and Bertha's distress turned to rage because she had managed to well and truly ruin the new dress. There followed a period of disgrace for Dianne.

Things never did turn out how Bertha expected.

At first it seemed as if the war wasn't really going to change things that much. Bertha refused to contemplate evacuating her children, despite the fact that Grays was right in the firing line, being on the eastern edge of London. 'I want them here with me,' she said, and that was that.

Meanwhile, with an echo of what had happened at the beginning of the First World War, William insisted on volunteering, and met with nearly as much horror from Bertha as Charlie had from Clara. However, William wasn't immediately sent into the army – he was put on the reserve list – and so, for the first couple of years the family stayed together, and William carried on building houses, while Bertha stayed at home bringing up John and Dianne, and found ways to adapt to the rest.

Once it became difficult to buy fabric, due to rationing, Bertha just cut things up – like the old orange blanket out of which she made John a double-breasted coat, with matching floppy flat cap – it was huge, due to the size of John's head and crowned with an enormous button.

On its first outing, Dianne and John had to take a trip across town to see their grandparents. As they walked along the road, Dianne could see a gang of rough boys waiting at the bus stop, and she could see by John's face that he had seen them too, and they were both thinking the same thing.

They might have crossed the road but they had already been spotted.

'Oi! Look at this poofter!'

'The sun has got his hat on, eh?'

'Oi! Can you hear me? Nice hat, mate.'

'Yeah, give us a twirl, darlin'!'

'Oooooo, right little Fauntenroy, ain't ya?'

The children walked faster but the boys started following them. A stone whistled past Dianne's ear and then John jumped as one hit him in the back. They were trying to knock John's hat off his head. Luckily, just then the bus turned the corner and the boys ran back to the stop, otherwise who knows where the large, orange, flat cap might have ended up?

Entertainment opportunities also carried on as before. Being a Swain, Bertha loved to get dressed up and take a trip into town to the theatre. Just as the Blitz was really getting under way, William managed to get tickets to see Noël Coward's new play, *Blithe Spirit*, which had just opened at the Savoy Theatre on the Strand.

At the start of the war the government had closed the West End theatres, but such was the distress of the population that the government changed its mind, and decided that bombed theatres were a risk worth taking. Bertha agreed with this policy of refusing to let the Germans get the better of them, and gleefully got dressed up in her old fur, left John and Dianne with her neighbour, Pat, and went off on the train into London.

Which would have been fine, except there was an all-out Blitz that evening – not only in central London, which interrupted the performance, but also over Grays. And Pat the neighbour had no air raid shelter.

Mum remembers a long night spent crouching under next door's kitchen table with herself, John, Pat and her two children, and their crazy sheepdog, which insisted on howling all the way through and had to be constantly wrestled down to stop it dashing out into the street. As the house shook and plaster rained down, they could work out from the planes going over that central London was being bombed too, and Dianne prayed for her mum to walk back through the door all in one piece. But she didn't, and the bombing went on and the dog kept howling.

Eventually, hours after they were expected, Bertha and William came running in, grabbed John and Dianne and then ran out again. The bombs were still dropping, so William picked up Dianne and ran with one arm over her head to protect her from the red-hot shrapnel that was raining down.

Poor John was already too big to be carried so Bertha was shouting, 'Quick, John! Run, run! Quick, quick!'

Luckily they made it to their air raid shelter with no harm done, except a few frayed nerves.

'But still, Mum,' I said. 'What was she thinking of, leaving you in the middle of the Blitz in a house with no air raid shelter and then going right off into the thick of it?'

'Well, dear, times were different, then.'

'You're telling me. Was the play worth it?'

'She didn't say. I don't think they managed to get to the end of it. I think she was a bit cheesed off about that.'

We giggled.

'Oh, well, it puts my own rather exciting childcare arrangements into perspective.'

'Yes, dear. I suppose it does.'

And we gave each other a rueful smile. I know she thinks I'm a bit cavalier with my arrangements and she knows I know.

And then the time came when things did change. A letter arrived out of the blue, summoning William. It happened so fast. Within a couple of days a heavy uniform had arrived and then the order to report for duty early the next morning.

Dianne was woken up in the early hours to say goodbye to her father. He was dressed in his uniform. William was a small, wiry man and his army clothes were far too big. Underneath his black beret, he looked at Dianne with terribly sad eyes and then he was gone. They watched as he marched off down the side passage and into the street in boots that were far too big.

Dianne would not see her father again for nearly five years.

*

Dianne cried, but her tears were eclipsed by Bertha's utter desolation. Mum remembers my nanna with her head in her hands on the kitchen table, sobbing uncontrollably for hours, her children standing by, helpless.

Dianne never stopped missing her father. He had a soft spot for her which manifested itself in constant teasing. Dianne was tiny: 'If you step into the road your bottom will hit the kerb,' he used to say.

One day Dianne was crying because she had fallen over: 'Come on, snooky nose, be brave. I tell you what, I'll show you what being brave is.' William carried Dianne to his shed, put her down outside the door and said, 'Stay there.' He went inside, shut the door and there was the sound of clattering, and hammering and groaning. He emerged a few minutes later with a mouth empty of teeth, waving his dentures in his hands.

Dianne, knowing nothing of false teeth, ran inside and hid behind her mother's skirt.

Dianne treasured his letters. He made little drawings for her. I still have a cartoon he sent after he went to Egypt. It's of a distant pyramid and a dog in the desert with a look of anguish, scampering across the sand with a sign next to him: 'Next tree 100 miles'.

But letters weren't enough to fill the gap – which actually sometimes felt like a real, physical gap right in her stomach.

At night, Dianne would lie in the dark in her twin bed next to her big brother's and keep him awake with her questions.

'Don't you miss him?'

'Not really.'

'Aren't you scared?'

'No. Are you?'

'Yes.'

'Why?'

'I don't know. It feels wrong. Like something awful is going to happen without him here.'

'Like what?'

'I don't know. That's the point.'

'Well, we've got Mum.'

'But don't you feel as if we're looking after her?'

'No.'

Dianne sighed. Boys seemed to have much less complicated lives. And John seemed to have an easier relationship with Bertha. He was the boy. Dianne always felt as if she was not quite what Bertha had expected.

'Am I pretty?' she asked Bertha one day.

'Well, dear, you're quaint,' was the reply, which made her feel like a thatched cottage in a Devonshire village.

Dianne's feelings of unease weren't helped by the way the war was going. Every night they were woken by the wail of the sirens. They would dash to the kitchen and pick up their protective head gear: Bertha the big saucepan, Dianne the little saucepan, and John the frying pan because his head was too big for anything else, and then they would run across the lawn to William's shelter. Mum still remembers clearly the feel of the wet grass between her feet and the sound of the sirens in her ears. Inside the shelter it was freezing cold and dark, whatever the time of year, but nobody complained – it felt safe.

Increasingly, as Britain fought off the German invasion in the skies above their heads, the family didn't even bother to go to bed in the bungalow, but went straight to the shelter every night. And their shelterless neighbour, Pat, and her two daughters, and the crazy dog, joined them too.

It was during one of those nights that Bertha found herself confiding in Pat: 'I've found myself a job.'

'Really?'

'Yes. You know I used to be a shorthand typist? Well, I've got a position in the office at the munitions factory.'

'Oh. I'd have thought you'd want to stay home with the children.'

'Well, I don't know,' she said, pointing at the ceiling where the noise of dog-fighting planes could be heard over their heads. 'I feel I ought to be doing something.'

'Oh.'

Pat wasn't convinced. And she was right to be suspicious. Bertha was perfectly happy at home, but the moment William had been called up, building had stopped and his business had folded. Bertha now found herself trying to keep up appearances on an ordinary soldier's wages, and she couldn't do it. The house was expensive to maintain; in fact, their whole lifestyle was expensive to maintain. She thought ruefully of the beautiful white Lancaster car that languished in the garage for want of expensive petrol.

They could have sold the bungalow, downsized and lived off the capital until William got home, but Bertha was not ready to do that yet. Not at all. She was going to fight her own battle and hang on for as long as possible.

'Of course, John is at school. It's just Dianne,' she said.

'Yes, Mummy, who's going to look after me?' piped up Dianne from her bunk. She had been listening to the conversation very carefully.

'You know,' Pat said, 'I can think of someone who might well be happy to look after Dianne ... for something in return, of course.'

'Of course,' Bertha nodded.

And that's how Dianne found herself with ... let's call them the Barratts. First thing in the morning, Bertha strapped Dianne into the seat on the back of her bike and tore off –always slightly late – to the Barratts. Dianne would then be left there for the day until Bertha arrived around 5 p.m., strapped Dianne back into the bicycle seat and tore home again in time for tea.

The Barratts should have been the perfect solution to Bertha's childcare issue: they were middle-aged neighbours, recommended by friends, they had a teenage daughter, they had the time and they needed the money. But appearances can be deceptive.

Dianne doesn't know how long she went to the Barratts' house, but guesses it was between one and two years. One weekend, she had built a camp with Pat's daughters in the wood at the bottom of the garden. They were playing 'Secrets' and Dianne's big brother, John, was spying on them. Dianne told a secret about what was happening to her at the Barratts' house.

John ran straight to his mum and told her what Dianne had said. He was sent back to fetch her.

Bertha demanded: 'Right, stand here and tell me what you told them.'

Dianne must have been only about four and a half years old, but she knew there was something wrong about what had been happening to her at the Barratts', something wrong about telling Pat's children, and now something even worse about telling her mother. But somehow she stammered a little of what had been happening: something about being taken to the lavatory and touched by Mr Barratt in private places and him making her touch him.

Bertha lost it. She flung a rolling pin across the kitchen at Dianne. 'If you ever, ever, speak of this again to anyone, I will kill you,' she said.

There was more shouting and screaming, but Dianne was frozen. The fact that she could cause so much distress and anger to her mother, who, with their father away, had become everything to Dianne, was horrific. She had never seen her mother so upset, and she had caused it. And that's when the guilt started.

In the psychotherapy world there is a distinction made between actual abuse, and then secondary abuse, where further damage is caused by the world's reaction to the abuse. Once a child is made to feel that what has happened is not to be spoken of, that it is shameful, then they start to feel ashamed, and then guilty. They take on the perpetrator's guilt as their own.

Mum did what Bertha said, and never spoke of it again – not until over forty years later. She and I were sitting watching the launch of the charity for victims of childhood abuse, ChildLine, in 1986. It's easy to forget how the sexual abuse of children was something that was rarely publicly debated or spoken of, although clearly it was very much happening. But this launch started a revolution in talking about abuse and protecting children.

As we watched the presenter, Esther Rantzen, make her appeal for funds, and films of people's stories, I realised Mum was crying. 'That happened to me,' she said.

I was dumbfounded.

'When I was a child. A neighbour,' was all she said.

I was horrified. I didn't ask any more; I didn't want to know any more. I was young and this was way out of my comfort zone. But despite my own reluctance to engage with my mum's experience, it started her on a journey, which began as a correspondence with Esther Rantzen, and from there going to seek counselling, and then training to become a counsellor herself.

If anyone criticises Esther Rantzen in my mum's presence, they will get an immediate counter of: 'She saved my life.'

It was only much later, when I started on this journey into the sisters' past, that I felt ready to know more, and that somehow it was important to know. So I asked Mum to tell me what happened.

She described how, when she arrived at the Barratts' house every morning, she was seated at the kitchen table and given a breakfast of bread and butter. She sat by herself, eating in silence. She was then moved to the front room, where she had to sit on a chair by the fire and not move or speak, all day, every day, day after day.

'Didn't you even have a book to read?' I asked Mum.

'Nope. Nothing.'

'But you were three? Four? You must have been so bored.'

'Yes. But I was more scared than bored. They had a huge dog which used to sit and guard me, and if I so much as moved, he would growl and bark and show his teeth, and you know how much I'm scared of dogs.'

'I'm not surprised.'

'Yes. You know the scar on my forehead?' She pointed to a thin, white, horizontal line across the top of her forehead, which was usually covered by her fringe. 'That's where that dog bit me.'

'Mum! I had no idea. You never told me.'

'Didn't I?' She looked surprised. 'Well, anyway, one day I was sitting there and I needed to go to the loo so badly, I thought I was going to wet myself. I had to go, so I plucked up courage and stood up, and he leapt at me and bit me.'

'Oh, Mum.'

'And it was so hot in that room! They kept the fire on full blast, whatever the weather – I used to roast. It was so strange. Everything about that house and that family was strange. They had a big garden but I was never allowed out to play. I was never given anything – pencils, paper, nothing. They had a daughter who was at school, but when she came home, she never came in to see me. I don't even remember her ever speaking to me. She just went straight out into the garden and never came in.'

'Maybe she didn't want to bump into her father.'

'Exactly, dear. Looking back, it's hardly surprising. They were such an odd couple. She was hard, there was no love lost between them. I actually felt sorry for him. And I had this feeling, although it was based on nothing but a feeling, that the reason he did what he did was something to do with her.'

The only person who would come into the room was Mr Barratt, on the pretext of taking Dianne to the toilet.

'He used to pick me up and it was quite confusing, because it reminded me of being picked up by Dad. And you know how much I missed him. There's something special about being picked up by your daddy, isn't there? Those big, strong arms … you feel protected. I just trusted him … And I couldn't understand when he started to do things my dad never did.' She paused and then went on, 'The house was dark

– dark wood panelling. Horrible. And the toilet was at the end of a dark corridor. It was basic, just a loo. A room with no window, under the stairs. A cupboard, really. I can see it so clearly. All brown. He used to take me in there and lock the door behind and it was that sound, the heavy lock being drawn. That feeling of not being able to escape, there was nothing I could do. You know how much I hate small spaces to this day.'

Oh, yes. Mum's claustrophobia. Suddenly, her unwillingness to use public lavatories, her refusal to ever turn locks on doors in public places, a certain ride in an aquarium where we were sealed in a submarine and Mum had a panic attack, rifling through her handbag for Valium … yes, it made sense. Always, always that need to keep a light on. Her obsession with being broken into in the middle of the night which meant she locked her bedroom door and placed a chair under the handle for good measure – which I always forgot about, and would try and crash in, in the mornings and have to wait for her to unlock the door; the sound of desperate rattling on the other side.

In the loo Mr Barratt had free rein with Mum, to do what he wanted to do, all the time whispering to her, 'Isn't this nice? Doesn't this feel nice?'

And Mum couldn't speak, frozen.

'Even then, I didn't know why, but I knew whatever he was doing, it was very wrong.' She paused and then she said, 'What I don't understand is why I never went to Mum to tell her myself.'

'Well, I don't think that's unusual. I think even very young children can sense that something is wrong and want to pretend it's not happening and protect the people they love,' I said.

'Yes, I think that's right. Anyway, I didn't. But of course it came out anyway, and yes, I was right to be scared of telling her.'

Mum told me how Mrs Barratt was summoned to speak to Bertha. Mrs Barratt stood in the kitchen and Bertha pulled up a chair and, in a confusing contradiction to the rolling pin moment, said: 'Dianne, stand on the chair and tell Mrs Barratt what you told me.'

Mum stood on the chair and opened her mouth and nothing came out. She could not speak – it was as if her mother's command that if she ever spoke she would kill her had sunk right through to her bones.

'Right. If Dianne's not going to tell you, I will.' Bertha had then proceeded to relay to Mrs Barratt what Dianne had told her.

Mrs Barratt had screamed and put her hands over her ears. '*No!* She's lying. Liar, liar, liar!' she screamed, pointing at Dianne, who was still standing on the chair. And then she ran out of the house in hysterics.

Dianne got off the chair and it was never spoken of in the family again.

'Your Nanna never did say that she believed me.'

'Oh. So what happened next?'

'Well, she did give up work. And I never had to go to the Barratts again.'

'Perhaps that shows that, at some level, she did believe you.'

'Yes, I suppose you're right.' Mum didn't seem convinced.

So Bertha gave up her job and looked after Dianne for the last few months before she was ready to start school.

But going to school still involved a daily torment: the Barratts' home was right next to Dianne's new school, and she had to walk past their house every day.

And there was Mr Barratt watching the young girls going backwards and forwards. He would lean over his gate and leer at Dianne. There was no other way into school and there was only pavement on the Barratts' side of the road. Despite this, Dianne would run past on the other side, in the road, and was nearly knocked over several times.

What would happen today? Perhaps nothing different, but at least there is a chance that Dianne would not have been silenced; perhaps Mr Barratt might have been prosecuted and not been able to continue to leer over his garden gate; perhaps the damage my mum suffered might have been alleviated at least a little. Because knowing this, I now understand her much better. There are the obvious effects: the claustrophobia, the inability to speak in public, the hating to be the centre of attention, but then there are other things which I now know are common for someone who has had an experience like this. It makes me angry. I think about Mum: her cleverness and her humour, and how her fear of the outside world has held her back. That's not her, but what *happened* to her.

We went back to the subject of Nanna again.

'You know, she never spoke to me about it,' Mum said.

'I know. It must have been awful.'

'Yes.'

'I mean, Nanna never having had the relief of saying sorry,' I said, and then I thought that was disrespectful to my mum's greater trauma. But I needn't have worried.

'No, I know what you mean. I agree. All those years, because I'm sure she thought about it, don't you think?'

'Oh, yes.'

'She must have felt awful, and a terrible burden to carry to your grave.'

'Yes. There's a lot to be said for saying sorry, and meaning it and it being heard,' I reply.

And Mum gave me a look. 'Yes, indeed.'

There was a moment of tension between us. I immediately thought of the sorry I long to say to Poppy, and I wondered what sorries Mum might feel she wants to say. But I didn't ask, and the moment passed.


I think Mum has forgiven Nanna. It was a very different time: all keeping up appearances and stiff upper lips; a belief that the less said the better. It must have been really hard to be a single mum, struggling to make ends meet, keeping going with bombs dropping around you and no idea when and if it all might end, and whether you were going to have a husband at the end of it. And to have to part with the life you had always dreamt of, so soon after achieving it – well, you would fight to hold on to it, wouldn't you? I certainly would. And I did. For many years I knew something was wrong, and I asked the right questions but I allowed myself to believe the wrong answers, because the consequences of the truth would have been so catastrophic – it meant losing everything I had worked so hard to build. And when I had discovered the right answers, for a year I tried to make it work; I tried to forgive and make a new go of it, but living with someone you no longer trust and loving someone who has treated you so badly ultimately destroys your soul. Besides which he was still lying and cheating. And, actually, the moment when I faced the truth – that my marriage was over and he had to go, and I told my children and my family and friends, and I no longer tried to keep up appearances – was the moment when everything started to get better.

In Bertha's case, the price of trying to hold on and keep up appearances was very high. And the conversation with my mum got me thinking. About Bertha's house and what it represented and how much holding on to it had resulted in so much damage. Because I realised I hadn't let go of everything.

The girls and I were still living in our family home. It was beautiful, Victorian, double-fronted, with elaborate fireplaces, high ceilings, stained glass and mad, original tiles. We had bought it as a wreck and I had transformed it into our perfect home, with a kitchen extension and a penthouse in the loft. Like Bertha, I had filled it with chandeliers and old paintings, oriental wallpaper and bright colours everywhere. But it was expensive – it was the home of the family of a City lawyer, and we were no longer that family. In fact, we had never been that family, ever since we had moved in. It was a bit like walking through a field of flowers and then looking more closely and seeing it was a field of snakes.

I didn't have to move but, financially, it was a chance for me to have a clean break from the man who had hurt me so badly. Our new home would be smaller, but it would be completely ours, a new start for me and the girls: real, with no mistresses haunting it. And if I had made a home before, I could make one again. So I put the house on the market.

# CHAPTER THIRTEEN
# Staying Alive

It's the middle of July and as hot as it gets. I'm dashing through West London in my purple Mini with the roof down, shades on, music blaring, my hair – unfeasibly long (sorry, Nanna) – flying in the wind. I am hurrying to pick up Dora's twin daughters, Jackie and Angela, from the station. They may be nearly seventy-four, but they've come all the way from Stafford on the train and negotiated the rather fiddly tube journey with bravado.

'They're a game pair,' I say to my mum.

'Indeed,' she says, with eyebrows raised.

They've come to my house to have lunch with us. It's been years since the cousins have seen each other. In fact, they haven't met since my nanna's – Bertha's – funeral, ten years ago. As I screech into the bus stop outside the tube station, they are waiting for me, all jaunty scarves and big sunglasses. They wave enthusiastically and shower me with kisses. They are very stylish. Yes, the Mini definitely suits them and the occasion.

As we speed along by the banks of the Thames, the sun shining down on us, even more hair flowing in the wind, there is constant chatter and laughter. When we reach home and my daughter, Amber, meets them, she is fascinated by their exuberance, in tandem, like a walking soap opera. They look identical and say the same things at the same time. They hug her as if they want to break her: 'Ooooooo, aren't you lovely?'

Amber grins at me and shakes her head in disbelief. 'They're amazing!' she mouths.

*Mum with Angela and Jackie*

Amber witnesses a classic fit of the Swain giggles when I bring out the photos that I've collected from various cousins. My little mum is seated between these two tall, slender, identical ladies, but it feels as if she's just a smaller, older, toned-down version. And because they have the same intonation, the same expressions, the same humour, and it's infectious and reminds me of my nanna, it feels very comfortable. Am I like that too? I look at my eldest daughter who looks so like me, and I feel the shared mitochondrial inheritance. We are all at home here. And it manifests in the banter.

An example: a photograph of one of the uncles on the beach in his trunks.

'Oh, dear, he's rather letting it all hang out,' I comment, and pass the photo over to Angela.

'Ohhhh, I say!' The twins gasp in unison, their hands go over their mouths and they start giggling.

'Where?' Mum snatches the photo. 'Oh, dear, I haven't got the right glasses.'

'Shall I get the magnifying glass, Nanna?' Amber says, trying to be helpful.

'That won't be necessary,' I say.

'Oh, I say!' the twins say again in unison, at which point Mum is chuckling too.

'Oh, I wish I could see it.'

'Trust me, Mum, you're not missing much.'

'The photo, I mean!'

'Mother!' Amber says, but now we've all lost it and there's banging of heads on the table, and a bit of choking and eyes being wiped and swigs of pink prosecco being drunk, and I do wonder whether our departed ancestors can see us, and I send a little apology heavenward: 'Just a bit of fun … '

Meanwhile, the twins have picked up another uncle.

'I always thought he was a bit strange,' Mum says.

'Yes, but he had some nice suits,' says Jackie.

'Nice suits?' I say, and then we all lose it *again* and Mum, choking, says, 'Well, you know what your Nanna used to say about him?'

'No.'

'Ooooo, what did she say, Dianne?' The twins ask together.

Mum looks a bit abashed and I prepare myself for what's coming. 'Well, I don't know whether I should say this …'

'Go on, you know you want to,' I say.

'Go on, Nanna,' Amber says. 'You've started so you have to finish.'

Mum pauses for effect and then comes out with it. 'Well, she used to say he wasn't a *real* man.'

There's a stunned silence. And then we all burst out laughing.

'What on earth did she mean by that?' I ask.

'I have no idea! That was typical of your Nanna. She always made these cryptic pronouncements and then left the rest up to your imagination.'

Later, when the whirlwind that is the twins has departed, Amber says: 'I love them. Can't we keep them? Put them in the mini fridge?'

There is a running joke in our house: I have a mini fridge in my bedroom, used to house diet Cokes and half-bottles of champagne. Metaphorically, we put all sorts of people we like in the mini fridge too, someone for every occasion: the girls' jolly singing teacher, for when we need cheering up; my salsa teacher, with the perfect derrière, when I need to feel most like a woman; David Tennant in his *Dr Who* incarnation for those moments when the universe seems a bit frightening … it's getting a bit crowded in there.

But Amber is right. The twins are lovely, warm, kind, happy creatures that defy the way they came into the world. Because they made their surprise entrance in perhaps one of the darkest moments of our family story.

Jackie and Angela are the only children of my Great-Aunt Dora – the fourth child, third daughter, and therefore the middle Scarlet Sister. Dora was born within a year of Charlie Junior being diagnosed with polio, a bit different to the others. She didn't like dancing and she didn't like going out; she stayed home, close to her mother, Clara. She had always been a nervous child, and once Charlie Junior died, she suffered from terrible nightmares, waking her sisters at night with her screaming. Dora suffered from what they used to call, in those days, 'nerves'. Today there might be more scientific labels applied, but in some ways 'nerves' feels a kinder, looser and actually better description for Dora's general state of mind.

In families where there has been a trauma (Charlie Junior's death would definitely qualify), and there is a pretence that nothing has happened, one of the family members can start to act out the effects of the trauma; sometimes they become the black sheep. Dora definitely wasn't the black sheep, but she did seem the one sister who showed the symptoms of the family's bereavement; as if the family had made her the hired mourner at the funeral, to do the wailing for all of them, so they didn't have to. It was as if she turned all the pain in on herself.

I pondered why Dora should be the one who carried the family's shadow. And then I thought about my own daughter, Scarlett. Dora was the middle child, and it was my middle child who did the grieving for us when her dad left.

As Amber, Daisy and I concentrated on building a new life through gritted teeth, Scarlett looked at us in disbelief and wept. 'How can you all act as if nothing has happened?' she would shout. 'Because we have no choice,' I would reply. But Scarlett is nothing if not persistent. She ran away from home, she cried at school and failed exams she should have walked, she phoned her daddy at all hours and, waiting up for me to come home, she cut off her fringe.

Scarlett was like a lightning rod for the grief in the family, the wise fool at the family court, determined to point out that her mother was living in denial. Her grief was so bad there was little room for our own. But, gradually, somehow, the grief became a bit more evenly spread: Scarlett settled down and the rest of us became a bit more shaken up – Amber fell out with her friends and got into trouble at school, I had some filthy rows with my ex and injured my ankle, the six-year-old Daisy refused to see her dad with the immortal line: 'You can't just get sick of one and go and get another.' It all became more messy and probably a bit more healthy. We took turns to cry. We cuddled under a blanket late at night and tried to make sense of it all. It was better for all of us.

By the age of thirty, Dora still hadn't married, and she was the only sister left at home. Clara was only too happy to have one daughter to keep her company. Like many women of her generation, Clara's daughters were her best friends. Having Dora helped dilute the endless disappointment that was living with her husband. While Charlie spent long hours in the pub, Dora sat beside Clara next to the fire and entertained her with tales of the patent office and the women who worked there – what they were wearing, who didn't like who, who was kissing who. Dora had inherited the Swain ability to tell a story and could always make Clara laugh.

In turn, Dora would listen patiently as Clara confided her worries about her married daughters and their children: Alice's tiny cottage; Grace's husband Bill's erratic mood swings; Alice's struggle to make ends meet; the smallness of baby Dianne; Alice's over-working because that Tom Corbett was only a milkman – actually, almost every aspect of Alice's life, for which Tom Corbett got the blame.

As the sisters left, home became a very different place – it was transformed into a haven of space, order and harmony (as long as Charlie was out). Clara, who was naturally a maternal woman, finally had the time and means to enjoy (some of the sisters used the word 'spoil') one of her children. Clara made sure Dora went to work on a full stomach, and came home to her favourite meals every day. She kept Dora's clothes in the best condition: every loose button was tightened and pin tuck faultlessly ironed. When Katie got married, Clara bought Dora a pet Cairn terrier, called Suzi, so that she wouldn't be lonely.

Suzi was a pampered doggy – her hair was brushed every day and Dora made sure she was dressed in the latest pooch fashion with a big blue bow and jackets in a variety of colours that co-ordinated with Dora's outfits. Unfortunately, Suzi's jackets had to be altered because she was fed too many cakes. But Dora was a bit of a secret squirrel.

I have a studio portrait of her looking like a film star: long eyelashes, painted lips in an enigmatic smile, hair coiffed in rolls framing her face. She has signed it in the bottom right-hand corner: 'Love, Swainy!' Indeed. I wonder for whom it was destined.

Unbeknown to Clara, Dora didn't plan to live at home for ever – she wanted her own wedding, house and children, like the rest of her sisters. It was just that Dora was not going to marry the first man who

*Dora*

came along. Having witnessed the dramatics around her various sisters' relationships, she was determined to wait until she was sure she had found The One. And in order to make sure he would notice her, Dora always dressed immaculately – still elegant in black or navy.

And it was effective. She worked as the secretary to a top patent lawyer in Lincoln's Inn who was so taken with her that he asked her to become his mistress, even offering to set her up in a smart address in town – a request she turned down on several occasions: 'Thank you for your most generous offer. I am deeply flattered' – he was her boss, after all – 'but I must decline on account of there already being someone who has filled this position for you. If it becomes vacant, then let me know. But until then, I've always been hopeless at sharing!' And she would give him a coy smile that made it impossible for him to take offence.

Of course, being a married man's mistress was not going to be good enough – solicitor or no solicitor, she was not going to share her man with anyone, particularly a legitimate wife and family. Dora was smarter than that, and had more self-respect.

Years later, it was a lesson she was to pass on to her daughter, Angela, when she became entangled with her own solicitor boss. He was clever and charming, with a name that sounded like a hero from a Mills & Boon novel. He was already promised to someone else, and Dora warned Angela to stay away from him and insisted she moved back to the family home. Angela was a good girl and did as she was told, and waited, and in the end married Ellis, with whom she has been happy for many years.

The solicitor – married with children – was to turn up on her doorstep a few years later, asking to rekindle their affair.

'Well, I knew then I'd obviously done the right thing. He wasn't a nice man, was he?' Angela said.

'These sorts of men never change,' Jackie nodded sagely.

'Gosh, I wish I'd met your mum,' I said.

'Oh, Helen. Ahhhhh, bless you! You'll see, it'll all work out for the best … he's not worth it … you're better off without him … your prince will come, I know he will!' they chimed.

'If he hasn't already,' Amber murmured archly, and under her breath sang the cheesy seaside pier tune that she'd hacked into my phone and put as the ringtone for Mr D.

I shot her a look.

Meanwhile, the twins took my hands and squeezed them and I was overwhelmed in a wave of female Swainy love.

As if to prove that all good things come to she who waits, Dora's patience was rewarded when she came to the attention of one of her fellow commuters on the 8.10 train from Grays into Fenchurch Street.

Spencer Sier was a trainee manager for The Co-operative Bank, working in their Fenchurch Street branch. He was a clever fellow – a scholarship boy at Palmer's Grammar school in Grays – and he had always wanted to become a doctor but, like so many members of the family, there wasn't the money for him to continue his education. However, his excellent grades had got him a prized place at the bank.

Spencer was good with figures of course, and he used this to great effect on the daily commute, joining his carriage's card circle and playing for pennies. One day a member of the circle was ill and, having had his eye on the chic, yet slightly aloof Dora (actually, a rather shy Dora), Spencer plucked up courage and asked if she might do them a favour and make up the numbers.

Ordinarily Dora would have declined, but she had also noticed Spencer. She liked his kind, polite manner, while his round, heavy-rimmed spectacles gave him a serious, clever air, which she found attractive. And he always wore nice, dark navy suits with a subtle, thin pinstripe. Dora described him to Bertha as 'a cut above', something of which Bertha completely approved, and was slightly envious.

Dora and Spencer's courtship could hardly be described as a whirlwind romance – more of a slow burner, or even a mere tea light of an affair. The card games lasted for over a year before Spencer actually asked her out, and then it was many more months before Dora took him home to meet her parents and even longer before she met his. And then they just carried on as before.

Both seemed perfectly happy with their domestic bliss only extending as far as an hour there and back on the train every day. Indeed, things might never have gone any further if Hitler hadn't invaded Poland.

Spencer knew he was going to have handle this carefully. As the descendant of Huguenot weavers who fled to England from persecution in Holland, he felt a strong loyalty to the nation that had given them shelter, and a need to fight against tyranny. So, like Bertha's William, he enlisted straight away. But it took him a while to tell Dora. In the end, he did it over a game of whist as the train left Essex and started racing through the outskirts of East London.

'I think we should have a bet on this,' Spencer said.

'Do you now?' Dora arched a single eyebrow rather fetchingly. 'And what did you have in mind?'

'I think I would like to leave it as a surprise. If I win this hand, you have to grant me a favour.'

'And if I win?'

'Then your wish is my command.'

Dora smiled. She'd had these bets with him before and they usually meant all she had to endure was a particularly lingering kiss at the garden gate, which wasn't really suffering at all, if she was honest. And if she won, she wouldn't mind a new hat pin. She'd seen just the one in the high street.

'All right then, I'm game,' she said and dealt the cards.

Fate was on Spencer's side, as he had known it would be – he had a royal flush.

As he laid down his hand, she smiled. 'So, what's it to be, Mr Sier?'

'Your hand in marriage.'

'What?'

'Marry me, Dora. I want you to be my wife.'

Dora looked like she'd seen a ghost.

'Well, aren't you going to answer me?'

'It's just I wasn't expecting that.'

'Umm …'

'What?'

'I'm afraid I've got another surprise for you.'

Dora, always expecting the worse (although in this case she was right) said, 'Oh no!'

'Yes, I don't know how to tell you this, but I've joined up.'

'Oh, Spencer, no!'

'I'm sorry. I have to do something. But I won't go anywhere for a while, if at all. They've said it will take ages to train me, and in the meantime I want us to be married. Dora, please, I love you. I want you to be my wife.' And he took a ring from his pocket and put it on a sobbing Dora's finger.

Around them their fellow card players were clapping. After more than ten years' commuting, Swainy's rather Eeyorish disposition was well known: 'Go on, Dora, say yes!' they shouted.

All she could manage was a nod. For Dora did love Spencer and by now did indeed believe she had met the right man. And her amazing ability for catastrophic fantasy worked in Spencer's favour because, in her mind, Dora could see him by turns torpedoed on a submarine with the water rushing in and covering his face; stepping on a mine and bits of him flying through the air; or shot while caught in a piece of barbed wire murmuring, 'Dora' as his final breath. The thought of refusing to marry him, and then Spencer getting killed, was far too much for Dora to carry on her conscience, so that was that.

They gave themselves a couple of months, just enough time for Dora to make her gold, shot-taffeta dress, and then Spencer and Dora were married. Within a few months, Dora was pregnant.


We can never really know what other people are up to. In this case, while everyone knew about the dark forces gathering on continental Europe, no one (except for Charlie, perhaps) was aware of the shadow darkening in Dora's own family home.

Because, six weeks before Dora was due to give birth, her father, Charlie, died.

The official story was always that Charlie died from injuries to his lungs received when he was gassed during the First World War. However, after extensive research, it is now absolutely clear that Charlie was never, and could never have been, gassed.

And as my cousin Dennis pointed out: if he wasn't gassed, then what did he die of?

After I had made this unsettling discovery, there followed a period of extreme email communication between myself and various second cousins. One morning I woke up to a surprise email waiting for me from Katie's son, Barry, who lives in New Zealand.

'My mother always implied that Charlie committed suicide,' he wrote.

I emailed Dennis, who was shocked. His memories of his grandfather are fond: Charlie spending hours in his shed, secretly making Dennis a toy steam engine; buying Dennis fireworks on Bonfire Night; marching Dennis and his cousins round and round the dining-room table to the tune of 'Colonel Bogey' with a stick under his arm – it didn't seem like the same man.

When I went to see Alice's son, Brian, he told me that Barry's email had brought something back: 'I was getting into my bath and I had a kind of flashback. I seem to remember he hung himself at the neighbour's house. And the more I think about it, the more I'm certain.'

Dennis was now desperate to know the truth and I promised to get hold of Charlie's death certificate. But circumstances or fate, or something, conspired against me – I went online and ordered it, but when I came to pay, my bank card was nowhere to be seen. I then had to go on holiday, but when I got back I tried again. This time, the certificate got lost in the post. But I was not going to give up. The final time I ordered it, I paid for it, and I paid extra for it to be couriered to me.

It arrived a week later. I opened it nervously, but it said that while Charlie did indeed die at Brian's neighbour's house, the cause of death was a cardiac arrest. It stated that his wife, Clara Swain, found him. I emailed Dennis the news.

But then I thought a little more, and I had a conversation with a doctor friend, and I did some more research, and it turns out that depending on how the knot is tied, people who hang themselves can die of a heart attack, as opposed to asphyxiation. And as doctors used to be (and still are) very reluctant to put 'Suicide' on a death certificate if they can avoid it, it still leaves a question mark over how Charlie died.

It was just at this point that I went for a weekend to the North Norfolk Coast. As I strode across the marshes in the golden halo of a perfect August evening, I remembered the only time I had ever felt like voluntarily making an exit: it was on another magical late summer's evening, about three months after my first daughter, Poppy, had died.

There were days when the grief felt darker. I was like the Ready Brek kid – surrounded by a fuzzy aura, but instead of an orange glow, mine was more of a black fog. Everywhere I went, every time I came close to enjoying myself, my Siamese twin of grief would give me a nudge. I was like a highly strung racehorse: sleek and shiny on the outside, but ready to snap at the least provocation. Things that would have just amused me in the past now really got under my skin.

It was our friend, Ian's, wedding, one of those red-letter days that had been in the diary for a long time, long before Poppy was born. She would have been just a few weeks old. Ian had asked my husband to sing at the ceremony and we'd had long discussions about whether it would be practical with a new baby; but then if she cried, I could just take her outside – friends told us babies were much more portable when they were little. So we were really looking forward to it, as it would be our baby's first outing into society.

Now, the day only highlighted that we had lost not only our baby but also the new life we had planned as a family. There was a Poppy-shaped hole at our side all day.

Then there was our relationship. In the morning, we wandered around the little seaside town of Bude. I stopped at the window of an antiques shop. There was a small painting of a field of poppies. My husband and I stood staring at it in silence. Eventually I said, 'I've got to buy it.'

He sighed.

'What's the problem?'

'Oh, I don't know. It's just we can never escape, can we?'

'Escape? No, no! We can't escape, it's happened.'

'Why, Helen? Why are you doing this? It's too sad.'

I went in and bought the painting anyway. Not for the first time I thought, 'Why does this annoy him? Why can't he just humour me?' I felt very alone.

We arrived at the church early so he could practise. It was a little old church in the middle of a field. In the dark inside he started to sing.

I sat in a back pew and listened. He didn't look at me. It was the first time he had sung since Poppy died. His voice was beautiful and sad, a new depth to it. I wondered how he was going to get through the service. It was too painful, so I went outside and walked in the churchyard. I went in search of the children's graves. There were plenty. I read the gravestones and tried to picture what all the different mothers over the centuries would have looked like and felt. My husband's voice came gently through the windows. I could have been back in the 1700s burying my baby and nothing would be different. Except perhaps I wouldn't have felt so alone? Most mothers would have buried babies, surely?

After the service we went to a stately home. It was wonderfully crumbling, faded, bohemian. Drinks were on the terrace overlooking a lawn and a dark green lake surrounded by woods, overgrown and wild; it felt like nature was about to reclaim its property. I made polite conversation. No one said anything about Poppy. Already it felt like it had been a long day. We had a meal in the marquee and I made it through that too, but then the dancing started.

Ian took his bride to the floor and we all clapped and then he let go of his wife and picked up his daughter and started swinging her round – proud Dad with his beautiful little girl, dressed in her best party frock. There was another, bigger round of applause and everyone got out their cameras. His wife, Tara, looked on, wiping away a happy tear; a perfect ending to a fairytale day: Daddy dancing with his little girl.

I looked across at my husband and saw the most extraordinary look of pain on his face. An all-too familiar feeling of guilt and panic grabbed my throat. I strode into the house and locked myself in the loo.

I took deep breaths. After a while, all was quiet and I felt brave enough to come out. As I opened the cubicle, in swept a giggling Tara with a couple of her bridesmaids.

She stopped dead. I knew Tara – we'd spent many evenings together. Now she looked as if she'd seen a ghost.

She blanked me, walked straight past and locked herself in the loo.

I felt bad. It was her wedding day, and I was the spectre at the feast, the last person she wanted to see, as if my bad luck might be infectious. I thought it might be infectious too. I couldn't go back to the party, so I went for a walk.

It was a balmy, clear summer evening. I wanted to get away from the sound of music and laughter coming from the marquee. The moon hung over the lake and the frogs croaked. It was so beautiful, like a set for *Swan Lake*. I was drawn to the water, but as I got closer I realised I couldn't quite get to it: there was a ditch in the way. So I sat on the edge of the ditch and sniffed the breeze.

It felt good to be out there, surrounded by nature; I felt more in tune with the wild surroundings than the human revellers in the marquee. In fact, it was almost as if, if I could only get to the lake, I could find what I was looking for. This was the real world, but the lake was on the other side. Like the River Styx separating us, I could almost see Poppy there, waiting for me, if only I could make it over. I was so close I could almost touch her.

It wasn't that I consciously wanted to die or anything but, just for a second, an opportunity opened up for me to get to the other side and be reunited with my baby. I could so easily slip off my shoes and try to swim out there, just to see what would happen, lose myself in the calm darkness of the moonlit lake, submerge myself in the dark, black water, and disappear.

Wash the pain away.

If I left, I couldn't upset anyone anymore. My husband would be free to find someone else, someone who could have children.

I slipped off my sandals and dangled my toes in the cool water of the ditch, then started to wade across towards the lake. As I did so, someone flung himself down on the bank behind me.

It was one of the guests, out for a cigarette. 'Beautiful, isn't it?' he said, and offered me one.

I took it, inhaled deeply and marvelled at how close I'd come to doing something extraordinarily reckless. For a moment I'd found a gap in the hedge between this world and the next, and I'd been very tempted to fight my way through. I nearly, nearly did it.

Looking back now, it was about feeling not just alone but something darker – that people didn't want me around, that they would be better off without me. And, moreover, that there was someone who needed me and loved me on the other side.

Did Charlie feel the same way, too?

Just a few weeks later I felt completely different.

For the first few months after Poppy died I couldn't contemplate trying for another baby. After what we had done, it seemed the height of disloyalty. And I couldn't imagine ever having the courage to go through with another pregnancy, so I didn't even think about it. If my husband raised the issue, I blanked him.

Then I woke up one morning and everything had changed; the urge to go forth and multiply was overwhelming and all-consuming. All the arguments against seemed totally irrelevant when measured against a massive biological urge to reproduce. Just like that. There was no rational explanation. Pure hormones. I kept this as my secret and started making plans.

Blakeney is right on the edge. It's flat, with big skies stretching out over the freezing North Sea. I like it because on this mad, over-crowded island it's a place where there's space to think. Something about the endless horizon opens up possibilities.

So when the time came, I knew where to go. I told no one my plans. I had done my calculations, and the doctors told me I could start trying. I could think of nothing else.

My husband's birthday, his thirtieth, conveniently fitted. I lured him there as his birthday present. Everyone thought we were going to celebrate his birthday; what he and they didn't know was that we were off to make a baby.

I sneaked out of work early and travelled the tube across London to pick him up from his office. I remember waiting in reception, dreading meeting someone – there were so many people I hadn't seen since I lost Poppy. I thought the receptionist gave me a strange look. 'She must know,' I thought. '"Beautiful but can't have children."' I felt my tragedy wind like a shroud around my beautiful clothes and shiny hair.

My husband walked in with a client. Laughing, they both looked handsome in their expensive shirts. My heart sank. They were obviously back from a long, enjoyable lunch. I saw my well-laid plans go down the sink with three good bottles of Burgundy. Outwardly, I played the charming wife, while inwardly I was sticking pins in his image.

I drove to Norfolk while he slept. It was not the auspicious, romantic moment I was hoping for but, later, as the sun went down, and we walked along the harbour out to the marshes, my bad mood melted away with the soft evening breeze and my hopes rose. It was a perfect evening. Geese flew in arrows overhead. When we reached an old ruined boat we held hands and kissed.

On the day we came to leave we decided to take a picnic to the beach. We walked and walked, and eventually fell down exhausted in a perfect spot. We ate our picnic, drank warm wine and he fell asleep, his head in my lap. I looked down at him. He hadn't shaved all weekend and he was all shaggy and stubbly, with freckles and a sunburnt nose, his fleece smelling of Man. He was sleeping a wonderful deep sleep.

I felt a huge wave of love. Blakeney had worked its magic and built a bridge over the fault line between us. It was good to spend time away from London, our friends and jobs, just the two of us. We should have done more of it. I realised I hadn't put on any make-up for three whole days – unheard of.

I lay back and watched the clouds; out at sea, distant thunder rumbled, but the sun was shining, burning my cheeks. I felt overwhelmed with peace and happiness.

As we walked back, we passed a family struggling down the footpath: Dad carrying nets, Mum with deckchairs and a baby on her back, two young children tripping them, under foot.

For the first time since Poppy died I looked at a family and didn't feel bitter. I surprised myself, but I knew then – I didn't need to feel bitter, because that was going to be me.

My husband liked an adventure. I'm not really that keen, but it struck me that a balloon ride might be one thing we could both enjoy. I had booked one as a surprise birthday treat for our way home.

The weather wasn't promising as we left: the storm brewing out in the North Sea was coming closer. 'Surely they'll cancel?' we said to each other, as we raced to catch our balloon, the grey skies hard on our tail.

As we arrived, preparations to launch were in full swing. I was amazed but there was a huddle of aggressive customers surrounding the pilot. I could hear raised voices saying things like: 'This is the eighth time we've tried to get on a flight. They always cancel!'

'We've come all the way from Birmingham.'

'It's Gran's eightieth birthday today. She's always wanted to go up in a balloon.'

The pilot was under pressure. I didn't like it one bit, especially as he didn't look too convincing. How would you not like your balloon pilot to look – baseball cap turned backwards, grubby sweatshirt, mad look in his eyes …?

He licked his finger and held it up to the wind. 'I think we'll be OK. There's a patch of blue over there – we'll head for that.'

I did what I was told even though all my instincts were screaming 'No!' I climbed into the basket and before we knew it we were shooting up in the air, basket swinging wildly as the wind blew around us.

'Ha ha! Hold tight,' he cackled, as we travelled at high speed into the eye of the storm. 'I'll bring her down a bit. She should start going the other way.'

So we started to go down, and then down some more. Now I could see the pretty gardens of the houses below – there was an old couple standing pointing at us, and we were so low I could even make out the green embroidery on the lady's top.

We were plummeting. The pilot desperately yanked the rope to power up the heat, but with one gust of wind the fire went out completely. We came down like a stone, just missing the roof of the house. The old couple ducked as the basket clipped the top of their hedge.

'Brace yourselves,' yelled the pilot.

We hit the ground with a thump, and everyone screamed. I was thrown half out of the basket but my husband caught me and hauled me back in. We bounced along the field one, two, three times, then a gust of wind, the burner reignited and we took off again – straight into the path of a massive electricity pylon.

'No! No! No! I don't want to die! How dare you kill me after everything I've been through, you tosser!' I screamed.

The others looked at me with a mixture of fear and bewilderment, except my husband, who knew exactly what I meant.

My mind was racing, a million thoughts at once. I felt so angry. This whole summer, all the pain I'd been through, the hard work I'd put in just to carry on: working, my marriage, my friends, trying to get my life back together; all those lessons I'd learnt, and for what? I may as well have died on the table of the operating theatre.

At that moment I could have wrung that pilot's neck. Just three weeks before I'd been on the brink of drowning myself, but now something fundamental had changed: I'd gone from not caring, even wanting to die, to feeling there was stuff on this earth I still needed to do.

And a tiny thought said maybe I didn't want to die because I was pregnant.

Two weeks later I found out I was indeed pregnant. This was Amber's beginning.

In those few weeks between the wedding and the balloon ride something fundamental had changed. And the difference was that I was a mother again.

Now, I feel an unbelievable imperative to remain on this earth, because however much I might have moments of despair, I know I am loved and needed by three precious people, and I cannot bear the thought of leaving them to face the world without me. They literally keep the balloon of my existence tied very firmly to this life.

In theory, Charlie should have felt the same. He had five beautiful daughters and by this stage six grandchildren, with more on the way. But others in the family are not as surprised as Dennis with the suicide theory.

For many years Charlie had felt a bit of a spare part. As his daughters grew up, and his wife's business flourished, there seemed to be no role for him. Even the money he brought into the house was increasingly overshadowed by the success of Clara's grocery. The girls seemed to follow their mother's lead and have little love or respect for him, or that's how he felt, anyway. When he walked in from work, they ignored him.

Charlie still regaled everyone with the fact that he was surrounded by so many daughters: 'They drive me mad,' he would say. 'All these women.'

The birth of his grandsons was bittersweet. While filling him with joy, Dennis, Brian and John also reminded him of his own lost son. Charlie drank, but there were times when it just made him feel worse. And when he had one of those fits of melancholy, he would remember the night he fell in Marlow lock: the peace and the sense of relief he felt as the water washed over him and the oxygen left his body.

Bertha, Katie, and Dora used to tell how, on occasion, they came into the house to find Charlie with his head in the gas oven.

'For goodness' sake, Charlie. Stop being so stupid and get yer head out,' Clara would say and march over and turn the gas off. Nanna used to tell this story laughing. But now it doesn't seem like a laughing matter.

Perhaps the outbreak of the Second World War was the last straw – watching all his sons-in-law go off to fight. Perhaps he had that feeling of being a failure too. But, more than anything, perhaps the outbreak of war pushed Charlie over the edge because it gave Clara the excuse to leave him.

When war was declared in September 1939, there was a hasty Swain exodus west into London, and then out the other side. Everyone knew that the German bomber planes would approach the capital from the east, down the Thames Estuary, following the river into the heart of the city. There was a good chance therefore that even if they weren't dropping their bombs on the docks or airfields around Grays on purpose, sometimes they would drop them by accident, or if they had any bombs left after raids in central London, they would off-load them on their way back. The sisters couldn't be living anywhere more unsafe.

But there was one sister who was not living anywhere near the firing line, and that was Alice.

By 1939 Alice had moved from the Welsh valleys to High Wycombe, where Tom had found a job as a delivery man and Alice was working as a typist in an office. Alice now had two children: Jean, who was six, and Brian, who was four. They lived in a tiny cottage, with just two bedrooms, a kitchen and a front parlour. There was no running water.

Instead, they had to draw their water from a well in the back garden. It was a source of endless fascination for the local children.

'How no one ever fell in and died, I'll never know,' Jean said. She reckoned it was so deep you could throw a stone down and never hear it hit the water. A lot of time was spent hauling that bucket up and down. And there was still no running water when Jean got married in the late fifties – as a present, she was invited over to the neighbours on the morning of her wedding so she could have a bath. No wonder the gold taps in Bertha's bungalow caused a bit of a stir.

When war was declared the Swains downed tools, walked out of their jobs and left their homes. It wasn't very well thought through, but I suppose it's a measure of just how frightened people were.

Alice was so delighted to find herself back in favour that she welcomed them all with open arms, despite the fact that she had no room for them. But, ever resourceful, she managed to organise for them to stay with various neighbours, for a small fee. Dianne remembers the cousins having a riot running around the woody hills behind Alice's house, and the adults hanging around smoking and gossiping. The sisters sat around Alice's kitchen table swapping stories about their children, relations and neighbours.

After the first few weeks, when it became clear that Hitler wasn't actually going to bring Armageddon on the capital straight away, the Swains gradually trooped back to London having had a bit of a holiday.

'We may as well go back, then,' Charlie said to Clara.

'You can. I'm not.'

'Eh?'

'No. I've been here long enough to know where I'm really needed. I'm staying with Alice. Tom's off to war. I'm going to look after the children. Sometimes you still need your mum.'

Charlie was momentarily speechless. 'What about me? Who's going to look after me?'

'You're a grown man. I've looked after you for forty years. Little thanks I've had for it. Now you're on your own.'

Charlie stared at Clara, looking for any signs of regret or apology. But she stared right back at him, her expression defiant. Charlie was too proud to say anything else except, 'Have it your way, then.'

'I will, Charlie, I will,' Clara said, and finally it was her turn to march out of the room.

She felt no remorse, only a light-hearted elation.

Ever since Dora had left, Clara had missed her daughters. An unbearable loneliness had descended during the long nights sitting by the fire by herself. The hours dragged and there didn't seem to be any point, even her enthusiasm for her shop had gone. It was like being homesick in her own home. No daughter to confide in, to gossip with, to smile and admire and see love reflected back in their eyes. Clara had spent her life surrounded by six sisters and then five daughters, and it felt too late to try and reconcile herself to being on her own now. Especially when she was so needed.

The first day she had arrived at Alice's and seen her struggling to draw water up the well, cook something hot for the family, keep her children out of trouble – all the while holding down a full-time job – Clara knew she was not going back to Grays. And when she heard the shouting late at night between Alice and Tom, it brought back memories. As she had prophesied, Tom had turned out to be hard and rough with Alice. It felt like history repeating itself. But this time Clara resolved it would be different. Alice would have her mother there, in the same way that Clara wished she'd had her own mother to support her in her battles with Charlie. No, Charlie could lump it. He deserved nothing. And she shut her shop without looking back.

So Charlie was forced to go back to London by himself. For years he had bemoaned being surrounded by women, but now the house seemed empty, eerie. He had never lived on his own and he couldn't bear to be there by himself. He stayed longer in the pub.

Dennis remembers coming across him swaying along the road, drunk in the middle of the day, hardly recognising his grandson.

And then, on his first visit back to High Wycombe, Charlie was found dead at the neighbour's house by Clara.

No one remembers a funeral, any grieving or, indeed, Charlie's death being talked about at all. But, years later, my mum and her brother John were spending the afternoon with Clara when she said, 'Put on your coats. There's somewhere I want to take you.'

They trotted off down the street and across town. The children were intrigued. Clara was almost furtive. They went right through to the very edge of the cemetery, where it was all wild and there were some graves overgrown with grass.

Clara pointed to an unmarked grave and said, 'That's where your grandpa is.'

She looked very sad. John and Dianne didn't say anything. They walked home in silence.

So Charlie seemingly disappeared from the family consciousness. Unmentioned and unmissed, except by his young grandson, and his daughter Dora, who true to form seemed to take on the shock for all the rest of the sisters put together.

When Charlie died in August 1940, Dora was in the final six weeks of her pregnancy. Spencer had been sent to South-East London to train for the army and Dora was living with his parents in Grays. When she heard the news of her father's death she went into her bedroom, drew the curtains, got into bed, pulled the covers over her head and refused to get out. The world seemed more dangerous than ever. If her father could just disappear, what next? Spencer's removal from existence seemed only a matter of time, and then what would become of her? Dora could not eat, and only managed a few sips of the endless cups of tea her mother-in-law brought her.

Spencer's mother was a stoical woman who was nonplussed by her daughter-in-law. She tried gentle encouragement: Dora's favourite supper, her favourite radio programme, her doggy, Suzi, was missing her. Then she tried more brutal methods: marching in, opening the curtains, turning on the light, ripping back the blankets, telling her her baby was in mortal danger if Dora didn't move herself and eat something – a counterproductive tactic which resulted in sobs and shaking.

After a couple of days, Mrs Sier sent for the midwife. This only compounded the problem. The midwife gently coerced Dora into a routine examination, paused long and hard listening with her stethoscope at different points on Dora's surprisingly large bump, and then started feeling around and listening again. It was dreadfully uncomfortable, and there was a sudden feeling of tension in the room.

'She can't find the heartbeat,' Dora thought to herself. 'Bad news comes in threes.' And then, 'It's dead.'

'It's twins!' said the midwife.

Which was not what Dora was expecting, but still qualified as the third piece of bad news as she rolled over to one side and threw up over the side of the bed.

The midwife went downstairs and had a word with Mrs Sier.

'I really think for all sorts of reasons your daughter-in-law needs to come into hospital and be looked after by professionals.'

Mrs Sier heaved a sigh of relief. The next day an ambulance came and spirited Dora away into the City, to the London Hospital in Whitechapel, and right into the middle of the Blitz.

Most of the London hospitals had been evacuated to the home counties; however, a few were left open for emergencies and the casualties of the bombing. The London Hospital in the East End had anti-splinter glass put into the windows. When the air raid warning sounded, the babies in the maternity unit were put into little gas chamber carrycots and taken into a concrete room. The mothers had gas masks placed over their faces and were wheeled into the corridor, where they were given a cup of tea and encouraged to knit for the troops until the raid was over. How they were supposed to drink tea with their gas masks on, I don't know. But it was all very necessary because the London Hospital was hit several times by bombs and patients killed.

Of course, this environment did nothing to dampen Dora's state of anxiety and nervous exhaustion. She longed for Spencer but he was only allowed to visit her a couple of times, and then seeing him in uniform and not knowing if this was the last time they would meet left Dora crying and clinging to his sleeve. Bertha came to visit but she wasn't much help. She refused to discuss anything that really mattered, such as Charlie's death or the impending birth, with the fashionable view that it would only cause more upset. She didn't even have anything good to say about being a twin ('Carnation milk' summing up how she felt about that whole experience), so she avoided that subject too. It has to be said my nanna was very good at discussing distressing subjects as long as they had nothing to do with her or the person she was speaking to. This was the way she'd been brought up. On this occasion it left Dora feeling even more abandoned.

Every night Dora lay in bed waiting for the sirens to start, aware that she was far from home, surrounded by strangers. There was always noise and upset. The shouts of pain of mothers in labour, babies crying, doctors and nurses rushing backwards and forwards from one emergency to another. It was unfortunate that only really extreme obstetric cases made it into hospital. Dora saw and heard some terrible tales. She got no sleep.

Finally, after a month, Dora went into labour. Through the night, as the hospital shook with bombs, she was in agony and terrified. A message had been sent to Spencer, but with the Blitz all around, his ability to make it across London was severely hampered. Eventually, though, the twins Jackie and Angela were born, and Spencer made it to see them.

This turned out, however, to be just the beginning of Dora's nightmare.

Two months later, she found herself in an unknown small town in North Wales with her newborn twins in her arms, knocking on doors, looking for shelter.

'Really?' I asked the twins.

'Yes,' they said in unison.

'Surely they didn't just put her on a train with no idea where she was going?'

'Yes, they did. It was different in those days,' Angela said.

'It was the war,' said Jackie.

'She had to leave London. There were too many bombs, so they put her on a train, and she got off at the end of the line somewhere in North Wales.'

'Dad was sent away, you know. He went to fight.'

'Yes. Poor Mum, it was hard. She literally had to walk through the town knocking on doors, asking for a room.'

'And no one wanted to take her. Well, you can't blame them, really. Two new babies. It was a bit of a handful.'

'Luckily she went into a sweet shop and Dolly took her in.'

'They were marvellous. We stayed with them for the whole of the war.'

'And they brought us up. Mum suffered with her nerves terribly at first.'

'What do you mean?'

'Well, she wouldn't get out of bed.'

'So they bathed us and changed us and fed us.'

'And then Nanna came down.'

'Clara went to Wales?'

'Yes. It got so bad someone sent for her and she helped too, for a bit. Mum couldn't be left alone with us, you see.'

'No, she didn't trust herself.'

It started to feel a bit dark and I wondered about poor Dora. Today I'm sure she would be diagnosed with post-natal depression – in those days, particularly during the war, post-natal depression was not recognised or understood. Which is tragic, because research shows that early intervention can be very effective at a time when the establishment of a mother's relationship with her baby is so crucial.

Any new mother can succumb to post-natal depression but there are factors that make it more likely – bereavement, trauma, a lack of a support network, absence of a partner, a history of depression or mental illness and, of course, Dora had all of these.

Hearing about Dora took me back to the first months of having Amber. It's the only time in my life I have been depressed. What I know now but wished I'd known then (it would have saved a lot of guilt), is that 80 per cent of mothers who lose a baby experience depression after going on to have a healthy child.

I started waking up in the mornings and feeling as if my life was over. I could see no future, just a horrible grey fog. I was also feeling guilty – if I loved Amber, I felt I was being disloyal to Poppy, and I felt ashamed because I couldn't feel the love for Amber I felt she deserved. By day I could feel no joy and by night I couldn't sleep. And when I did sleep I had a recurring nightmare that I was in a hot-air balloon and Amber was there but there was also a skeleton and the skeleton was Poppy. She was crying because I couldn't feed her and she was withering away. I would wake up sweating, terrified of going back to sleep. I couldn't tell anyone because it would seem so ungrateful, shameful, when I, of all people, knew how lucky I was to have a live, healthy baby.

I tentatively asked my husband if he was feeling a little confused, ambivalent – guilty, even? But he said emphatically, 'No'. And I really think he wasn't. There was no conflict in his mind, and I resented him a little for being so uncomplicated and, well … so damn all right! He also didn't seem to twig that I was in trouble, and to be fair I didn't tell him, either.

On my second day back from hospital we took Amber for her first spin in the pram. I walked gingerly along the pavements around our house with my husband. Suddenly it started to rain and then it started to pour. We tried to put the hood up but it jammed and we didn't have a rain cover yet. Our new baby, tiny, slightly jaundiced, in theory still premature, was getting wet.

'Quick ! Get her home. Don't wait for me. Run. Please run!'

'It's OK, Helen. She'll be OK. She's got an enormous blanket.'

'Just do it. PLEASE.' My pleas turning desperate.

He got the message and took off. A few minutes later I got home, soaked and sobbing. I grabbed Amber from my mum, and hugged her tight, saying over and over, 'Poor Amber. I love you, Amber, I really do. Mum, I love her, really I do. I couldn't bear it if anything happened to her. I'm so sorry, Amber, I'm sorry.'

'Of course you do, darling, of course you love her. We all do.'

'Do you think she'll be OK?'

'Of course she will.'

'I don't want her to die.'

'No, of course not. But she won't.'

I knew I was acting weird but I couldn't help it. All around me I seemed to be surrounded by new mummies who were intoxicated with their babies and their new role as mothers. I went out on long picnics with my antenatal group and I realised I was not in the same place.

It didn't help that people seemed to think that now I had a baby everything must be better. I tried very hard not to show what I was feeling and even if I had felt free to express what I felt, I couldn't have, because I didn't understand what was going on; I didn't have words for it. So we all colluded in the charade.

Things came to a head at a friend's wedding. Amber was exactly twelve weeks old. She cried all the way through the service and all the way through the reception. Halfway through dinner I gave up and carried her, still screaming, to our bedroom. A horrible thought occurred to me – was I being punished for what I did to Poppy? Was Amber punishing me? Was Poppy punishing me through Amber? Was God punishing me through all of them? I put a screaming Amber down in the travel cot and backed out of the room and was just about to go somewhere – I didn't know where – when I bumped straight into my friend Heather, carrying two glasses of wine.

'Want a drink?'

She thought I might need some moral support. And then, one after the other, my girlfriends came up, taking turns to keep me company and my glass filled, and Amber finally stopped crying and fell asleep.

It was under the influence that I confessed my shameful secret – that despite having been taught the hard way just how precious a baby is, I did not seem to have the capacity to love my new baby.

'It gets better,' Sarah said, and put her arm around me.

'You don't seem surprised.'

They laughed and exchanged looks.

'God, I cried for the first six months when Louis was born. I was so miserable.'

'Really?'

'Yes.'

'You never told me.'

'You never asked.'

'Gosh, I'm sorry … I just presumed – you looked really happy when I saw you. Although, now thinking about it, I don't think I did see you. Only the once after Louis was born.'

'Well, it's really difficult to get out when you've got a baby, and then it's not really the done thing to moan about them.'

We all paused and drank some more and gazed at the fire.

'But you know, I think it's more than that. Every time I feel a bit of love towards Amber this great sledgehammer of guilt comes down and I find myself apologising.'

'Have you ever thought of hypnotherapy?' Heather asked.

'No, strangely enough, I haven't.'

We giggled.

'This sounds a bit weird but there's a lady I know who gives hypno-therapy classes. She's really special. I think she's worth a try.'

That night was a bit of a turning point. Amber slept through for the first time and carried on sleeping through. I felt a bit better but I still couldn't sleep myself; I was still trapped in my nightmare balloon ride.


And so I found myself in the house of a hypnotherapist. I was quite nervous and more than a little bit sceptical – I mean, if my whole problem was I couldn't sleep, how was anyone going to hypnotise me?

The hypnotherapist said that she would first like to demonstrate the power the mind has over the body.

'Stretch out your arm and say to yourself, "I am strong, very, very strong," over and over. Now, I'm going to try and pull down your arm and I want you to resist saying to yourself, "I am strong." Let's see how difficult it is.'

So I stuck my arm out and said to myself, 'I am strong, very, very, strong,' and she leant on my arm and it took some effort but eventually she brought it down.

'OK. Now let's do the same thing but I want you to say to yourself, "I am weak. Very, very, weak."'

My arm buckled under the first bit of pressure. It was like a feather. I was impressed.

'So you see how powerful the mind is in controlling our bodies? It's the power of positive thought. Now I am going to demonstrate the power of the subconscious mind. I'm going to hypnotise you.'

It was just like in the movies.

'I'm going to count down from ten and you're going to feel more and more sleepy and by the time I get to one you will be at perfect rest. Aware of what is going on around you but perfectly relaxed.'

I was aware of what was going on, but relaxed. She told me to open my eyes, stand up and hold out my arm.

'This time your arm is made of steel. Look at it. It is a steel pole. Like on a scaffold. It is so strong. Nothing, nothing is going to make it bend.'

And the hypnotherapist put all her strength on my arm and my arm wasn't going anywhere and then she lifted herself up on it. I was standing there supporting a grown woman on my outstretched arm. It was as if it was completely detached from my body.

She brought me out of the trance. And asked me what I thought.

'That's amazing,' I said.

She nodded, smiling a little. 'OK, you can't sleep, but what's the real problem?' she asked.

And I told her everything about Amber and me, and most of all about Poppy. I confessed everything, even those things I had trouble admitting to myself.

She hypnotised me again and she took that image of the hot-air balloon and told me I was there with Amber and Poppy and the three of us were together and we were healthy and happy. Then we were landing in a beautiful field full of flowers and we got out and played.

When it was time to leave and Amber and I got into the basket, but Poppy was left in the field. But that was OK. Poppy wanted to stay in the field and it was the right thing to do and Amber and I were happy to leave her. Loving her, but knowing she had to stay and we had to go and that was right. And Poppy was happy that Amber was with me and we were together. As we sailed up into the air, Poppy waved goodbye and we waved back. As we went up she looked smaller and smaller, but we felt happy because Poppy was in a beautiful place, where she wanted to be. And we would see her again one day when the time was right.

Then the hypnotherapist asked me to go to my favourite beach. I was suddenly lying on that beach in Norfolk and I felt the warmth of the sun on my face and could see the gathering storm clouds in the distance and she asked me to look at the wide, endless ocean and believe that my love was as big as that endless expanse of blue, infinite, and big enough to love Poppy and Amber and indeed any other children I might have, because my love was a mother's love and a mother's love is infinite.

I don't know whether hypnotherapy works. What I do know is I walked out of that house and I never again had any problem loving Amber, and I have never felt guilty for loving her. Whatever the hypnotherapist did, she erased all those complicated, negative feelings I had about Poppy and Amber and me, and I was finally free to start loving my new baby.

Amber and I got off to a tricky start, but I don't think that matters. Yes, for me, she will always be in some way connected to Poppy, but that doesn't mean I love her any less. In fact, I think that it has given us an extra-special bond. She helped make me happy again. She is my special girl. Who knows what travels down that umbilical cord? I can't help feeling that her powers of perception and empathy might have come from those long months of grieving and tears when she was in the womb. I was right in the middle of a huge, personal journey and she was there with me, hanging on for all it was worth. And she is still there with me, together forever travelling through life in the basket of our hot-air balloon, my precious Amber.

According to some theories, post-natal depression makes a difference and leaves an imprint. But I'm not sure. My experience is that despite, or even *because* of, what Amber and I went through together, we are very close. I wonder whether Dora too eventually saw her twins as the sunshine after the tragedy of her father's death, and felt closer to them because of that. Because while I don't know how or when Dora started to feel better, there is no doubt that at some point the twins bonded with their mum. They describe their childhood as very happy, and the family

*Angela, Jackie and Dora*

all agree how contented the twins were and adored by their mum. They stayed very close to her always. I have a photograph of them, at probably about four years old. Dora is smiling at her girls, who sit immaculately dressed, with huge bows in their hair, staring confidently at the camera. It's a happy photograph. I don't think the camera is lying.

I guess the lesson I take from this is not to give up, and the resilience of love, particularly maternal love.

And I begin to start seeing this story in a different way.

Much of my work as a psychotherapist is about rewriting narratives (which is not unrelated to what the hypnotherapist did with my nightmare). I had a client who seemed so hopelessly sad. She could not see one good thing about her past, there were no happy memories, she never smiled. After many months of her saying she had achieved nothing in her life, nothing good had ever happened, I challenged her to a rewrite.

'You know, we are constantly choosing how we tell our story. You give a different version to a prospective employer than you would to an aunt, or a new lover.'

'No, I don't.'

'Really? Because it really is the way you tell it,' I said to her.

'No, it isn't. There's only one way you can tell my story and it's the way I've told you. Many times,' she said to me.

She was right in that she'd only told her story one way so far.

'OK, I bet I could write it in a different way.'

'No, you couldn't.'

'Don't bank on it,' I said. 'I'm good at telling stories.'

So we agreed that we would spend the next session having a go at rewriting her life story. This client popped into my mind at this point, and I started to wonder whether I was in danger of falling into the same trap.

*Me, Amber, Mum and Nanna*

The more I have got to know the twins, and think about what they and my mum and indeed all of my kind, funny, clever second cousins faced, the more I begin to see the story of the Scarlet Sisters not as a tragedy, but as a story of survival. The 'in spite of' tale of resilience. What strikes me most is how open and loving they are. I think I have been looking at this the wrong way. When I first started uncovering the family story, it left me feeling a bit hopeless. There was an inevitability to it – how could I or my children ever hope to find a happy, stable life with those layers of trauma as our foundation?

But *is* it inevitable, are we predestined? Yes, it might make life harder, but actually might it not make us deeper? Do we not have some choice and agency in our lives? Do I not have the ability to break the spell myself?

I think about my relations, and I start to think I can.

# CHAPTER FOURTEEN
# The Heroine and The Boyfriend?

I am standing in a park in Glasgow at four o'clock in the morning. It may be August but I'm absolutely freezing. No matter. I am kissing Mr D, our cold noses brushing, and I have an Elbow song going through my head that is so loud, it threatens to take over:

'We took the town to town last night. We kissed like we invented it.'

Indeed, it was some party we had been to and I love the way we kiss. I could stay here for ever, even if it means I freeze. No past, no future. It's enough. I'm happy. I'm also merry on a cocktail of warm, cheap prosecco drunk from a mug (sorry, Nanna, not classy), shouty conversation and that feeling of smiling brown eyes watching me from across a crowded room. Just checking.

I had made up my mind that we should part – a noble sacrifice for the greater good of myself and my girls. I needed to prove I could survive on my own.

But my friends were horrified: 'Don't be daft!'

My girls were horrified: 'But we really like him!'

And a wise old psychoanalyst friend said: 'Why are you trying to write the end of the story when you are barely at the beginning? Hasn't he got some say in this? What would be wrong if, for once, you let the story write itself?'

And I thought about it and I remembered all the years I had told myself a story about my relationship with my ex-husband. That we were childhood sweethearts who grew up together, went to London, made our fortunes, and had three beautiful daughters and then shared our grandchildren. I thought we would be buried together. I had held on to it for too long, because I loved that story and it blinded me to what was really happening. I had written the end before it had actually happened, and that's dangerous.

And now was I not writing an end to my story with Mr D? It was the opposite – a negative end, but still, I was just making it up. That 'gap' was still driving me. Before, it had kept me in a relationship; now it was driving us apart. Could I not work at growing up, and being a heroine, and still have a relationship? Is the heroine not allowed a boyfriend?

I decided it's all about the difference between need and want. As long as I am with Mr D because I want to be with him, rather than need to be with him, then that's OK. Besides, every time I see him, all resolutions quickly evaporate. He disarms me. Yes, I want to be with him. For now. Another song keeps going round my head called 'It Is What It Is'. It's country and western, on an album full of trailer parks; early, disastrous marriages; love and loss. The lyrics are so darkly humorous I chuckle and somehow it seems to fit the story of the Scarlet Sisters. But that one line has become my mantra: 'It is what it is, 'til it ain't anymore'.

For now, with Mr D, all stories are banished.

# CHAPTER FIFTEEN
# Sisters at War

Grace sat on the train from Paddington to High Wycombe seething. Something had got inside her head and was driving her mad. Like an annoying and potentially lethal hornet buzzing in her ear, she would have no peace until she squashed it. So, after opening the letter from the ministry, Grace had grabbed her bag and run for the station.

Alice, her sister, indeed her closest sister and best friend, had been conning her. It took her breath away. She was so angry that the train could not travel fast enough to confront her. She got out the letter and read it once again.

It was a hefty bill from the government demanding money to pay the expenses they had been giving Alice to look after Grace's children for the last two years. Which would have been fine except Grace had already been paying Alice directly and generously, which meant that it looked as if Alice had been deliberately taking money (which Grace could barely afford, and Alice knew that) both from her and from the government.

What really wound Grace up was that she felt she had had no choice, and Alice knew that. The bombing had got so bad in Essex that her children, Dennis and Glenda, had ceased to have any recognisable childhood, their lives had been in real danger and both children, even robust, bubbly Dennis, had shown signs of psychological damage, or, as Grace put it, they were 'starting to go round the bend'.

Of course the first few months of the war had been a deceptively damp squib, which is why Grace and her family had left Alice and High

Wycombe and gone back to their new home, just down the road from the rest of the sisters, in Hornchurch, Essex. There was no bombing, and as for the rest of it – well, it was scary, but not in a real way; more in a what-might-happen way, and it did provide a bit of excitement.

There were many good yarns through the chaos of people not knowing where they were going. There were no street lamps, all the windows were blacked out and cars and bike lights had to have masks over their lenses. Then the signposts were taken down, and finally plastic protection was put over the windows of buses and trains. One time, Grace had set off with her children to see an old Crisp aunt in Walthamstow and ended up in Epping Forest.

These minor upheavals drew everyone closer together in a spirit of united purpose and shared sacrifice. Being Grace's son, Dennis relished the excitement – he was delighted with his new identity card and freaky gas mask. He watched, fascinated, as gas decontamination centres were built – concrete buildings where you went for treatment if you were gassed. Then white wooden posts appeared at regular intervals around the town. They were about one metre in height, with a metal plate on top, coated with a special mustard-coloured chemical. The children were warned to keep an eye on them as they would turn red if there was gas about. At first Dennis was always nervously checking them, then almost wishing them to change colour, and then forgot about them as the Germans failed to unleash that horror on the population.

Dennis was particularly excited that his dad was involved in the nightly fire-watching activities. Best of all were the huge brick water tanks that were built at strategic points. Dennis and his friends used them to sail their homemade boats, getting soaked in the process. Then there was the hilarity of the local Home Guard. The men who were deemed too unfit or old to go into the Armed forces were drafted into platoons and trained to be part-time soldiers. At first they were a rather comical bunch, marching down the street on Sunday mornings, some with no uniforms and sticks instead of rifles. Dennis and his friends, seeing them coming, would rush home and grab brooms and march behind them in a column, trying to keep in step, only to be shouted at by the sergeant, 'Clear off, or you'll get a clip behind the ear!' which sent them running with jeers and peals of laughter.

The Home Guard had their uses, though. One day, one of the silver barrage balloons that hung over the town came loose and landed in telephone wires at the end of their road. Dennis watched in delight as the Home Guard battled to bring it down.

By 1941 things had started to get more serious. Bill was called up. There was much anxiety in the Smith house because Bertha's husband, William, had already been told he was off to fight the Germans in a tank in the Egyptian desert; everyone was relieved when they heard that because of his qualifications as an accountant, Bill was going to be drafted into the Army Pay Corps. He was first sent to Kent and then Oldham, near Manchester. But still, from then on, Bill hardly ever came home.

And then, of course, the bombing started. It was bad. Every night they ran to the shelter, Grace clutching Dennis and Glenda and hiding their faces in her dressing gown. She put on a brave face even though she was terrified.

Like continental plates, the dynamics between the sisters were always on the move. Growing up, Grace had been closest to Alice, but physical distance had forced a kind of separation. Dora, of course, had been evacuated, while Katie was married and running a household, but she still hadn't had any children. However, Bertha, like Grace, was also struggling to cope with two children and a husband away, and she was just down the road. So they spent a lot of time together comparing notes and sometimes indulging in a kind of strange, anti-competition as they sat in Bertha's posh kitchen drinking cups of tea, while their children ran wild outside.

'Poor you. You must have it worse, what with the docks and all that,' Grace said.

'Well, I'm not sure – all those white, concrete roads around you. You must look like you're living slap-bang in the middle of an airbase when Herman comes over! I'm not surprised you've had a battering,' Bertha said, in her most sympathetic voice.

This was true. The estate the Smiths lived in was only a quarter built, but all the roads had already been laid, criss-crossing the fields over a wide area. Being made of white concrete, it did look like an airfield.

'Well, I don't know about that. All I do know is I'm absolutely amazed the house is still standing when I come out of the shelter,' Grace said.

'I know what you mean.' Bertha nodded.

'But my goodness, the children! How are the children coping?'

'Fine. Well, Glenda has always been quite nervous but Dennis is fine. I guess it's all a big adventure for them, isn't it?'

And then Grace started what the sisters called 'going off on one': 'I tell you what, though, I'm fed up with all those bleedin' pieces of shrapnel. He's got nearly a cupboard full. Lord knows – if this war goes on too long, he'll end up filling the house – out there, first thing in the morning, with his friends. He doesn't even wait to have his breakfast. He found a whole silver nose cone yesterday. Oh, he was the envy of the street! Does John do that?'

'No, not so much. You know what he's like – more interested in his own company. Serious. But he's very interested in planes. Him and Dianne stand on top of the shelter and count the bombers going out and how many make it back. He's keeping a record.'

'Yes, he's quite special, John, isn't he?'

Bertha looked keenly at Grace, trying to detect any sarcasm. Yes, John was a bit different, but Bertha was very proud of him – he was clever, no doubt about that. That unusually big head stored an enormous brain. Anyway, he was a lovely-looking child.

'He does wonderful drawings, you know. Really detailed, of the planes. Bombs and things coming down on parachutes, stuff exploding, German bombers crashing in flames, crews bailing out with all guns blazing at them. Sometimes a bit too detailed, if you know what I mean …'

'Oh, dear.'

'Hmmm.' They grimaced at each other, and Bertha wondered whether she had not done John any favours.

'I think he was very upset by that squadron crashing into each other.'

'Well, he would be, yes.'

They both thought back to the month before, when Dianne and John had been watching a squadron of Allied planes. One of them had flown too close to another, their wings had touched and then, like a row of dominoes, they had all toppled into each other and went spiralling down in flames. It hadn't seemed real. Little parachutes had emerged with tiny men attached and there was a huge bang as they crashed. John and Dianne had joined the other local children, shouting to their parents and running off down the road. Luckily, the planes had crashed in woodland, with the wreckage all tangled up in the trees. The children had been kept at a distance as the adults tried to see if they could rescue anyone. Mum was pretty sure that she could see a couple of men hanging from the trees in their parachutes and another in the cockpit of the plane, all burnt and tangled and dead.

'Why on earth do they fly so close together?' Bertha asked.

'So they can't get picked off by the Germans, I suppose.'

'But they're not going to be picked off in Essex, are they?'

'That's what comes from showing off.'

'Grace!'

'You've got to laugh.'

'No, you haven't.'

'No, I suppose you're right. Sorry.' And then, looking up at the heavens and putting her hands together beseechingly, she said another, 'Sorry!'

They smiled ruefully at each other, and Grace changed the subject. 'Dennis is missing his food, though.'

'You'd think they'd come up with something other than those dreadful cough sweets in the shops just once in a while.'

'Hmmm. Yes. Miserable bastards, aren't they?'

'You can tell it's men in charge.'

'Hmmmm.'

'I think you did a wonderful job with Dennis's birthday cake, though,' Bertha said brightly. Grace looked at Bertha carefully. Was she mocking her? 'I think the turnip worked.'

'Oh, Bertha, stop it!'

'No, really!'

'Bertha, you always were a big, fat liar. Your nose is going to get so big it won't fit in this room.'

'No, really – it was moist, and ... chewy, and ...'

'Tasted like a gran's knickers?'

At which point they succumbed to one of those fits of giggling.

'Do you always have to take everything down to that level, Grace? Honestly, what would Mother say if she could hear you?'

Which only made them laugh even more.

'Anyway, I think it was very clever to cut the turnip up into chunks and soak them in pineapple essence.'

'Now you're just being patronising. Just because you've become a whizz with prunes and carrots. And don't think I don't know you got those nuts from the hedgerows.'

'So what? Dennis told John you've been eating whale meat.'

'Well, it had to be better than corned beef.'

'And was it?'

'No! It was bloody disgusting – pardon my French.' And they were laughing again.

'No, but seriously, there's something I want to talk to you about – Christmas.'

Which set Grace 'off on one' again. 'What about it? No, actually, I don't want to talk about it or even think about it. Dennis has been worrying about the tough time Father Christmas is going to have getting through the aircraft guns and search lights. Perhaps I should just tell him the truth and be done with it. There's no place for fairytales in this war.'

'No, indeed,' Bertha said, shaking her head.

'It's going to be miserable – Bill can't get leave and the children are going to have to make do with a couple of wooden toys knocked together in an old man's shed down the road.'

'Well, hang on. I've been thinking about it. Obviously we're in the same boat – William won't be here, so why don't you come round to us? The children can play with each other and you and me can put our rations together and share a bit of sherry …'

So on Christmas Eve, Grace, Dennis and Glenda came to stay. The two boys went head to toe in John's bed; the two girls went head to toe in Dianne's bed, and Grace had the luxury of the spare room and a bath with running water.

Four stockings were left out at the end of the beds.

'Do you think Father Christmas is going to make it?' Dennis whispered.

'Of course he is,' John said loftily. Unlike his older cousin, John had his suspicions about the existence of Father Christmas and thought it was either his mother, in which case the stockings were going to be full in the morning, or if he really did exist, then he would have to have such amazing supernatural powers he'd make it whatever.

'Look, a small matter of anti-aircraft guns and search lights are going to be nothing to a man who has the capacity to deliver presents to every child in the world in twenty-four hours, is it?' he said, a touch dismissively.

'No, I suppose you're right,' Dennis said.

The next year, when John had proved definitively that Father Christmas was in fact his mother, he took great delight in telling my mum, who to this day tells the story of how her big brother ruined the magic of Christmas for her.

In the morning the stockings had definitely got something in them, but they were rather uneven – Dianne's and John's were stretched to bursting, whereas Dennis and Glenda had to root around hard to find something down at the toes. In fact, not only did the Kendall children have full stockings, but there was a beautiful painted wooden dolls' house for Dianne and an engine house for John at the end of the bed.

'Gosh, Father Christmas must think you've either been very good, or perhaps I've been very bad,' Dennis said, gulping back tears.

'Perhaps it's both,' John said.

So poor Dennis spent the rest of Christmas feeling awful. In later years he found out that it was not a vengeful Father Christmas, but William's Old Uncle who had made these presents for John and Dianne. He was of course a master carpenter, now retired, and had lots of wood off-cuts at his disposal. And John and Dianne were the nearest thing to grandchildren he'd ever have. Nothing personal. But it did mean Bertha's well-meaning suggestion had rather backfired.

As the new year got underway, things became increasingly difficult for Grace. School had become intermittent, with daily interruptions when the siren went off and the children trooping backwards and forwards in and out of the school bomb shelters. In the end, the government closed the school and replaced it with 'travelling teachers', who came to certain houses once a week to give a small group of children a few hours' tuition. It wasn't very effective, especially as it was a different teacher every week and the children were all different ages. Grace tried to supplement this by hiring a teacher to come to their home for an extra lesson, but she knew Dennis and Glenda were falling further and further behind.

Glenda stayed close to home but because he wasn't at school, and Grace was out at work all day, Dennis was free to get into all sorts of mischief – bomb-chasing was a favourite. He scoured the area on his bike looking for unexploded devices and tracking the movements of the local bomb disposal unit. He loved watching the squad cordoning off the area and carefully excavating around the bomb. Once it was exposed they used a doctor's stethoscope to listen for a ticking sound. If there was an unexploded bomb, they had to remove the detonator, which often had an anti-tamper device attached. Sometimes they used a steam generator to dissolve the explosive out of the bomb casing. Which was very exciting, but didn't help Grace's nerves. Every time Dennis was late for tea, she wondered whether he'd been blown up.

Then one day something like that happened. Grace had asked Dennis to run to the farm shop with a sixpence to buy some potatoes for tea. As the old shopkeeper weighed them, the air raid warning sounded. 'You'd better run along, son,' she said. 'This might get bad.'

So Dennis grabbed the bag and ran out, but just as he came around the corner into his road, he was deafened by the sound of a low roar behind him, and he looked up to see a German bomber, flying very low following him, with flames and black smoke pouring out of its engines. It was obviously about to crash. In fact, it was so close he could see the faces of the two pilots as it flew past; then, at the back of the plane, he saw the rear gunner staring at him, eye to eye. The gunner swivelled his protruding gun right at Dennis, who was rooted to the spot, unable to move. Dennis remembers the roar of the gun over the sound of the labouring engine as a stream of shells struck the ground, hitting the road and making small craters. Splinters of red-hot concrete went into Dennis's legs, cutting them. He thought he'd been hit and went all weak and dizzy. But the gunner had missed Dennis. Why? Was he just a bad shot? Or did some humanity stop him from killing an eight-year-old boy? Eventually, Dennis came to his senses and jumped over a low wall, almost immediately hearing a loud explosion as the plane crashed with its bomb load. He sat behind the wall shivering, still holding the potatoes; even after the all-clear sounded, he still couldn't get up.

At home Grace had heard the noise, and with Dennis nowhere to be seen, she feared the worst. She ran out and gathered the neighbours, who started searching for him, calling out his name, at which point Dennis finally managed to get his wobbly legs together and emerge from behind the wall.

After that, Dennis became a lot less keen on the war. He was haunted (and still is) by the faces of the crew, and couldn't stop turning over in his mind what it must have felt like knowing they were about to die, and did that gunner mean to hit him, or did he deliberately miss him? It still seems important.

Now Dennis only had to hear the first sound of the air raid warning and he would scramble for the shelter. Then, only a week later, a rare type of incendiary bomb filled with a highly inflammable oil exploded in their street less than 80 yards from their house, and blew the shelter door down on top of Grace and the children.

They weren't physically hurt, but their nerves were shattered. Grace had had enough. Bill had refused to let the children be evacuated, believing the rumours that evacuated children were being used as little more than farm hands or servants or worse. But Grace was lucky, she had her sister. She wrote to Alice:

'It's bad here and getting worse with raids every night, and most days too. I really think the point has come where the chances of Dennis and Glenda getting killed are high and even if they are saved, they will have no life as they are receiving no education. We cannot afford for me not to work, but if you could look after Dennis and Glenda for me and keep them safe while it is so dangerous here, I will be for ever grateful. I can bear it, or at least I can bear it if I know the children are safe.'

And, by return of post, Grace received a letter in Alice's wonderfully familiar, flowery handwriting:

'It's cosy here! They will have to share a bed with Brian and Jean. And I'm out at work, but of course Mum is a brick, looking after them. But I'm guessing by the sounds of it these are minor inconveniences compared with the peril they're facing in London. Of course send them over and I will keep them safe until they can come back to you.'

And Grace had cried tears of relief, which fell on the letter and made Alice's beautiful handwriting all smudgy.

Which made the arrival of the letter from the ministry so particularly hurtful and shocking.

Grace's visit was a complete surprise. She arrived at teatime. When she walked in the door her children were overjoyed and ran into her arms.

But Grace couldn't pretend with the niceties. 'Dennis, Glenda, all of you – go upstairs. I need to have a talk with Auntie Alice.'

They got the message. The children trooped out sombrely.

'And you, Mum.'

Clara looked affronted. 'What are you going to say that you can't say in front of me?'

'I'm sorry, but I don't want you to hear this.'

Clara was shocked. She walked out of the door, shaking her head.

'What is it, Grace?' Alice said, seriously worried. 'Is it Bill?'

'No, it's not Bill. It's this.' Grace scrabbled in her bag, and with shaky hands brought out the letter and handed it over.

Alice sat down and read it. She took her time and then put it on the table. 'What about it?'

'What about it? How *dare* you! You've been cheating me. Cheating your own sister. Making money out of me and my children. Money I don't have.'

'I had no idea they were going to charge you for it.'

'Oh, didn't you?'

'No, I didn't. Who do you think I am?'

'Well, I'm seriously beginning to wonder.'

'Now hang on, I took your children in without a second's pause. You asked, and I said yes. Even though I had no room for them and no means to feed and clothe them. My children have had to share their bed and have I complained? No.'

'No, you jolly well haven't because my children have been a nice little earner for you, haven't they?'

'I told you I had no idea you were going to be charged too. And what if I did make some money? Would that be such a bad thing? Why would you begrudge me that? I needed the money you gave me and I needed the money the government gave me. Look at how I live. I'm hardly living the life of a princess, am I? Where do you think I sleep at night?'

Alice had a point. She'd even taken lodgers in her front room. In the cottage, there were four children sleeping in a double bed, head to toe in the main bedroom; Clara had the back room; and there were two adults, a child and a dog in the front room. The only place left in the house for Alice to sleep was a chair in the kitchen.

'I don't ever remember Mum sleeping,' her daughter Jean said to me.

When I asked Brian he seemed perplexed. 'Do you know, I'd never thought of that. I don't think she ever did sleep. She worked during the day and then she had a shift at the local parachute factory every night. She used to bring home the beautiful material and make white silk underwear out of it. If she did sleep, then I don't know where she did it.'

Is it possible that Alice just didn't sleep? In a family renowned for its hard-working women, and also for its insomniacs, who can exist on unfeasibly small amounts of sleep (I'm one of them), perhaps she didn't. They were all driven, but Alice most of all. Clara was very proud.

But Grace had been spending time with Bertha, and at this point was so enraged she couldn't resist ... 'Well, that's an interesting question, where you sleep, isn't it?'

'What do you mean by that?'

'I think you know what I mean.'

Alice blushed bright red. 'I think you had better leave. I have always counted you as my best sister, the one I love the most, but you have insulted me in too many ways, Grace.'

'Likewise. Don't worry – I'm going, and I'm taking the children with me. You won't get another penny from us.'

Alice sat down in a state of shock while Grace marched out of the kitchen and shouted to the children to pack their cases, they were going home.

As they came to leave Alice kissed them goodbye. Glenda looked nervous but Dennis was holding back tears.

Clara was crying. She loved her grandchildren, especially the boys. She hugged Dennis tight and kissed him and whispered, 'Stay safe, young man. Remember your Nanna loves you.'

On the train back to Essex everyone was quiet. Dennis had a horrible lump in his throat. He'd been happy in High Wycombe, as the bombs never reached as far west as their peaceful patch of Buckinghamshire. Sometimes at night they could see the distant flash of gunfire from the direction of London, and he would say a little prayer of thanks that he wasn't caught up in the middle of it.

Now he was travelling right back into the eye of the storm, and it felt all wrong. As Dennis stared out of the window watching the trees and fields turn into houses and roads, he felt slightly distraught.

Grace was not distraught – merely furious. She had expected an apology and couldn't believe it when none had been forthcoming. She was so angry she hadn't got to the point of wondering what on earth was she going to do with Dennis and Glenda; she was still stuck on Alice telling her how hard her life was. There was a big, 'Yes, BUT!' that Grace hadn't got around to saying and was kicking herself for that. She'd gone off on a bit of a tangent with the, 'Where was Alice sleeping?' line, and she hadn't really meant or wanted to go there. What she felt she should have done was say things like at least you're not being bombed every night and at least you've got Mum there to help you. Basically: 'Yes, you've got a hard life, but so have I. So have we all.'

Back in High Wycombe, Alice was replaying the row in her mind too. In a state of shock at the sheer force of Grace's anger, she had had to pour herself a drink. She didn't drink as a rule, but she felt like she'd been hit by one of those German bombs. As she first gulped, then slowed down and sipped the drink, her mind raced. She was hurt that Grace could think she was deliberately misleading her about the money, but that last thing that she'd thrown at her – about where she was sleeping, that was niggling too.

All she could think of was Bertha, because, just a month before, she had turned up on Bertha's doorstep with a tall, dark, handsome GI in tow, asking for a room for the night.

Alice remembered the moment when she started taking Mickey Edwardes Junior seriously. It was lunchtime on a Monday morning. She was sitting at her desk at work when she heard a plane flying low overhead. It was very noisy, and seemed to be going backwards and forwards over their roof, almost as if it was dive-bombing them.

'What the blazes is that plane up to?' said Mr Allsop, the manager.

Suddenly an idea popped into Alice's head. 'Holy Mother of God, it can't be!' She leapt up from her desk and ran outside onto the street, her bemused colleagues following behind.

Alice shielded her eyes with her hand and looked into the sunlight. And there he was, just as he'd promised – in a little Tiger Moth plane – looping the loop over her office. Her spirits soared with the little plane as it rose and her stomach lurched as the plane then fell, nose pointing to the earth. Everyone had stopped in the high street and there was a collective intake of breath as, just in time, he brought the plane steeply out of its tailspin and started to rise again.

And he was close enough for everyone to see him turn around and blow a kiss in Alice's direction.

Alice realised she was biting her nails. She took her hands out of her mouth and, grinning from ear to ear, waved back and blew a theatrical kiss.

'Mrs Corbett, is this flying circus anything to do with you?' asked Mr Allsop.

'Certainly not. As if!' she replied. She winked at her fellow lady typists and then turned on her heel and strutted back into the office.

Of course it was everything to do with Alice. It was the result of a giddy wager made late on a Saturday night when, on the long walk home from the dance hall in High Wycombe (made longer by the frequent pauses to kiss in the moonlight), they had fallen into bantering about how much Mickey loved her, and what he might do to prove it.

'If you love me you'll fly that plane of yours over my office on Monday lunchtime,' she said.

'I'll do more than that. I'll loop the loop over your office, sweetheart.'

'Really?'

'You betcha! But if I do, what will you give me in return?'

'Hmm … I know. You keep asking me about where I come from. If you loop the loop, I'll take you back to my home town.'

'OK. You're on, cupcake. Start finding us somewhere to stay in that town called Blue.'

'Grays, Mickey. It's Grays, and I'm not going to take you if you keep getting the name wrong.'

'No, I've got it now – Greens. Yes, I can't wait to go to Greens.'

'Stop it!' She hit him playfully and he grabbed her arms, suddenly serious. 'Only … only if you kiss me, beautiful Alice.'

She went giddy at the sudden intensity in his eyes and surrendered to a slow, lingering kiss, while asking herself, 'For goodness' sake, what's wrong with me?'

But Alice knew exactly what was wrong – she'd been living in something of a love desert for years, and now she had no ability whatsoever to withstand the onslaught of Mickey's courage, certainty and charm.

I feel it's time for me to say something about wagers – you may have noticed they are a bit of a theme in my family. Actually, until I started researching the sisters I had no idea: Alice and Mickey's loop-the-loop moment was the first wager I was told about. But when I was told, I couldn't help chuckling to myself. Because ever since I'd met Mr D, we'd been engaged in a series of wagers.

The next time I saw him I asked: 'Do you always make wagers with your girlfriends?'

'No. In fact I think you're the only one I've ever made a wager with,' he replied, grinning.

I had thought it was just him, but actually it looked as if it might be me. When I 'fessed up to my mum she said, 'You're a chip off the old block,' and gave me a meaningful look.

I'd had a moment with Mr D, just like Alice had had with Mickey Edwardes Junior. It was early on and we were sitting at his kitchen table, drinking some kind of spirit and shooting the breeze as the dusk turned to night. He was describing someone to me: 'Yes, she's very good at turning on the charm beams.'

'Ooooh, what a great phrase! "Turning on the charm beams",' I said. 'I must remember that. Mmmm. Although it's not the sort of thing you can use in your reports, I suppose?'

'What? Of course I can.'

'Really?'

'Yes!'

'Bet you can't.'

'OK, what do you bet me?'

I took a sip of the terrible spirit he'd given me and pondered. 'I will give you a surprise if you do it.'

'A surprise? Is that it?'

'Yep.'

'Well, it had better be good.'

'It will be. So if you manage to get the phrase "turning on the charm beams" into your next report, I'll give you a surprise. And if you don't think the surprise is good enough, I'll have to try again.'

He giggled like a girl. 'Really? Now you're asking for trouble. I'm just going to say it's not good enough and make you try harder and harder and do more and more ridiculous things, aren't I?'

'No, I know you won't do that. I trust you. I think you're a man who plays fair.'

'Oh, do you?'

'Yes, I do.'

At which point he stopped teasing me and smiled a different kind of smile, his eyes turning soft and gentle.

And no more was said about it.

A few days later he sent me a text: 'Switch on TV NOW'. So I did. He was doing a report on changes to the benefits system. 'Surely not?' I said to myself. But there he was, talking in all seriousness about a prominent politician 'turning on the charm beams' to bring his party behind him. I was impressed. In fact, I texted him: 'You win. Respect!' And the next week I did surprise him in a way that should probably remain between the two of us, and I was indeed right to trust him because he declared himself suitably surprised for the debt to be paid off.

And something about that bit of playfulness made me take him more seriously. From then on we always had at least one wager on the go, as if, if we stopped making them, our relationship would stop too. They kind of locked us in – there was always a dare to be done and a prize to be awarded – future commitments booked in, if you like.

What I couldn't understand was why I lost every single one of them. It was almost as if unconsciously I wanted to lose. Why? Sometimes I had to give up small things; sometimes I had to do small things; and then sometimes I just had to do the daftest things – dressing up as a

Korean airline stewardess was one of my favourites. Then there were the downright risky: a naked run through a public building was one of them, which I nailed after months of planning and the help of a friend.

And then there is the romantic one, the one that was his idea, an idea he had on the first night we met, when I said I'd never been to New York and he exclaimed, 'Oh God, I'd love to take you to New York!' even though we'd only known each other for a couple of hours and yet already I found the idea quite attractive too. But it would be a year later, during an Easter Saturday spent entirely in the pub, and we were talking about the forthcoming Scottish Referendum and arguing about the likely outcome, and he said: 'I tell you what. If the "No" vote wins by ten percentage points or more, I'll show you New York.'

At 6 a.m. on the morning after the vote I cuddled up with Amber and turned on the television. I was a bit blurry-eyed, so it was Amber who screamed: 'It's ten points! They've won by ten points, Mummy! You're going to New York!'

I squealed and hugged her and I texted him: 'Ten points, eh?'

And he simply replied: 'A bit over, I think you'll find x'

So I said: 'Is it Destiny?'

And he replied: 'We'll see …'

It's interesting how being with someone new can bring out all sorts of things in each other that neither of you knew existed. And Mickey Edwardes Junior brought out something in Alice. Maybe it's to do with where you are in life. When she met Mickey in 1943, Alice was forty-one years old, pretty much the same age that I was when I met Mr D. The last time I'd started a relationship I was seventeen. Now I felt more comfortable in my skin, like there was less to lose, and much more confident all ways round, really.

Alice must have been ready to play. For too long she had been trapped with a man who made playing difficult. Tom was serious and silent, tough on his wife and his children. He locked Alice in the downstairs cupboard in anger. He later locked his daughter in there too. When he went off to war Alice didn't want him to go, but she soon found it was something of a relief. It was hard work, but without the fear of his disapproval there was room to start being more like herself again. And it was a situation that felt uncannily familiar. Once again, with a war on, Clara and Alice were left to bring up the children and run a household together; and, just as Alice had been Clara's general, Clara was now returning the favour.

The day Tom left, as he closed the door behind him, Alice and Clara were left staring at each other.

'We'll be all right, won't we, Mum?'

''Course we will. It's just you and me again, and we'll do fine, just like we did the last time. You'll see!'

Clara took Alice's hand and squeezed it and this caused Alice to fling her arms around her mum and give her a massive hug.

And that's pretty much how it was – most of the time, anyway.

Their one point of disagreement was over Alice's dancing.

In 1943 the Americans came into the war and set up their head-quarters just outside High Wycombe. There was a huge influx of young men who needed to be entertained. Every Friday night Alice would put on her make-up, her best dress and her old dancing shoes (the ones that had helped her to catch two husbands), and she tripped off into the night.

Clara would try and stop her. 'Going out again?'

'Yes.'

'I don't understand you, Alice. Why do you have to keep on going out?'

'You don't have to understand, Mum. It is what it is.'

'Well, what is it then? You've got two children and a home and a husband. All right, he's not here but he's out there somewhere. Surely there's no point in you going out?'

'You're never going to understand. I'm different to you. Things are different.'

'You can say that again.'

'It's not about getting a husband.'

'Isn't it?'

'Not in this case. I'm going to have fun, to meet people, to dance, to escape. How many times, Mum? I. Love. Dancing. It's the only time I really feel alive.'

'Eh?'

'Look, it doesn't matter what you say, I'm going. The children are fine. This way I'll be fine. I've earned it.'

Clara wasn't sure about that. She knew how hard Alice worked, but for her generation that's just what being a wife and mother meant. That was reward enough. She had never gone out dancing and wouldn't dream of it. Respectable women didn't do such things. But even by 1943, things were a little more liberated, especially in those war years, especially once the Americans had arrived. Many people just turned a blind eye, whatever their private feelings. And that went for Bertha too.

When Alice turned up on her doorstep, Bertha was not happy. She had absolutely no idea about the existence of Mickey Edwardes Junior. To fling open the door and find a sister who was supposed to be 200 miles away looking after the next Swain generation, holding the hand of a tall handsome soldier – well, Bertha was completely lost for words.

'Bertha. Hello. This is my friend Mickey Edwardes Junior. I've been showing him around. I wonder whether you could give us a bed for the night?'

'Ah. Oh. Um … well, yes. Um … I mean, obviously I wasn't expecting you.'

'Well, Mickey has heard so much about you and your wonderful bungalow, he really wants to meet you.'

'Does he?' Bertha found that hard to believe.

'Absolutely, and you are just as beautiful a woman as your sister said.'

'Oh, really,' Bertha said in a tone which was supposed to imply that she wasn't going to be taken in by any of his American soft soaping.

'Do you know, you really remind me of Rita Hayworth?'

'Oh?'

'But a more refined, English-rose version.'

'Really? And you remind me of James Cagney.'

'Oh?'

'In *Torrid Zone*.'

'Oh … something else Alice was right about. Your English humour.'

Just at that moment Pat the neighbour walked past: 'Afternoon, Bertha!'

'That's all we need,' Bertha thought. 'Come on, you'd better come in … before the whole of Grays gets to meet you,' she added, under her breath.

They trotted in. Alice was practically skipping. Mickey, so unusually tall and American, looked completely out of his natural habitat in Bertha's parqueted hall.

'And isn't this just as wonderful as Alice told me. It's like a film set.'

'Well, I wouldn't know about that, never having been to Hollywood and never likely to go, either. Anyway, we were just having tea,' Bertha said breezily.

'Oh, of course,' Alice said.

'Now you mustn't go to any trouble for us, Mrs Kendall,' Mickey said, his strong white teeth shining.

'No! Absolutely no trouble at all,' Bertha said, glaring at her sister. 'That's what family is for, isn't it? These unexpected emergencies. One can never turn away one's family, whatever the circumstances, eh? Oh, well, come through. I guess you're going to have to meet the children. Hmph.'

And with that Bertha shook her shiny red locks (which happened to be hanging in ringlets tied with an enormous bow round her head, very impressively) and flung open the door of the kitchen, where John and Dianne were tidily eating their meat-paste sandwiches.

'Look what the wind's blown in!'

John and Dianne watched their Auntie Alice bounce in, looking all made up and glamorous, which in itself was a shock, but then a tall, dark, handsome American soldier walked in, holding her hand.

Both their jaws dropped wide open.

'John, Dianne, close your mouths. If you're not careful you'll catch flies!'

At which they both clamped them shut immediately.

It wasn't as if this was the first time that the children had seen an American soldier in their kitchen. The GIs had disembarked at Tilbury and they'd been living in tents on the pavements all along the roads in Grays for months. The Kendall family, like most families, had welcomed the American soldiers with relief and joy. Everyone knew their arrival was almost certainly a turning point in the war. And Dianne's memories of the soldiers are fond – they gave her chewing gum and sweets and told her about their daughters at home. Bertha made them cups of tea and she was given the odd pair of nylon stockings – oh, the joy! Their arrival was a bit of fun in the dreary wartime world. Then one day they woke up and all the soldiers had gone and they knew France was about to be invaded. But the street seemed empty. They were missed.

However, with children's perceptiveness, John and Dianne immediately realised that Mickey Edwardes Junior was something different. They watched the dynamics between their mother and Auntie Alice, their mother and Mickey Edwardes Junior and Auntie Alice and Mickey with fascination. They had hardly ever seen their mother so angry, unless it was with their father, but then it wasn't this kind of pinched, icy sarcasm. But then they'd never seen anyone flirt like Alice and Mickey before.

It was quite clear that Auntie Alice had the hots for Mickey, and he couldn't seem to take his eyes (or his hands) off her. John and Dianne were dumbfounded. In their world men and women never touched each other – they barely even looked at each other. It all felt terribly racy and exciting and they were a bit disappointed when they were shooed out into the garden by their mother.

Bertha braced herself to ask the question she really didn't want to ask, but had to, just so she had things straight: 'You did say *a* bed?'

'Yes,' Alice said, looking her straight in the eye.

'As in one bed.'

'Yes.' Alice was still looking her straight in the eye.

'And did she give them a bed?' I asked my mum.

'Yes, I think she gave them hers.'

'Really?'

'Well, she wasn't happy about it, that was obvious. But you know your Nanna. She never could say no.'

Every summer holiday, John and Dianne were sent away from the capital to safety at Alice's until they had to go back to school.

The next time they went to visit, the cousins – John, Dianne, Jean and Brian – had all been put to bed together. They were lying in the dark, chatting and John piped up: 'We've met your mother's boyfriend.'

'What?' Jean and Brian said together.

'Yes. He came to stay with us in Grays. They came together,' he said.

'He did not. Our mummy hasn't got a boyfriend,' Brian said.

'Oh, yes, she has. He's a tall, American fella,' Dianne added.

'You just shut up and don't you ever say that again!'

At which point John and Dianne realised they'd said something they shouldn't and did indeed shut up.

*

When I went to see Brian I asked him about his mum and the GI. Brian didn't know anything about it, and couldn't remember the conversation with John and Dianne in the bed. But he did laugh and say, 'It's not impossible,' and then he said, 'Come to think of it, I *do* recall someone. Yes, there *was* someone around.'

He remembered going to the VJ celebrations, which were particularly big because of the American headquarters down the road.

'I remember Mum taking me with a very tall, dark American soldier and he took me by the hand and there was a huge bonfire. I guess that must have been him.'

I don't know what happened to Mickey Edwardes Junior. What I do know is that after the war Clara left the Corbetts and moved back to Grays, Tom came back in one piece and Alice picked up her life as Tom's wife.

I imagine that it must have been difficult for her, after the relative freedom and excitement of the disruption of war; what I know is that Alice carried on dancing whenever she could, winning competitions and buying colourful dresses that sometimes got her into terrible trouble with her husband.

Alice seems to have been the only sister who was particularly interested in men. It's not that the sisters weren't interested in getting married, but men as desirable for their own sakes? Because they're rather sexy …? The topic of sex never came up when I was with my nanna, and Mum says that she only ever referred to it in a way that made it clear that she didn't have much time for it – it was something slightly distasteful that had to be endured if one was to be a wife and have children. And a good husband was one who didn't make too many demands in that department. It wasn't that Nanna was a prude – far from it. She loved a filthy joke, and she had no problems with her grandchildren's exciting love lives – witness her joy and collusion with my frolics with the student boyfriend!

It would be easy to point the finger at Charlie and say the sisters had been put off men by the antics of their father. But actually I think they were simply women of their time and brought up with a completely different attitude to sex. Clara was typical in teaching her daughters that respectable ladies didn't enjoy physical relations – there was something unseemly about that. But men were different and had their needs, and therefore within marriage these must be tolerated.

There is a noisy consensus among all of us Swain survivors that the only Scarlet Sister who had a happy marriage was Dora. And yet however unhappy, there is not the slightest hint that they ever looked at any other men (except for Alice). Leave their husbands, yes: Bertha, Katie and Grace all tried that one – but not for another man. Katie and Grace went to live with Clara, and Bertha wandered around the Kent countryside until it got dark and she had to concede defeat and go home. All the sisters survived their husbands by many years and none of them remarried, or even had a special male friend, again except for Alice. So why was she the exception? I can't help feeling the answer might lie with the tragic death of her first husband, Joseph, barely a year after they married. If someone was taken from you so suddenly, and you remarried so quickly and so unhappily, wouldn't there be a part of you that was always looking for that first love?

Something that never was quite the same was Alice's relationship with Grace. Tough times can unite a family or tear them apart. Perhaps when everyone is struggling, when there is too much to deal with, fault lines rupture. At this moment in their story, I think the sisters didn't have the capacity to be kind and give each other the benefit of the doubt. Because while Alice was struggling, Grace was too.

It took everyone, not least Grace, some time to realise how difficult her husband, Bill, really was. In fact, 'difficult' is the wrong word – in the end he was diagnosed with schizophrenia. The very intensity and possessiveness that had attracted Grace developed into a kind of mania and paranoia which was directed at Grace, and also Dennis. He was unpredictable and cruel to his son, and beat him terribly. Grace would step in and try to stop Bill and in the process would be hurt herself. In the end, she left him and turned up at Clara's house in Grays, with her children. She lived there for a while but, in the end, she went back to Bill.

Dennis would always wish she hadn't and didn't understand why she did, except it was different in those days – divorce was not an option, except for the very rich.

Finally, Bill was sectioned. He came out again when he was better, and then he got worse and was sectioned again. This time, when the doctors said he was ready to come out, Grace refused to have him back. He stayed in hospital and refused to eat. He starved himself to death.

Grace was a favourite aunt among the Scarlet Sister children. They talk of her fun, kindness, and total lack of pretence. They all enjoyed going to see her. It must have been a constant battle for Grace to keep hold of her sense of self under the assault of living with such a sick husband, especially when so much of his darkness was directed at her and her son. My hope is that today if any of us find ourselves in this situation, things have changed enough that we could extricate ourselves, with some level of help and security, and without society being so judgemental. It must be easier now.

# CHAPTER SIXTEEN
# Least Said, Soonest Mended

My Uncle Nigel could never quite work out how he happened.

Bertha gave birth to Nigel on 8 April 1945. Which is fine, except my grandfather, William Kendall, had not been home for two years. He'd been in Yorkshire training to fight in tanks, and then at around the time that biology says that Nigel must have been conceived, William was sent to Egypt. It had been a slow realisation for Nigel, and he didn't like to ponder it too much, but every so often a moment of insidious doubt would creep in. It doesn't help that he looks nothing like John and Dianne. In fact, he isn't like them in many ways. John and Dianne are slim, small-boned, and dark – they looked like their father. Neither of them are extroverts, and they were both swots at school.

Meanwhile, Nigel could be described as a typical Swain: fair, broad-faced, funny, sunny, gregarious. He loves to keep a room entertained with his many stories; Nigel worked in magazines in the sixties in the bit of London that really was swinging, so he has plenty – like being offered an unidentified pill by a beautiful stranger, and taking it because, well, she was beautiful, and then waking up on platform two of Bournemouth station a week later with no idea what had happened in between. My favourite are his tales of racing Minis across the New Forest. I'm sure he told me that they drove them through the legs of New Forest ponies; although, as Mr D pointed out, that's physically impossible, especially as New Forest ponies have particularly short legs.

Nigel is a natural charmer. He's a hoot – but that's the last word you would have used to describe William. However, Nigel always felt like William was his father. There is evidence for the defence: they shared the same interests – walking and the natural world – and Nigel is a gifted writer, photographer and artist, making detailed paintings and drawings of wildlife and plants. He has sold pictures, had books published and spent many years as a graphic designer. This talent is certainly something that could have been inherited from William and the Kendalls.

But the dates just don't add up.

It wasn't until quite recently that Nigel finally voiced his doubts. The person he chose was his big sister, my mum, Dianne.

He was somewhat surprised by her reaction, 'It's funny you should say that, Nige, because I've always wondered about that myself.'

'Really?'

'Yes. But I never wanted to say anything. I didn't want to hurt your feelings or stir things up. There never seemed a good moment to bring it up.'

'Well, I can see that.'

'But you know, it may be a blessing in disguise that you haven't raised this before, because I've only just remembered something which might explain how you came into the world. And I'm very glad I have remembered it, because it's the only explanation I can think of … other than the 60th Division of the American Army that was camped outside our front door.'

And here she giggled, and so did Nigel, because he never loses his sense of humour.

'Well. that's what I was thinking …' and he broke into an American accent: 'Although people have always called me a bit of a cowboy …'

'Oh, stop it, Nigel. You are awful!' Mum said, laughing affectionately, which is how a lot of their conversations go.

'No, but being serious now, Di, that's the only thing I could think of as well. But I just can't imagine it. Mum wasn't really like that, was she?'

'No, she wasn't. I don't think she was ever really into men.'

'Di!' Nigel pulled a face.

'Oh, that's not what I mean, you know what I mean. Oh, stop it!' and they were off laughing again.

But when they'd sobered up Mum went on to tell him the only explanation that anyone can think of for Nigel legitimately appearing on this earth.

Dianne was always a sickly child and in 1944 she got pneumonia. At the same time she also got a kitten.

Dianne had wanted a pet for ages and had been pestering her mum and, finally, Bertha bought her one: a beautiful, fluffy, black, mewling thing called Lucky. Despite the fact that Dianne was quite poorly, with a cough that wouldn't go away, she stayed outside playing with it in the front garden with Pat the neighbour's daughters. Lucky the kitten was adorable, and they were taking turns to hold her and tease her with a ball of wool, but then Dianne suddenly felt terribly weak and couldn't breathe and had to go inside and up to bed. That night Bertha kept vigil beside Dianne's bed as she lay in agony with pains in her back, in her ribs and around her lungs. She was slightly delirious. Bertha watched her anxiously, the ghost of Charlie Junior hovering. She seemed to be having trouble breathing, and was deteriorating fast, so as soon as morning came Bertha rang for the doctor. He rushed over in his car and said it looked like pneumonia and she must go straight to hospital.

Unluckily, as he leaving, he managed to back over and kill Lucky the kitten – which cast a shadow over the whole of Dianne's illness, Bertha seeing the death of Lucky as an omen of Dianne's inevitable passing. Lucky was never replaced, not by a kitten anyway.

Dianne remembers waking up in a hospital bed in a plastic bubble. She was surrounded by empty beds, and there was no one about. She could hear the sound of bombs dropping close by and she felt the room shake. Dianne was actually in intensive care, in an oxygen tent, and the other patients had been put under their beds for protection. But Dianne was too poorly to be moved. It was strange and frightening, so she just closed her eyes and went back to sleep and hoped someone would appear when she woke up.

Dianne was in intensive care for three weeks. The patients who were very sick were put on something called the danger list. This was an actual list that they used to put up outside the doors of the hospital, so anyone passing could check the status of their loved ones. Needless to say they only put up the names of those whose lives were hanging in the balance – I suppose today's equivalent would be being described as in a 'critical condition'. Dianne's name was on the list for ten days. And it was during the time that my mother nearly exited this world, and actually because she nearly exited this world, that Nigel must have entered it: when William's superiors were informed of his daughter's condition, they gave him one night's compassionate leave to go and see his daughter and say goodbye.

Bertha told Dianne how William arrived in the middle of the night and came into the pitch-black, sleeping ward, and stood for a while beside her bed looking down at her, and then kissed her, and in the morning he was gone. The next week he sailed for Egypt.

Bertha only told Dianne this story when she was close to her own death. Which is a bit worrying, because of course if she hadn't, then the conversation between Nigel and Dianne would have taken a different turn, and Nigel may well have come to the conclusion that William was not his father. Which just goes to show, it's good to talk.

I was having tea with Mum and Nigel and they were discussing this very issue: 'Of course, I don't remember him coming because I was asleep. So we can only take her word for it. But I'm sure that's what happened.' Mum raised her eyebrows. 'Don't you think?'

'Yes, Mum,' I said and then we giggled. I don't know why we are so playful except that, like our running joke about Grandpa being half-Egyptian, it's so unlikely.

And then Mum looked a bit sad. 'But if that is the case then I can't help but be a bit shocked, because there I am fighting for my life – I mean, they really did think I was going to die, and what were they doing? Having a good time. It's a bit hurtful, isn't it?'

'No!' Nigel and I chorus together.

'Think about it, Mum! They haven't seen each other for what, two years? He's going off to Egypt next week, maybe never to return. What are you going to do? Wouldn't it be a bit strange if they didn't?'

'Yes, definitely,' Nigel agrees.

And then a bit like a cloud going over the sun, I feel a shadow as I'm back in the neonatal unit and remembering the nurses telling us to be careful, how having a sick baby or child seems to make people go off and conceive, as if nature pushes us to secure a replacement just in case. And I remember the strange, aphrodisiac effect of those days: totally counter-intuitive, and engendering feelings of guilt, as if it was slightly disrespectful. But the nurses were right. I think we often underestimate the strength of the primeval forces working underneath.

Obviously Dianne didn't die. She came out of intensive care and was sent to a convalescent home for sick children in the Surrey countryside for six months. She learned how to sew, and on fine days she had lessons outside, sitting in a wheelchair.

When she came home it was to find her mother wearing an uncharacteristically unfashionable smock. Dianne stared in horror at her mother's normally svelte stomach. 'Mummy, what have you been eating?'

'Dianne, this is a baby!' Bertha said, patting her bump triumphantly. 'You're going to have a little brother or sister.'

At which Dianne, still not entirely 100 per cent, looked as if she was about to faint and had to be sat on a chair and given a glass of water. But when she'd had a few sips and got her breath back Dianne said, 'Really?'

'Yes, really!' Bertha nodded.

And Dianne leapt up and threw her arms around her mum. 'Oh, Mummy. Just what I've always wanted – a baby! Thank you!'

And that pretty much summed up how Dianne felt – this new baby was a personal coming-home gift from her mother, and nothing could have made her more happy. (Lucky the kitten was forgotten at this point, a baby being a much better replacement.) The only downside was that in order for this baby to be born, Dianne would have to lose her mum for a few weeks again.

Bertha had had a difficult pregnancy. Everything was swelling up and she was booked to go into Chelmsford hospital around her due date and then stay there recuperating for a couple of weeks afterwards. Dianne was particularly nervous about being left and Bertha struggled with what on earth to do with them. They were supposed to go to Alice's but Dennis and Jean were still there, and Grace had come round and read the riot act: 'You can't do this to me! You can't force my children out of their home.'

'But what am I supposed to do? Look at me!' Bertha was over eight months pregnant.

'Well, not send my children back to be bombed.'

'But I'm booked to go in next week! Who's going to look after them?'

'Not Alice. She's already busy looking after mine. You find someone else.'

Bertha was the only Scarlet Sister who had three children – the others had their two and then were careful. (Dutch caps were prolific and surprisingly effective. Mum remembers Nanna keeping hers in a box under the kitchen sink. Although obviously not always used …) Bertha had a feeling her sisters were had taken umbrage at her nerve, or perhaps fecklessness, to produce this baby out of nowhere in the middle of a war.

Grace stormed out and slammed the door. Unfortunately Dianne had been standing quietly in the corner of the kitchen and had witnessed the row. As Bertha sat at the kitchen table with her head in her hands, Dianne crept over and stood in front of her. With her time at the Barratts very much in mind, she asked, 'Mummy, who's going to look after me now?'

'I have no idea, darling. No idea.' And Dianne watched as her mother, huge with child, sobbed in despair.

But when Old Uncle and Mrs Beesom heard of Bertha's plight they immediately offered their services, and a few days later they moved in. Bertha went off on the bus with a little suitcase full of tiny knitted romper suits to have Dianne's baby.

It was a satisfactory arrangement. Mum remembers Old Uncle and Mrs Beesom being very kind to her and John. Of course, they were well-behaved too. It was a happy few weeks, although Dianne missed her mum terribly: 'With Dad gone, Mum had become everything to us,' she said.

Then, one morning, Mrs Beesom told John and Dianne that they'd had a call from their mother and she would be home that afternoon with their new baby brother. The morning dragged as the excitement rose but, finally, John and Dianne reckoned it was almost time for their mum to arrive.

For reasons best known to himself, John said, 'Quick, let's hide, so she can't find us when she gets back.'

And Dianne, being the little sister, did what she was told.

'Look, Di, come in here,' he said, pulling her into the bushes by the front gate. 'This way we can see her, but she can't see us.'

They crouched and waited. Finally, they saw an ambulance draw up outside and their mother step down carefully, holding a bundle which must have been the baby. She walked to the door and Mrs Beesom let her in and the door closed and then ... nothing. They sat in the bushes and waited, and nothing happened. There was no great commotion or search party as John had hoped.

'Oh, I've had enough of this,' he said and got up and went indoors and Dianne was left alone.

Over seventy years later Mum says she can still remember the piney smell of the laburnum branches, the prickles of the leaves, and the staring at the door, waiting – for what? She didn't know. With them in the house and her outside hidden, she felt cut off and a suspense and a suspension, a feeling of the moment before. It was one of those rare occasions when you can sit and relish the feeling of that last moment before your world changes for ever.

In the end Dianne got up and walked inside too. She could hear them all in the sitting room. The first thing she saw was Mrs Beesom, sitting on the sofa holding the baby, who was all swaddled up in a crocheted blanket – the blanket that Dianne had watched Bertha knitting as her bump grew.

'Come here, Dianne,' Mrs Beesom said, patting the seat next to her. 'Sit down beside me and hold your new baby brother.'

Dianne sat down and Mrs Beesom carefully passed her the baby Nigel and got them settled. Dianne held him for ages. He was asleep and peaceful and she couldn't take her eyes off his face.

Mum had never told me the story of Nigel's homecoming before and I was struck by the emotion in her voice. Mum is not given to crying, even under the most extreme circumstances, but as she told me this story there were tears pouring down her cheeks. I couldn't make out whether they were tears of joy or sadness. I was confused, but she said: 'I just couldn't believe how beautiful he was – this baby, and he was mine.'

Joy, then, I think? But her words seemed tinged with sadness too.

From then on Dianne doted on Nigel. To her mind he was the most perfect baby, and then little boy. Bertha needed Dianne's help, and Dianne was only too delighted to oblige. She nursed him, bathed him and fed him. She was a little mother to Nigel. Not that Bertha wasn't equally entranced. Throughout her life, Bertha called Nigel 'her sunshine'. As Bertha lay dying in hospital, Mum remembers Nigel walking into the room and Bertha waking from her final sleep and holding his hand, her whole face lighting up, and gazing at him with the most enormous love.

Apparently, in those last days, my nanna had only two things on her mind: when was Nigel coming, and how on earth was Helen going to cope with three girls …

Dianne first heard that she had a new baby brother while having tea at a neighbour's house. Auntie Katie walked in. 'Dianne, John, I've just had a telephone call from the hospital. Your mother has had a little boy.' And then she turned to Dianne and said, 'Bet you wanted a little sister. Well, you haven't got one. Naaaah,' and pulled a face.

Dianne was upset. 'I really don't mind what it is, Auntie. I just want a baby.'

Which was true. Dianne couldn't fathom the sudden unkindness from her aunt. But in retrospect it's quite understandable.

*Mum, Nigel, Nanna and John*

*Katie*

Katie met Horace Smith when she was fourteen, kicking her heels in the air, doing a particularly enthusiastic Charleston. Like her sisters, Katie loved dancing. She was good at it and always in demand as a partner; she was also in demand in other ways: she had a pink and white complexion, shiny brown hair with red lights streaked through it, and a cute rosebud mouth – neat, pretty, doll-like perfection. She matched this with a bright, business-like, confident air and she did well at work. She'd had a job in Fleet Street as the secretary to one of the editors of the *Daily Express*. He was always, in her words, 'pestering' her, begging her to let him install her in a flat in Mayfair and become his 'fancy lady'. It seems that Dora was not the only Scarlet Sister to receive special attention from her boss! But the sisters were never attracted to the role of mistress, and Katie changed her job. She did hang on to Horace, though.

After courting for nine long years, they married in 1936. Horace had trained in retail and they shared a dream to run their own shop, which they duly opened after the war – a grocery store in Grays High Street, rather larger and better appointed than Clara's shop down the road. Until then Horace worked as a rather skilled engineer. Indeed the Smiths had a somewhat swanky lifestyle. Somehow I've managed to inherit Katie's fur coat – it's huge! A whopping, luxurious, dark brown, full-length affair. It drowns me and I'm quite tall, much taller than Katie. I could never wear it because it's so obviously REAL – a large number of animals died to create it. My daughters get it out occasionally and gaze at it in awe – and dismay.

But it wasn't just clothes. Like Bertha, Katie loved her home and she put a lot of effort into getting it just right. She made scrapbooks of cuttings from home decoration magazines. Katie and Horace made the most of their leisure time too. They belonged to a tennis club and played in a league. They mixed with the 'top drawer' of Gray's society and went to balls in the grand ballroom of the Queen's Hotel. They travelled a lot with their friends, and before the war they even went to France, which was quite unusual. They were probably a bit grander than even Bertha with her bungalow and white Lancaster. But, however perfectly set up they were, there was something missing, and that was a child.

It must have been difficult for Katie to watch her sisters get pregnant, one after the other. There was no one in the family who had had difficulties having children. And there was so little known about fertility, no options other than adoption, and so much social pressure.

The idea of a couple marrying and not having a family did not sit comfortably in 1930s Britain: people talked about you behind your back, and Katie would have known that. A wife and mother commanded great respect, more so than today. And respect mattered a lot to the three youngest Scarlet Sisters. Right from a girl's wedding day, 'well-meaning' people would be dropping hints about the 'pitter patter of tiny feet', and looking for the slightest signs – if you put on a bit of weight, felt a bit under the weather, developed a sudden liking for aniseed balls, they'd be nudge, nudge, wink, wink and, 'Have you got any news you'd like to share ...?'

Katie was on the verge of being able to give some news several times, but each pregnancy ended in a miscarriage; again, something her sisters had never experienced. Katie felt as if she was abnormal, broken, especially as in those days there was an automatic presumption that it was the woman's 'fault'.

Katie was proud and didn't talk to her sisters, so they stayed off the subject and merely resigned themselves to gentle gossiping behind her back. But she did talk to her mum. Clara came out with all sorts of weird and wonderful suggestions such as wearing a corset, growing her hair and avoiding exciting pictures, quarrels and hot baths.

After her third miscarriage, Katie was lying in bed, very shaken. Clara came to see her and sat on the edge of the bed and took her hand.

Katie plucked up courage and said how she was really feeling: 'Mum, what's the point? What's the point in all this if I can't have a baby? I feel useless.'

But Clara had no truck with this. 'Come on, Katie. The best thing you can do is stop crying and keep trying. Worse things happen at sea. Anyway, you have no choice, so best get on with it.'

After that, Katie kept her feelings to herself. Inside, though, she was seething at the injustice, but that was better than the fear that crept up on her in the dark hours of the night, because she didn't know what she would do if she never had a baby. Every pram was a rebuke, and the noise of her nieces and nephews went right through her head. When they were invited round to Auntie Katie's immaculate home for tea they knew they had to be on their best behaviour, and woe betide them if they dropped crumbs.

After more than seven years of trying, just at the point when Katie had given up hope, she fell pregnant again and this time the pregnancy was successful. Katie sailed through, passing all those crucial stages:

twelve weeks, twenty weeks, thirty weeks. She looked and felt really well, very different in fact, to how she had felt in her previous pregnancies. She relaxed, her hair thickened and grew redder, she grew kinder and invited her nieces and nephews around for tea and ignored the crumbs dropping under the table. She started to see more of Bertha again, especially when her twin announced that she was expecting a baby too: 'A bit of a surprise!' Indeed …

'What do you think? Boy or girl?' Katie asked Bertha.

'What, me or you?'

'Both.'

'Hmmm … do you think we ought to have a bet on it?'

'Why not?'

'I bet you …'

'Hang on. Let me write this down.'

Katie got up and found a bridge scoring card and pencil in the drawer of her dresser. She sat down and turned it over, pencil at the ready, and said, 'OK, off you go, then.'

'I think you are having a boy and I am having a boy too.'

'Really? You think we're both having the same?'

'You know I'm good at sniffing out the flavour of the bun in the oven,' Bertha said.

'OK. Well, the proof will be in the pudding, won't it?'

'Or the bun!'

'Yeah, yeah … ha ha!' She started scribbling: *Bertha = two boys*.

'So, your turn then, madam.'

'OK. I think you're having another girl and I'm having a boy.'

'Do you? Why's that?'

'Well, let's look at the evidence. You, my dear, are all horizontal, while I'm all vertical.'

It was true. And according to generations of witchy folklore, ladies go spready with girls, and neat and spherical with boys; although all the midwives I've spoken to (and I've spoken to a surprising number) say this is nonsense.

'So I say Bertha girl, Katie boy. There. So whoever wins has to buy the other lunch at the Queen's Hotel?'

'Oh, Katie, top idea, but I can tell you've never done this before. I don't think either of us is going to have time for lunch.'

Normally that remark would have made Katie bridle, but she was feeling at peace with the world and she let it float off like a bubble in the breeze. 'All right, then. Ooooh, this will hurt – how about whoever loses has to give the other some of their clothing coupons?'

'Oooooh, that's quite a serious bet, then! Oh, heavens, why not? What could be more serious than the flavour of a baby? I'm game!'

'Right.' And Katie scribbled: *Prize = five clothing coupons.* And she got up and waddled over to her mantelpiece, where she rested the paper in front of the framed photograph of her wedding day.

'Now I'm up, come on, let me show you the nursery.'

'Oh, goody, yes, do!'

They both climbed slowly up Katie's stairs, into the small back bedroom which had been her sewing room.

Bertha was struck by how light it was. The dark, florid wallpaper had been taken down and it now boasted a layer of simple, fresh lemon paint. The sewing machine was stowed in a cupboard, and the sewing basket had been put away. Instead, there was a pretty white chest of drawers and a brand new cradle.

'Grace offered me hers, but you know I wanted to get new.'

'Well, that's all right, if you can afford it,' Bertha said, slightly pointedly, 'And a new nursing chair?'

'Yes. It was a special present from Horace.'

'He must be over the moon.'

Katie uncharacteristically blushed. 'Yes, he is.' And then she changed the subject quickly: 'Are you all ready, Bertha?'

'Oh, no need yet. I've still got a way to go. I always feel a bit superstitious about these things … And, anyway, I don't need to buy anything. I just need someone to get the stuff down from the loft for me. For some reason I never gave it away.'

'No. I wonder why that might be?'

Yes, Bertha's third baby was controversial with her sisters.

When the time came for Katie to give birth, because she was having her first baby at over thirty years old, she was considered high risk and she went into hospital. It was a long labour, but straightforward. But when the baby was delivered the midwife picked him up and turned him over and then her expression went very serious. Everything was happening quickly for Katie, but she still managed to notice that. The midwife told her assistant to fetch the consultant. The atmosphere in the room changed. Katie heard a gurgle and then a little cry working into a scream as her baby found the use of its lungs. But other than that everything was very quiet.

Despite the sound of her baby being very much alive, Katie's instincts were telling her that there was something wrong, but she'd never done it before, so she didn't know what was supposed to happen next. The midwife was examining the baby.

Katie asked, 'Please, can you tell me, is it a boy?'

'Yes,' the midwife replied but didn't give any more information or offer to show him to Katie. Then the consultant came in, and a few other people in white coats. They went outside the room and then came back in. 'Mrs Smith, we are going to take your baby away now. Then, when the final stage of your labour is finished, we need to talk.'

As the doctor was saying this, Katie saw, out of her corner of her eye, the midwife's assistant walk out of the room, carrying her baby in a bundle.

That was the last time she ever saw him.

Later, Katie was visited by the doctor, who explained that her baby had spina bifida – a congenital disorder where the spinal cord which connects the body to the brain hasn't developed properly and leaves a gap in the spine. It meant that he had no chance of surviving more than a few days and for that reason it was best she didn't see him. Katie called him Clifford.

But Bertha did see him. As Katie's twin sister, she was the only family member who was allowed a visit. She was taken to a small room where there was nothing but a cradle. Lying in it was a baby wrapped in a blanket. Later, she told my mum that it was heartbreaking: 'He looked like a normal baby. He was all wrapped up so all I could see was his face and he looked like a perfect baby. He opened his eyes and looked at me. It seemed impossible that there was anything wrong, and it was awful to leave him. I just wanted to pick him up and walk out with him.'

When a baby was deemed unable to survive in those days, it wouldn't be fed. It was left to die in its own time of natural causes or, in other words, starve. Clifford lived for ten days. Nobody knows where he is buried.

In those days it was commonly believed that, 'Least said, soonest mended'. No one ever mentioned Clifford to Katie: not her husband, nor her sisters. Bertha couldn't bring herself to tell Katie about her visit – too heartbroken to tell her how perfect he had looked.

When Clara came to visit her daughter in hospital, she talked practicalities, except her final words as she was leaving: 'It was meant to be, Katie. He wasn't meant to live. I'm sorry. But now you have to pick yourself up and get on. Be thankful for the things you do have. The best thing you can do now is get straight on and have another baby.'

And, much as it made her want to scream, Katie did what her mother advised, and just over a year later she had another baby. He was a son, Barry, and he was healthy. Katie never tried again.

But it wasn't easy. Just three months after she lost Clifford, Katie had to endure her twin having a healthy boy, when she already had two children. And she had to watch everyone being happy for Bertha and excited about the baby, and she had to pretend to be happy herself, all the time aware that no one ever said anything about her baby, as if he had never existed. She couldn't bring herself to open the door to that back bedroom where the cradle lay empty, still waiting, and she never gave Bertha those clothes coupons. The bridge card was scrunched up and thrown in the bin as if it was toxic.

In the evenings, at home with Horace, because they couldn't talk about Clifford and share their loss, there was nothing left to say.

And there was no relief during the day. Katie's baby had been a source of much talk among her neighbours, both to her face and behind her back. All through her pregnancy there was hardly a meeting which didn't involve some discussion of how she was feeling: the size of her bump, when the baby was due, was it a girl or a boy? Did she want a girl or a boy? What did Horace want? And she'd engaged happily with all of it, revelling in the excitement after all those years of waiting.

Now she was back, no longer pregnant, but without a baby. Most of her acquaintances had heard about Clifford, and by the time Katie returned it was never mentioned. Which was difficult, but nothing like as difficult as the odd person who hadn't heard and said cheerfully: 'Oh, hello, Mrs Smith. How's the baby?'

At which point Katie would have to say, 'He's passed away.' And then, in the face of their reaction, she would feel as if she was having to comfort them for her loss with statements like: 'It's for the best.' 'It wasn't meant to be.' 'We've all got our crosses to bear.' None of which she felt or believed. Never mind the 'helpful' platitudes along similar lines that came back, and made her want to spit.

I met Katie just once, as she went to live in New Zealand where her son, Barry, had married and settled. This was her only visit back to England. Katie and Nanna came to stay with us. It was fascinating to meet this twin of my nanna's who was so different. Katie seemed quite taken with me. She gave me a beautiful necklace when she left: big, sparkly, paste diamonds, very glamorous for a twelve-year-old, but I've worn it on posh nights out since, thinking of her.

Later, I wondered whether her fondness for me was an unconscious premonition that we were going to have something in common.

I have also only met her son Barry once, and that's when I was sent to New Zealand to do some filming. I took some holiday and I took my mum. We stayed with him at his beautiful farm outside Auckland. Katie had died some years before, but Mum was eager to know about her last years.

'It was very upsetting. You know she had dementia?' Barry said.

Mum nodded.

'Well, she lived with us, but she became very withdrawn into her own world. And the most distressing thing was that as she got more sick, she seemed to care less about us and all she would talk about was the baby who had died. You know about the baby? A little boy?'

Mum nodded again.

'She'd never talked about him before, but now he was all she would talk about. It was as if she didn't care about leaving us, she just wanted to go to him. It was as if she didn't love me at all.'

I was haunted by this story, particularly by how upset Barry was. And when I lost Poppy just a couple of years later, it preyed on my mind. I didn't want to carry that burden of grief so silently, for so many years that in the end it took over. I was fortunate – I had bereavement counselling. I joined a support group. I had friends who were brilliant and put up with long, tear-soaked evenings. I have felt people alongside me in my darkest moments. And that makes all the difference. Even more importantly, I held Poppy, I was able to know her and love her, and then I was able to bury her and mark her grave. To be able to do something, anything, for your child feels so important. I have photos and, best of all, a lock of her beautiful golden curls. I hold that lock of hair sometimes, because more than anything that makes her real.

Poppy's photograph is always close to hand. Actually, these days her photograph has been stolen by the girls and tends to move between their bedrooms. It's interesting where she is to be found. Who is the keeper of Poppy today?

Freud wrote about the mourning process and the work of mourning, and that involves experiencing the grief, living it, talking it, feeling it, marking it. If you cannot do that, you are stuck and it's impossible to move on. His writing on it was first published in 1917 and yet when Clifford died in 1945, Freud's ideas on bereavement tragically still hadn't become mainstream, as they are today. Well, that's the theory, but my experience suggests it's true.

Out of everything that happened to the Scarlet Sisters, Katie's loss is the most difficult for me. Even more than Charlie Junior. It was so hard after Poppy died, but when I think about Katie, what she faced, and how much harder it was for her, it takes my breath away and I wish I could tell her how sorry I am and how much I respect her for simply surviving and going on, when she really was on her own. It's so difficult that I have to stop and find my breath again outside in the fresh air.


I'm in Cley in Norfolk and I walk to the old church. They have a prayer tree inside, where you can write a prayer you would like the church to say for you, and pin it to the leaves of the tree. The girls and I come here every summer and we always leave prayers. The church keeps a scrapbook, where they stick each year's prayers and we look up our old ones and think about them. It's useful. In the last few years I've asked for inspiration, then courage, and last year, healing. This year the girls have given me their prayers. I read them before I write my own. Essentially they all ask for the same thing – help for our family to stick together and be strong. And then it's obvious what I should ask for. I write:

*Dear God,*

*The waters are stormy. It's difficult, but I know with your help I can find a way through to safety on the shore. Guide me, lend me your hand.*

*Stand at my shoulder and whisper in my ear. Show me the way to be a good mother.*

Because actually, in the greater scheme of things, in terms of the footprint I make on this earth, nothing else is as important. What I do and the way I am has a huge effect on not only my children's happiness, but on their children's too, and so on. I don't want to pass my losses on. I have never felt that as strongly as I do today.

Just as I am leaving I turn back, and I pick up the pen at the foot of the tree and I write one more prayer:

*Dear God,*

*Please look after Charlie Junior, and Clifford, and Poppy. Please can they know that they are much loved, and never forgotten.*

# CHAPTER SEVENTEEN

# The Beginning

When the announcement came that the war was over, Dianne expected her dad to walk through the door the next day. Unfortunately, he didn't. It was hard. She couldn't understand why he didn't come home. And the missing didn't lessen. With the war over, it became very urgent.

One day she was out in the front garden with John and the usual gang of children in their road. They had a beautiful tree, heavy with flowers, known as the Butterfly Tree. That day it was living up to its name and the children were running around with nets trying to catch them. As they laughed and chased the butterflies around the lawn, the telegraph boy stopped outside their house and knocked on the door. Everyone watched as Bertha took the telegram and went inside. Five minutes later the door opened and she came out again and called out, 'Children, can you go home, please. I need John and Dianne to come inside.'

Anxious, the two children went into the kitchen, where she beckoned to them to sit down. 'I've just had a telegram. Your father is coming home today.'

They squealed and hugged each other, and then they sat and waited, eyes pinned on the window where they could see the front gate. About an hour later they were still sitting watching, but William had decided to surprise them and came along the side passage instead. But Bertha saw the top of his army beret and screamed, 'He's here! He's here!'

Bertha and John ran into the hall, flung open the front door and rushed into his arms. Dianne was left in the kitchen on her own with the baby Nigel, who was in his seat. 'They've forgotten the baby,' she thought.

She was aware that William had never seen Nigel before and Nigel hadn't met his dad. She didn't quite know what to do and once again had that sensation of time suspended, a time lag, a gap – in the hall the next chapter had started, while she was still in the old one. It seemed like she sat there for ever, and then she knew what she had to do.

Dianne picked up Nigel and took him into the hall where her dad was standing, in his uniform, skinny but fantastically tanned, with a whiff of the Sahara desert about him. 'Hello, Dad,' she said. 'Look, this is our baby.' And she walked over to her father and handed Nigel to him.

Nigel immediately screamed, not having the faintest idea who this stranger was. And that just about sums up William's homecoming.

It would be lovely to write 'And then they all lived happily ever after', but this is no fairytale and life is so much more complicated than that.

The problem William faced when he got home was a family who expected, and indeed longed for, everything to go back to how it had been. What they didn't expect was for William to come back fundamentally changed, and because they were dependent on him, that meant their life changed too.

'It was as if my husband left his ambition behind in the Sahara Desert,' Bertha used to say. Like a changeling that had been blown in by the wind, he appeared the same (albeit even thinner and darker), but the look behind the eyes was different. The reason for this is completely unknown. William, like many returning soldiers, declined to talk about the war. When he did, it was only ever in passing and to say how much he enjoyed it. Which is curious because all the reports of life fighting Rommel in Egypt, especially in tanks, are horrific. However, William didn't go to Africa until quite late on, and he claimed he didn't see actual combat. Apart from one day, when he was sitting in a tank, in the gunner's seat, in the middle of the desert having his lunch, when he looked up and saw a Messerschmitt about to dive. So, with a sandwich in his left hand, he pressed the trigger with his right and, 'Blow me down,' he said, 'I hit it.'

Tanks were designed to fight in Europe and William found himself as part of an experimental unit trying to adapt them to fighting in the desert. I can see how messing around with huge vehicles would suit him – he came from a family of engineers after all – and he loved racing them across the sand. All the photos from that time show him and his friends smiling, looking tanned and healthy in shorts and short-sleeve shirts, as if they are at a tennis tournament, except there's a great big tank in the background.

What's obvious is that being in Egypt gave William a taste for sun and adventure, and he couldn't settle back in his old home town. Grays now looked exactly that – grey – to him, and the thought of living the rest of his life there filled him with gloom. William's ennui was not helped by the disappearance of his company. His building empire had ceased to exist and his business partner, Sparky, who somehow had managed to avoid having to go off and fight had disappeared, along with the money.

So, when he arrived back, William sat down with a newspaper and answered advertisements for casual labourers. What frustrated Bertha was that he seemed to be fine with this. She had thought that when he came back he'd start a new business, especially as there were plenty of new houses to be built after the Blitz. But William didn't, and Bertha started to seethe. She had thought she would be able to give up work and resume her old lifestyle, which used to be comparable to, if not better than, her sisters, Dora and Katie's.

But as the days rolled into weeks and then months, it gradually dawned on Bertha that this might be it, and she felt a little acorn of resentment taking root and starting to spread.

*

Change is a cheeky fellow who can wear all sorts of disguises. Sometimes he creeps in the back door, but every so often he's just barefaced and knocks at the door and demands to be let in.

For Bertha, change came to the doorstep in the form of Mr Jackson at ten o'clock on a Sunday morning in the spring of 1948. There was a loud knock on the door, Bertha went to answer it and ushered the visitor in the sitting room.

Mr Jackson was the self-appointed head of the residents' association of the last estate that William had built, and now William faced him with a sense of unease. This impromptu visit could only herald bad news, and he was right.

'We're still waiting for the road to be built, Mr Kendall. When we bought our houses it was with the proviso that there would be a proper road connecting all the houses. We've lived with an unmade road for eight years now. Of course we understand nothing could be done during the war, but the war has been over for nearly two years and there is still no sign of it being built. We need to know – have you any plans?'

William was an honest man, and had to give a direct answer. 'No, I haven't. My business no longer exists. I have no means to finish the road.'

'In which case I've a letter to give you. We've been to see a solicitor and he's advised us that you are legally obliged to build this road, whether your business is still in existence or not. Here.' He handed over the letter and William read it carefully. 'As it states, if you don't start work on the road immediately, then we will have no choice but to start legal action. We will have that road even if we have to hire the builders ourselves, Mr Kendall, and you are going to have to pay the bill.'

Mr Jackson got up to leave. 'I look forward to hearing from you … or, indeed, your solicitor.'

They shook hands – William was always polite – and he showed him to the door.

After he had gone William sat for a long time thinking, until Bertha came to find him: 'What was all that about?'

'They want me to build the road to the estate.'

'Well, you can't.'

'I know I can't.'

'Did you tell him that?'

'Yes.'

'And what did he say?'

'You'd better read this.' William handed over the letter.

Bertha sat down and read it, and then dropped it. 'Oh, no! Oh, William, what are you going to do? Surely they can't make you? There's a very good reason why that road wasn't built. It's called the war. I hope you said that.'

'No.'

'No? Why on earth not?'

'Because it doesn't make any difference.'

Bertha looked as if she was going to explode into one of her fiery red-head rages. 'Of course it makes a difference! It's the reason for practically everything. There's half-built stuff, half-ruined stuff everywhere! They've just got to lump it like everyone else. At least they've got houses to live in, unlike some people. Honestly, the nerve of it! Selfish blighters! I've got a good mind to tell them myself – "You haven't got your bleedin' road because my husband was risking his life running around the desert to keep people like you alive!" The nerve of it! I mean, my children went without their father for all these years, for what? So some miserable, wet bloke can say, "I want my road."!' She pulled a face.

William almost smiled. She was magnificent in her fury, but this wasn't going to help.

'Bertha, please, calm down. It's not that I don't think you're right but we've got to face reality. Legally, they may well be right.'

'Well, the law's an ass.'

'Yes, but it's an ass that can get me thrown into prison.'

That stopped her. 'You don't seriously think you could end up in prison? I mean, if you haven't got the money, you haven't got the money. It's not as if you've committed a crime or stolen something.'

'Well, in a way I have stolen the road, because I have got the money.'

'Well, where is it?'

'Here,' he said, and swept his arm around their luxurious sitting room.

'No! You can't be serious. The house?'

'Yes. There's enough money in this house to build the road and they probably know that.'

'But your children can't be left without a roof over their heads, while they're sitting in their brand new houses – houses that you've built! There's no court in the land that would make you do that, that's madness!'

'I think it might. Anyway, let's not get carried away, we wouldn't be left homeless. We'd probably just be left with a home that's a bit smaller.'

'I am NOT leaving my home!'

'Well, you might have to. But let's see. No point in worrying about it yet. The first thing I've got to do is find myself a solicitor.'

'No, William, the first thing you've got to do is find that crook Sparky and get the money back that he owes you and then you can build their bleedin' road.'

'I'm not going to find Sparky.'

'Why not? He can't just have disappeared into thin air. I don't understand why you aren't out there scouring the county looking for him. Someone must know where he is. I don't understand why you're so … so … *limp* about it all.'

William knew why he hadn't looked for Sparky – he hadn't looked for him because he didn't want to find him. He didn't care about the money: money wasn't important; in fact, he felt it got in the way. The root of all evil. Stuff just pinned you down. He had no fondness for Bertha's soft furnishings – it was her vivacity he loved, everything else was a distraction. He didn't want to start a business again, he didn't want to go back to his old life. He didn't want to be *there*, in that bungalow, in Grays, at all. It's not that he didn't want to be with his family, but he wanted them all to be somewhere else, starting out again, together, out in the wild, in the hot sunshine.

William was now acutely aware of the shortness and arbitrary nature of life and it just seemed a waste to sit there in Grays doing the same old thing for the rest of it. But at that moment he couldn't see a way out; and until he did, he felt it best to keep these thoughts to himself. He was in no doubt they would not be appreciated by his wife.

Instead, William felt with a heavy heart that he would have to try and find Sparky, or at least be seen to be trying to find him. To that end, he walked into a few of his old competitors' yards and asked where he was, but was more than happy to take them at face value when they shrugged their shoulders.

Bertha wasn't convinced. 'Grace has heard that he's been seen around Romford.'

'Don't know anything about that.'

Bertha looked at him through narrowed eyes.

'But I'll ask,' he added quickly.

Meanwhile, William received a letter from Mr Jackson letting him know that the residents' association had hired a builder and work had started on the new road. He reluctantly went to see a solicitor.

'I think it's an interesting case, Mr Kendall. Your contract states quite clearly that you undertake to make the road, and even though your company is closed for business, you are still personally liable to fulfil the contract. However, there are a number of complicating factors which might mean that a judge might sway towards leniency – not least a disappearing partner and a World War, where all sorts of contracts have not been fulfilled for good reason. It is a bit of a test case. It depends whether you're up for the fight.'

'Well, I'm not sure. I need to think about it,' William said.

Bertha didn't see what there was to think about. 'But surely that's good news. We've a chance of keeping the house. The judge *must* be lenient. The reason that road didn't get built was not our fault. It was bloody Hitler's and if that thieving so and so Sparky hadn't run off with the cash, it would have been built. You just need to put your case in front of the judge and he'll come down on our side, because we're right.'

'I'm not going to court,' William said quietly, bracing himself.

'You're joking.'

'No, I'm not. I undertook to make the road and therefore I will make it and we are just going to have to sell the house.'

At this point the biggest row of William and Bertha's marriage commenced. It started with the court case and mushroomed out into the wider issue of William's refusal to, in Bertha's words, 'get off his backside and earn some money'.

It ended with Bertha shouting: 'If you're not prepared to act like a proper husband and provide for your family, then I'm not prepared to stay here and be your wife.'

And she grabbed Dianne and Nigel and marched out of the house. For some reason, John was left to fend for himself.

They took the ferry to Margate and then a train into the Kent countryside. Bertha had no idea where to go. The exit had been completely spontaneous. After the war ended and Tom Corbett had come home, Clara had left Alice and come back to Grays. Bertha might have gone to her mum's, but she knew that was the first place that William would look. Really, she just wanted to get as far away as possible.

As she sat on the train she seethed. She was furious with William but, more than that, she was furious with herself for having married him. She thought he was one thing and he was turning out to be quite another, and as she looked at her sisters Dora and Katie – well, particularly Dora, because she seemed so in love, she felt they'd made better choices. 'Fool!' she kept saying to herself.

She got so cross she couldn't sit on the train any more and as it drew into a station, she leapt up, hauled Nigel over her shoulder and grabbed Dianne's hand: 'Come on, we're getting off.'

'Where are we?' Dianne asked.

'Where we're meant to be,' Bertha said.

'Where's that, Mummy?'

'Wherever we find ourselves. Now, quick, off you get.'

They found themselves in a typical Kent village. There was a large village green where a group of formidable ladies were preparing a small fête: trestle tables were being assembled, bunting put up in trees, and cakes laid out on stalls. To Dianne it was a bit confusing – had Mum meant to bring them there? It was a long way to come for a fête.

Bertha bought some food from a shop and they sat on the grass eating as the crowds started to gather. She became aware that they were being watched by a rather handsome soldier. Bertha did stand out – she was wearing that red and green, giant plaid coat with her bright red hair and her white-blonde children. The soldier caught her eye and she couldn't help but smile back at him.

'What beautiful children you have,' he said.

'Thank you,' replied Bertha.

He smiled again, as if requesting an invitation to join them and, suddenly, Bertha felt vulnerable. What was she going to do? She wasn't really going to go off with a random soldier, was she? The thought terrified her. But if she wasn't going to do that then what was she going to do?

Bertha considered the options. She could move in with her mum, but she knew Clara would not approve: 'You've made your bed and now you've got to lie in it' – that's what she'd say. Clara didn't love William, but he didn't drink, and he didn't hit Bertha, and he didn't see other women. She could just hear her mum saying, 'You've always been a bit of a princess, Bertha.'

But what were the other options? Her sisters had their hands full and she couldn't see much sympathy there, for the same reasons. The only money she had was what she had left in her purse, and that would barely stretch to a room for the night. The rest was all in a bank account in William's name and they didn't have any savings, anyway.

And that was just the problem of the next few weeks. In the long run, what would the future be? William would never divorce her and the only way she could get a divorce was if she proved William had been having an affair – the phrase 'Pigs might fly' came to mind – or if he was cruel to her. And while making her move out of her bungalow did feel like the height of cruelty, Bertha realised she would probably be alone on that one. No, she would be forced to live as a single mother, on one income, with few legal rights – she would not be able to get a bank account or a mortgage – and, worse still, lose all her standing in the community. Compared to that fate, losing the bungalow seemed like a small sacrifice. She was trapped.

As the fair started to pack up and darkness drew in, Bertha knew she had no option but to go back. They all got up and walked to the station and started the long journey back home in silence.

When she walked in William was waiting for her. He didn't know whether to be angry or relieved. 'Where have you been? I've been looking for you everywhere.'

'I've been thinking.'

'Well, I've been thinking too – I'll go to court. Let's give it a go. But if we lose, I want you to accept the outcome with good grace. You will have to get behind me, and we will have to move. Agreed?'

Bertha nodded. 'Agreed.' She had to admit, you couldn't say fairer than that.

It took six months. Everyone in Grays knew about the case, and it divided local opinion – there were many houses on that estate, and the residents all had friends, but the Swains had been a presence in the town for a long time too. It was the subject of gossip although people were careful what they said within Katie and Grace's earshot. The sisters might fall out with each other, but when threatened by an outsider, they were a united force.

Behind the family's back, however, there was some glee, even from so-called friends. Driving around in a white Lancaster and having a house with marble pillars did attract a certain amount of envy. By achieving this 'perfect' family, Bertha had rubbed a lot of her neighbours up the wrong way, and the prospect of her downfall caused some to say that it served her right. It's unfortunate but human. And Bertha knew what people were like, she could be like it herself.

Added to this, John and Dianne were teased at school.

'Your dad's been arrested.'

'Your dad's going to jail.'

'Your dad's a thief.'

It was not pleasant for anyone, especially William. Nothing could have been more alien to him than this legal fight, but he knew his marriage was at stake in some fundamental way – that Bertha would never forgive him if he hadn't at least tried to save the home that he had given her as her wedding present. And he loved her.

In the end, it only took a few hours to lay the evidence in front of the judge. After a short deliberation, the judge came back and announced to the court that he had decided that a contract was a contract, it was legally sound and binding, war or no war, partner or no partner, and that William did indeed have to pay for the road.

Within a couple of months Bertha had packed up the bungalow that had been her wedding present, and moved a couple of streets down the road to a 1930s semi-detached house. It was fine, but ordinary.

She would go on great detours to make sure she never had to go past her bungalow ever again.

*

I remember when I was training as a psychotherapist and I was worried about someone, I said to my supervisor, 'It's like watching a car crash about to happen,' and she said: 'Helen, sometimes the car has to crash. Sometimes that's the only way a person's life is going to get any better. You have to have the crash, and write off the old car, before you can get the new one. Get it?'

And I did get it. In fact, I've seen it happen quite a few times since. And I wonder whether this judgement wasn't William's car-crash moment. The nadir of their fortunes. The impetus and excuse to actually get out of his grey gloom and start a whole new life.

In the months following the trial, William carried on working as a jobbing builder. One day, he was sent off to Tilbury to pick up some materials. They weren't ready for him so he lit a cigarette and took a little wander along the docks – and there, right in front of him, was the answer. He watched as the *New Australia* liner got ready to leave with her cargo of people bound for a new life in Australia. Hundreds were on deck waving goodbye, bunting everywhere, a band playing, relatives on the quay waving and crying. The boat's horn sounded, ropes were cast off and it slowly started to move away. William was surprised by the wave of emotion hitting him, slap in the solar plexus. For a moment he had imagined what it would be like to be on that deck, waving goodbye to grey, dull Britain for ever, and travelling to some destination he had never been to before. Somewhere warmer, fresh, new, with space to breathe and to be.

William remembered how, as a boy, he had longed to get on one of those liners. And then he thought, 'Well, why not? Why don't we do that? What have we got to lose?' And in a way he was right: now they'd lost the court case, they had absolutely nothing to lose.

He also remembered some soldiers from New Zealand he'd met out in the desert, who had told him that the building industry in Britain was finished – the new land of milk and honey was their home, New

Zealand. As a master builder he would have no problems finding work – it was cheaper, safer, sunnier, happier.

Of course, Bertha didn't see it that way. She argued with William, but he had an answer for everything.

'I am not leaving my family and dragging the children to the other side of the world.'

'You won't be dragging them. It will be a wonderful adventure for them, a new start.'

'I'll miss my sisters.'

'You won't miss arguing with them.'

'Leaving poor Mum living on her own …'

'She's not on her own. She still has four daughters.'

'What about Old Uncle?'

That was more difficult, but William was resolute. 'He's my concern. If I'm prepared to leave him, then you should be too. There's nothing he has ever wanted more than for me to be happy and settled. He'll be behind me.'

'What about the children's school? I bet they don't have grammar schools in New Zealand.'

Dianne and John were the only Scarlet Sisters' children to get into grammar school. This was a matter of great pride for Bertha, and a first for the children to actually be able to go.

But William did not set much store by formal education: 'They'll have plenty of opportunities. They're clever enough to do well wherever they go … if that's what they want.'

'But we don't know if we're going to like it there. What if we go all that way and we find out we hate it?'

'We'll come back, I promise.'

But Bertha was not convinced.

I caught a radio programme about 'home'. People were asked where home was for them. The answers varied – for some people it was a solid, physical location: a house, a town they were born in; for others, it resided in another element – it was wherever their parents were, or their lover, or their children. But for some it was inside themselves, not dependent on a place or another person, but a feeling – contentment, security, love.

For Bertha it had been a place. It was a nest that she had created and was an expression of her; for William, who had lost all his close family by the time he was ten, a home had to be built inside. That made him rather mobile, certainly more mobile than Bertha.

I remember the feelings I had after my parents divorced and my mother finally sold the family home. I hadn't lived in it for a few years – by then I was living with my boyfriend, who would become my husband. But it hurt. In my head, whenever I went back I was still 'going home'. Now, when I stayed in Mum's cottage, I would not be in 'my' bedroom, but the 'spare room'. My father had emigrated to the other side of the Atlantic, and home had gone – I felt destabilised without somewhere to go back to, 'just in case' – as if someone had pulled out the rug from beneath me. Unexpected, but that's really what it felt like. It's not that I don't like travelling, I really do. It's just I need a home to go out from and come back to. If I have that, I can go anywhere. Otherwise I'm not travelling, I'm a refugee.

So I worked hard to build a new nest. My relationship with my husband and the house we shared became my new home, and when I had children one of the things I wanted to give them most was something I felt had been taken from me: a home, in my sense of the word – a physical place of security and love, in which they could grow up, and move away from, but always come back to. I wanted them to be part of a community. I wanted them to have roots. My husband was offered jobs in the Middle East, and he dearly wanted to go. He didn't want roots – to him they sounded boring, a jail, like giving up, a full stop, the end. It was probably one of the bigger things that separated us. A fundamental.

But, a bit like Bertha, I've had to reassess. Do you have to grow up in the same house? Do you have to have two parents? What are the essentials to have a sense of home and foundations?

When I first found out about my husband's infidelity I asked him to leave. In the months that followed, I felt like I was falling through space, spinning through the abyss, with no foundations. I had started going out with him when I was seventeen and I had been with him for over half my life. Now I quoted Nietzsche at my psychoanalyst supervisor:

'What did we do when we unchained the earth from its sun?'

'Are we not perpetually falling? Helen, you need to find your own inner plumb line. Centre yourself.'

I couldn't quite pull it off though, and I gave my husband another chance. But the next time it happened and the full extent of his unfaithfulness was uncovered, and I showed him the door again ... it felt different. This time it *was* for ever.

For about a week I was falling again. I couldn't eat and I couldn't sleep. The prosecco sat in the fridge untouched. All I could do was drink cups of tea and smoke cigarettes. I smoked in the kitchen. The girls didn't complain.

'Whatever you need to do to get through, Mum' – wise words from Scarlett (aged nine).

But then I started to feel better. I stayed up late with my girls watching reality TV, all of us snuggling under a duvet, arms wrapped round each other, like puppies cuddling for warmth. We shouted at the appalling people on the telly, placed bets on who was going to be voted off, and giggled. I started to eat and go out and I opened the prosecco and stopped smoking in the kitchen. I had a night out when he should have been there, and he wasn't, and I realised I was actually having a better time without him.

I think that was the moment when I knew that I was going to be all right. It had taken just six weeks, but I was so ready, and he had been so bad for me. Without him I started to laugh again.

This time, the world didn't come to an end.

To go back to Nietzsche, I had unchained myself from the sun and I had survived. Nietzsche also said, 'That which does not kill us makes us stronger.' Maybe, but what it feels like is that I have finally grown up. And as the girls and I look at new houses, just for the four of us, and start to get excited, I'm beginning to think we can make a home wherever the four of us are.

I think Bertha gradually came to the same conclusion. It was a long process – the sticking plaster wasn't ripped off but peeled back slowly. But the final tug came when William came home early one day. Bertha was surprised to see the top of his head walking down the side passage before the small hand had even reached three on the kitchen clock. She was immediately suspicious. 'What are you doing home so early?'

As ever William, incapable of giving anything other than a straight answer, said, 'I've been sacked.'

'You've been what?'

'Sacked. I was caught smoking in the lavs.'

'Oh my God, William! How could you?'

He just stared back at her and shrugged. There was something defiant in the stare. 'It doesn't matter. It was just a job. The pay was rubbish, anyway.'

'But it was a job. What are you going to do now? Who's going to give you another job when they hear about this? Oh, God, it's so embarrassing!'

At which point Bertha slumped into a kitchen chair, put her head in her hands on the table and sobbed. Then she lifted her head and shouted: 'I'm ashamed of you!'

William hovered. His first instinct was to walk out but he increasingly wanted to stand his ground and fight back. It was beginning to feel like his very existence was at stake.

'I was smoking when I should have been working because I don't want to do this job any more. I've told you, I don't even want to be *here*, and it's killing me because I feel like I'm wasting my life, when there is something so much better waiting for all of us. If only you could open your mind and let go of whatever you're trying to do here. What are you holding on for? What are you trying to prove?'

'I have no idea what you mean. I'm not trying to prove anything.'

'Are you sure? I think you've spent your whole life trying to prove something to those sisters of yours and, Bertha, I tell you now, it's not worth it. You're wasting your time and your life … and mine too, for that matter.'

'What I don't understand is how you've been sacked and somehow I'm the one to blame.'

'Think about it, Bertha. Just think about it. I think maybe you *are* the one to blame.'

And this time William did walk out.

But, finally, he had said something that had got through. Because Bertha did think, and started to wonder how much she had been trying to prove something not just to her sisters but, more importantly, to herself.

A couple of weeks later Bertha asked William to go for a walk. They strolled along the seafront promenade, with the gulls sweeping by and the fresh sea air playing havoc with Bertha's neat red ringlets. They stopped and looked out across the estuary to the open sea and she said, 'It's taken me a long time but I now realise how unhappy you've been. I can see you no longer feel at home here, but it's been hard for me to understand – this is where you were born, where you grew up. But there it is. And if you don't feel at home then it's difficult for the rest of us to feel at home. So I agree. I think it's time to look for a place which can be a home for all of us.'

William stared at Bertha, hardly able to believe it.

'So this means you'll move?'

'Yes.'

'Abroad? Emigrate? Get on a ship and sail a long way from here? Probably for ever?'

'Yes.'

And William flung his arms round her and hugged her and spun her around.

William subscribed to a monthly geographical magazine and at the back of it were advertisements for jobs all over the world. He applied for a job in New Zealand and got it. He had just enough money for the passage for all of them.

It would take three months to sail down and through the Suez canal, round India and across to Australia, with New Zealand as the final destination. It was only once their passage had been booked and they had their departure date that Bertha told her mother, Clara, and then her sisters in turn.

They were horrified. Clara's first reaction, and indeed what she kept saying to Bertha over and over was: 'But I'll never see you again.'

And the problem was that Bertha couldn't argue with that. The chances were that none of them would ever see her again. The passage to New Zealand cost £350 for the family, the equivalent of over a year's wages for William, and took six weeks. Flights only went to European cities.

Clara was now seventy-two years old. 'I can't believe you're really going and leaving me. You may as well be dead.'

'Mum!'

But in a way Clara was right. It wasn't even possible to telephone New Zealand. Letters took months to arrive, if at all.

Clara had lost one of her children already. She felt a familiar, horrible tug like she'd experienced when Alice had eloped, but which actually stretched back through to those first terrible days and months and years after Charlie Junior had died.

On their last visit to her house, Clara gave my mum a silver cross. It was delicate, engraved with a pattern. 'Here, Dianne. Something to keep you safe,' she had said and put it around her granddaughter's neck with tears in her eyes.

Years later, Mum was in intensive care, having had a heart attack. I took the cross in to hospital and put it around her neck saying, 'To look after you,' because it felt, and still feels, like a talisman. When I went away to boarding school she gave it to me, and I wore it through my A-levels and at critical moments through my life. Something blessed by Nanna's love – the most, unconditional love of all – must work. And Mum got better and is still with us at the age of seventy-seven. It works. The problems come when I haven't been forewarned and it's been left at home in a box.

Bertha's sisters were unimpressed. Katie was the only one who dared to voice what they were all thinking (and saying to each other): 'England not enough for you, then?'

Bertha was rather at a loss what to say, but Katie continued: 'You always want more, don't you?'

Of all the sisters, Katie could understand Bertha's move the least, and was the most hurt. Katie's whole life was embedded in the community – with her shop and social life, with her mother around the corner and now her son. For her twin to leave felt like some sort of comment on the life she'd built for herself.

'I don't expect you to understand, Katie. But I hope you can still wish us well,' was all Bertha could say in the end.

Katie nodded and they embraced, but Bertha had a feeling that, deep down, it took Katie a long time and many more things to happen before she would forgive her.

1952, and the Kendall family stood on the deck of the SS *Otranto* in Tilbury Docks. On the quay a brass band was playing patriotic tunes.

Hundreds of people had come to see their loved ones go. For many this would be a last goodbye. No one was more aware of this than Old Uncle. With faithful Mrs Beesom at his side, tears poured down his face as he took his last look at the family that was the closest thing he had to having a son and grandchildren. Beside him stood Clara and her remaining daughters and their children.

Jackie and Angela, by then almost teenagers, remember the occasion vividly, especially Old Uncle's tears. Bertha waved her flag at them, trying to smile, while battling with a streamer that had got caught up in that elaborate red hair.

She turned to William. 'You know the first thing I'm going to do? I'm going to change my name. From now on, you're all going to have to call me Betty.'

And the ship's horn sounded, the ropes were thrown, and with a chorus of shouting and cheering, the boat started to move off slowly, out into the estuary, towards the open sea. It was the first step on a new journey, a new beginning and a new home.

# CONCLUSION
# Breaking the Spell

I started this rummage in the family's attic looking for patterns and spells. I think I found them. What's harder is the question – can they be broken?

I'm sitting at my desk again. It's early morning, my favourite time of day. I've tiptoed past my girls' bedrooms – I can hear Scarlett gently breathing, the Little One snoring, and complete silence as ever from the Big Girl. I've left Mr D sleeping like a cat in my bed. A new day. I've put the fire on but the sun is coming up. I'm feeling optimistic.

The other day I happened to find myself at a party, seated next to a biologist. I was telling her what I'd found.

'Well, of course,' she said, 'it's hardly surprising when you think that a woman's eggs are formed pretty much as soon as she is conceived. We are literally carried by our grandmothers, and experience everything our mothers experience until we are born.'

In which case, part of Nanna experienced the disgrace and bereavement that Clara suffered when Alexander Crisp fell from grace, and watched as Charlie Junior fell ill. And then my mum in some way witnessed Charlie Junior's death and the violent, alcoholic arguments between Charlie and Clara. And it could be said that 50 per cent of me actually lived through the war. And, of course, that means that some part of me was present when Charlie Senior died – however he died – and I was there for those years that Mum was sitting on the chair at the

Barratts. And I guess that also means that the girls were in some way witnesses to the death of their big sister, Poppy, and my grief. And if they have children, they will have already been through the trauma of their grandparents separating.

I no longer underestimate the pull of these undercurrents and their consequences.

I love the Norfolk coast, striding backwards and forwards across the marshes looking out to the North Sea. I feel at home there. And yet I have no connection with it. Or at least, that's what I thought. Now I've found out that, on my dad's side, we come from generations of fishermen based in Greenwich who used to sail out into the North Sea and up that East Anglian coast to catch wives as well as fish. Perhaps, as a salmon returns home to mate, I'm being drawn by some ancestral pull to wander the North Norfolk coastline, scouring the sea looking for a man to sail past and take me home to be his wife. Which, eerily, is exactly how my dad met my mum: following in his forefather's footsteps, sailing the seas with a twinkle in his eye, but in this generation she was standing on the quay of Auckland harbour in New Zealand and he was an officer in the Merchant Navy and he saw her from the boat and took her back to England with him.

Which had huge consequences for the family: my Nanna, Bertha, said to her husband William, 'I cannot live halfway across the world from my daughter.'

So, after eighteen happy years in New Zealand, the Kendall family followed Dianne and came back to England and settled where Dianne was living, in the New Forest. Betty became Bertha again. The pull of her daughter was too much.

Years later, in a strange twist, Katie's son, Barry, went travelling to New Zealand, fell in love and settled there. Like her twin sister, Katie could not be separated from her child, so she went the other way and emigrated to New Zealand. Bertha and Katie had a complicated relationship, but I witnessed my nanna's real distress and sense of bereavement when Katie left.

I have one more photograph above my desk. It's a photograph of Clara holding her first great-grandchild. It is Alice's granddaughter, Audrey. Clara seems oblivious to the camera. Her gaze is fixed on the baby she gently cradles in her arms; it is a look of delight and love. When Brian gave it to me I was deeply moved. For me, that look holds an answer. The sisters said that Clara never got over losing Charlie Swain Junior, but that photo is telling me something different, or at least something more complicated – that whatever Clara's grief at losing her son, and I'm sure that was enduring, this did not stop her being able

*Clara and Audrey*

to experience great joy with her surviving children, and grandchildren and then great-grandchildren.

After the war Clara went back to Grays. She never remarried, or reopened her shop. Instead, she spent the last fifteen years of her life moving between her daughters, helping to bring up their children and their children's children, including her great-granddaughter, Audrey. 'She was a kind, gentle, loving soul,' was how Alice's son, Brian, described her to me.

Of course that's just how I remember my nanna too. She was hugely loved by all her children and grandchildren. She was right at the centre of us all, leaving a lasting feeling of love.

And that has been one of the most striking things that has come from my encounters with the Scarlet Sisters' children – how much Alice, Grace, Dora, Katie and Bertha were adored by their children, and made their children feel loved in return. All of them were widowed at a relatively young age. None of them remarried, but they all dedicated the rest of their long lives to helping their children and looking after their grandchildren.

I write a letter to my daughters, but it could just as well be to myself.

*Dear Amber, Scarlett and Daisy,*
   *How to Break the Spell*
   *A bit of Ecclesiastes: 'To every thing there is a season, and a time to every purpose under the heaven: A time to be born, and a time to die….a time to weep, and a time to laugh; a time to mourn and a time to dance'.*
   *Which is fine, but just be aware what ghosts might be leading you in your dance. Find out what went before. Keep it in mind. Be vigilant, so they don't haunt you and you can push them away: you can dance a new dance to a new tune, your own dance, in your own time and not someone else's.*

*Socrates encouraged men to 'Know thyself.' But I think this must include knowing your ancestors too, and this knowledge gives you the power to make a choice. Because I think it is a choice – it's not just about knowing the facts, it's what you make of them. In theory trauma keeps repeating when it hasn't been worked through. To work something through requires uncovering it, exploring it and taking some meaning from it, and then moving on. But it might be that the meaning you take is just as important as the uncovering in the first place.*

*Clara and her daughters may have had difficult marriages and traumatic experiences, but they survived in spite of them. They always picked themselves up. They created homes for their children and they worked hard. In the end they were undefeated and I feel privileged and proud to have such resilient, loving female ancestors. This is something I want you to remember and hold on to when life throws difficulties at you, as it most surely will. Whatever has happened in the past, what you take from it is up to you, and you have a choice where to go next. And, goodness, that is another thing that has struck me – how much greater our choices and opportunities are as women in the twenty-first century.*

*In a way, everything follows from this. I could say all sorts of things about the specifics – don't settle down too young, don't look for a hero, be a heroine and don't try to keep up appearances – but, actually, as long as you use your knowledge and use it wisely, all these things will happen by themselves.*

*Love,*

*Mum*

So, that's the girls, but what about me? What does this mean for me and Mr D?

Going back to the bet we had on the Scottish Referendum, the one where he said that if the 'No' vote won by ten points or more he would show me New York, and which (for once) I actually won … well, after the text exchange on the morning after it, there was complete radio silence. He didn't mention it again. And it was a bit embarrassing, because I'd told all my friends and the girls and they kept asking when I was going, and all I could do was shrug … and, if I'm honest, I was disappointed. After all I'd always honoured my debts – witness naked runs and Korean air stewardess uniforms – and it seemed symbolic, like more than just a trip to New York. I started to wonder where we were going – literally. Just how serious was he about me? Was he prepared to do as much for me as I was for him?

And then about a month later, on a Friday night after a long week apart, we were having supper, just the two of us, at my kitchen bench and he said, 'Are you busy in February?'

'Why?' I was feeling playful.

'I was just wondering. Is there any way you might be able to come to New York with me in February?'

I was enjoying the moment and so paused and kept a straight face. 'Well, I'm not sure …' And then I squealed, leapt up and showered the top of his head with kisses, and I swear he blushed …

So it looks like we are off to New York after all, and I'm aware that there is a perfect way to end this tale. If this was a novel it would be easy and I could tie it up to everyone's satisfaction, not least my own. But it's not. Life is far more complicated and subtle and deep. And if I did it like that, then I'd be ignoring another thing I've learned from the Scarlet Sisters, and that is that I've got to let things take their own course.

The story of me and Mr D has to be left to write itself.

*Bertha, Alice, Grace, Katie, Dora*

# ACKNOWLEDGEMENTS

I would like to thank my mum, her brothers, Nigel and John, and my second cousins, Brian and his wife Barbara; Jean, Dennis, Jackie, Angela and Barry for all their help in writing this book. Of course I couldn't have done it without them. Not only did they answer my questions with honesty, courage and humour, but they welcomed me into their homes and their lives.

I would also like to thank Professor Peter Clarke, formerly my supervisor at St John's College, Cambridge, who, as ever, answered my call with both seriousness and kindness, and guided my research into the context of my nanna's and her sisters' lives. I would like to say a special thank you to Rob Thompson of the Western Front Association and Chris Baker of fourteeneighteen. I'd also like to give a big cheer to the London Metropolitan Archives for their interest and enthusiasm in this project.

Thank you too, to Emma Heard and Sally Floyer, precious friends and unofficial editors, who have been with me all the way, and to Laurie Slade for his wisdom. I am also grateful to my editor, Charlotte Cole, who once again has been a joy to work with.

I'm deeply grateful to my daughters Amber, Scarlett and Daisy for all sorts of things. But in this instance you have tolerated endless streams of family anecdotes and I have appreciated your support and excitement for me and for the book.

Lastly, thank you to David Thompson, for being my special correspondent and historical consultant.

# ABOUT THE AUTHOR

Helen Batten is the *Sunday Times* bestselling author of *Sisters of the East End* and *Confessions of a Showman*. She studied history at Cambridge and then journalism at Cardiff University. She went on to become a producer and director at the BBC and now works as a writer and a psychotherapist. She lives in West London with her three daughters.